DJUNA BARNES (1892–1982) was born in ....-on-Hudson, an artists' colony north of New York. She was educated by her parents: her American father was an artist, her English mother a writer. In the early 1900s Djuna Barnes went to New York, studying art at the Pratt Institute and the Arts Students League. By 1913 she was a regular columnist for *The Brooklyn Daily Eagle*, illustrating her work with her own Beardsley-influenced drawings, also contributing to other newspapers. Her journalism enabled her to support her mother and three younger brothers after her father's remarriage. In 1915 Djuna Barnes published her first poems, *The Book of Repulsive Women*. She married the editor Courtenay Lemon but this lasted for little more than two years. After their separation in 1919 she travelled to Paris with letters of introduction to Ezra Pound and James Joyce. Here she continued to write, becoming a stylish figure of Parisian expatriate life, at the centre of the Modernist move-ment. She began a ten-year relationship with the silverpoint artist Thelma Wood and when this ended in 1931 she was helped by Peggy Guggenheim, who gave her money and somewhere to live. She also stayed at Peggy Guggenheim's English home, writing *Nightwood* under her roof. Her friend, the writer Emily Holmes Coleman, was largely responsible for bringing this novel to the attention of T. S. Eliot, who published it in 1936 with his own introduction. *Nightwood* immediately became a cult novel, as did her last major work, *The Antiphon*, a dramatic poem inspired by her association with Eliot. Djuna Barnes also published *A Book* (1923); a novel, *Ryder* (1928); a revised and enlarged edition of *A Book – A Night Among the Horses* (1929); *Selected Works* (1962) and a book of rhymes, *Creatures in an Alphabet* (1982). Virago also publish a collection of her previously uncollected tales, *Smoke and Other Early Stories* (1985), and a volume of previously uncollected interviews, *I Could Never Be Lonely Without a Husband*.

This enigmatic literary figure, whose circle included Robert McAlmon, Natalie Barney, Kay Boyle, Gertrude Stein and Antonia White, became a recluse in 1940. She moved into a small apartment in Greenwich Village and from time to time her neighbour, e. e. cummings, would shout from his window "Are ya still alive, Djuna?" She died six days after her ninetieth birthday.

A collection of Djuna Barnes's letters is forthcoming from Virago.

NEW YORK

DJUNA BARNES

Edited with Commentary by
Alyce Barry

Drawings by Djuna Barnes

Foreword by Douglas Messerli

Published by VIRAGO PRESS Limited 1990
20–23 Mandela Street, Camden Town, London NW1 0HQ

First published in U.S.A. by Sun & Moon Press 1989

This edition offset from the Sun & Moon Press 1989 edition

These pieces were originally published in *The Brooklyn Daily
Eagle,* the *New York Press,* the *New York World Magazine,* the
New York Tribune, Bruno's Weekly, Pearson's Magazine, the
New York Morning Telegraph Sunday Magazine, and the *New York
Sun Magazine.*

A CIP catalogue for this book is available from the British Library

Printed in Great Britain by Cox & Wyman Ltd, Reading, Berkshire

Contents

There's Something Besides the Cocktail in the Bronx
[*New York Tribune*, February 16, 1919]

Foreword

Written over a six-year period, from 1913 to 1919, the 41 pieces of journalism that make up this collection we have titled *New York* further reveal the remarkable diversity of Djuna Barnes's writings. As with the early stories, *Smoke* and the *Interviews,* both published in earlier volumes by Sun & Moon Press, the works of *New York* carry with them Barnes's signature style, a style that is filled with radical metaphors ("Chinatown is a period over which the alphabet of our city has to step"), aphoristic sayings ("There are two classes of people: those who wear caps and badges and those who wear hats and canes.") and original quotations that make all her "real" figures sound as if they had just stepped from a *fin-de-siecle* play ("When I first struck this town . . . there was a low haze over the dock, but the streets higher up were full of confetti and gay women, and I didn't know whether I had struck paradise or hell.")

But in these short works Barnes also explores serious social issues, and presents figures as real as the streets they inhabit. Here the great interviewer of theatrical personalities explores the lives of tenement-dwellers, middle-class tangoers, squatters, suffragists, ordinary working men, and the literary Bohemians. In one of the most impassioned writings of her oeuvre, Barnes permits herself to undergo the torture of forced feeding, a practice of British prisons forced upon suffragists who went on hunger strikes in protest. And in these works Barnes

11

bravely enters the previously male enclaves of the boxing
match, an Industrial Workers of the World meeting, and
the Brooklyn Navy Yard.

From Brooklyn, where she began as a cub-reporter for
the *Brooklyn Daily Eagle*, to the Bronx, from a boat tour
around the hem of Manhattan to a tour of the City with
American soldiers, Barnes explores the excitement and
energy of a radically changing world, a world teeming
with new immigrants, and crumbling from the corruption
of the old, a world at once containing the wit and polish of
the Greenwich Village Bohemians and the terror and fear
of poverty and war.

One might argue that, as we have said of her early
stories, the roots of her writing can be seen in these
pieces. For here, as in her great novels and play, *Ryder*,
Nightwood, and *The Antiphon*, one of her major themes is the
simultaneity of the beastly and the saintly, of cultures
"high" and "low." In these still-fresh portraits, the City of
New York is perceived by Barnes as an enormous landscape of theater, of circuses, operas, street performances,
carneys, hawkers, con-men, clowns, and just a few saints.

Douglas Messerli

You Can Tango—a Little—
at Arcadia Dance Hall

Reginald Delancey—which really isn't his name at all but will do as well as any other to tack onto and distinguish this young man—lolled in a soft armchair in the window of his club on Clinton Street and scanned the evening papers. He was bored. The tips of his immaculate tan shoes shone brightly as ever; the creases in his trousers were like the prow of the *Imperator* in their incisive sharpness; but his mind was as dull as a tarnished teapot. His fashionable friends had all fled town after the international polo matches, and he was left alone to sun and solitude.

Reginald yawned and glanced carelessly at a newspaper beside his chair. "A Night in Arcadia" read the black headlines glaring at him from the floor. Arcadia? He thought a moment. He remembered now: it was all about Evangeline and broken hearts and—Longfellow, of course. Then he picked up the paper; but what he read had nothing at all to do with misfortune and shattered home. It told of the recent opening and subsequent success of a new Arcadia, a modern dance hall built under the auspices of the Social Centers Corporation—a body of men and women banded together for the absolute elimination of the old-style dance hall with its flickering gaslights and furtive faces. The Arcadia is at the corner of Saratoga Avenue and

Halsey Street, and on Wednesday, Thursday, Saturday, and Sunday evenings one may dance to one's feets' content. It is all quite—but hearken unto what Reggie did, and then do thou likewise.

First of all, he cut out the article about the Arcadia. Then he went home and had dinner. He was not quite certain how he ought to dress for such a place, but he finally selected a quiet, Balkan cravat and a harmless-looking suit and, armed only with a silver-handled stick, sallied forth. When he got off the Halsey Street car at the Arcadia, he was agreeably surprised. There were arc lights and electrics and even a respectable automobile chugging with satisfaction before the door. Reginald paid twenty-five cents and trotted inside. He checked his hat and stick and sat down on a comfortable chair.

"My word," he said to himself, "Longfellow's Arcadia couldn't touch this."

Which was very true, at least as far as the dancing goes. The new hall, a fireproof structure 150 x 200 feet, has a dancing space of 89 x 100 feet and a promenade twenty-five feet wide. It is a one-story building, splendidly lighted, with a seating capacity of 4,500, and it is everything that a dance hall should in every way be.

When Reggie arrived, it was about 8:29, and Bill Doxie was waxing the floor, which already shone like a mirror in sunlight. Reginald, however, was not certain of just what was in store for him, so he asked Sydney S. Cohen, a pleasant man with a welcoming sort of smile, who is secretary and treasurer of the Social Centers Corporation.

"I say, Mr. Cohen," said Reginald, "what about these dances—the turkey, the tango, and all the rest?"

BY 8.29 DOXIE WAS WAXING
THE FLOOR

"The turkey trot is absolutely taboo, along with the bunny hug," said Mr. Cohen. "But the tango may be danced in modified form; in fact, we will have a demonstration of it tonight by professional dancers. We are endeavoring to elevate the tone of dancing and to place the dance-hall business on a clean and wholesome basis. We want particularly to attract the girls from the dance halls where liquor is sold, evil acquaintances are met, and bad habits are formed. We have already opened a hall in Newark which has received the commendation of the civic authorities, and we also run one in Philadelphia. During the winter we will run dances here four nights a week and rent the hall the other three nights."

Mr. Cohen then gave Reginald a pink pamphlet containing a list of the rules for correct dancing and announcing a list of specialties, to include a "Snookey Ookum" party, a Coney Island night, a robbers two-step, and other marvelous accompaniments of a night of dance and song.

Suddenly the orchestra of eight pieces struck up a lively tune, and immediately hundreds of gaily dressed girls and happy-looking men glided onto the floor and were two-stepping with vigor and vim. But there wasn't even so much as a wiggle of the shoulders to suggest the turkey trot. Reginald found that the sight of so many swaying bodies was infectious. He looked about for an "introducer" but found none. He was just beginning to think he would have a poor time of it after all when way off in a corner he spotted Thomas Murphy, his father's office boy. Social barriers flew out of the window. Reggie almost embraced Tom, who was quite overcome by the unexpected and, in fact, quite unbelievable appearance of his employer's son.

"Don't ask any questions," said Reggie quickly. "Introduce me—that's all."

Tom grabbed him by the arm, and the two shied into a corner.

"What's your style, eh?" asked Tom.

"Anything at all, so long as she can dance. I'm not at all particular."

THE RULES PROHIBIT
CLOSE DANCING

As a matter of fact, Reginald was very particular—that is, with girls of his own set—but now it seemed that the one great desire of his life was to get on that floor and dance. "I know just the one," said Tom. "She sells perfume and such stuff at the Paris department store on Broadway." And before Reginald knew it, he was introduced and found himself dancing away across the floor. It was a waltz, and Reggie did know how to waltz; also, although he kept it dark under his shock of bushy red hair, he knew how to turkey trot and tango and all the rest. But Phil Post, censor, stood right in the middle of the floor. He wore a red carnation over a white vest, and although he seemed almost asleep with a sort of beatific look of delight, his keen eyes kept tabs on every couple. But there was little need. It was an awfully good crowd, Reggie thought, and the dancing was far more polite and graceful than that done on the previous evening at a fashionable society dance by girls of Reggie's own sort.

When the music stopped, Reggie took the girl, whose name was Delia O'Connor, to the soda fountain, where all sorts of wonderful mixed sundaes and frappés were served by white-coated attendants. Although it was probable they would never meet again, they sat and soda'd together.

"Where do you work?" asked Delia confidingly.

"I—I—that is—," and Reggie swallowed a huge piece of ice cream.

"I work at the Paris," said Delia, with the air of imparting a secret. "Perfume's my line. It's something fine, too. You smell the bottles day after day, and by and by you begin to think of beautiful flowers and shady paths and goldfish. And then, lately, I have been coming here at night. Before the Arcadia opened, we used to go to the hot and stuffy movie shows. But this has that beaten to a thirty-nine-cent bargain sale on a rainy Monday." She carefully stuck out one dainty foot and stretched a bit.

Reggie laughed.

"You're really dancing now," he said. "You know, the word *dance* comes from an old High German word, *danson* which means 'to stretch,' so that what you are doing now is really a sort of dance."

"Quit throwing them cashmere bouquets," said Delia, "and let's get to that two-step."

Reggie paid ten cents for the drinks and sailed forth on the waxen sea with Delia, as lightly and trippingly as two smart yachts tacking against the wind.

And so the evening wore on. Everyone had a glorious

time. The Arcadia was light and cool, the music was good, and best of all, the authorities were not too critical. One might even tango a little in a tame sort of way. The whole place was pervaded with an air of refinement and good behavior (and the men who are running it intend to keep it so). At last midnight came, the lights were lowered, and the dancers departed.

"Say, Mabel," said Delia on the way home, "I met the real frangipani sort of guy tonight. Uses three-for-a-dollar words and told me all about some Dutch dance. Never once tried to get fresh, either."

"It's the Arcadia," said Mabel, knowingly. "Everyone behaves there like a kid dolled up for Anniversary Day before the ice cream is passed."

And Reginald, back in his club, resolved to go to the Paris department store on the morrow and buy a bottle of perfume, a thing he had always considered one of the seven deadly sins of manhood.

IMPRESSIONS OF "TWINGELESS TWITCHELL" AND HIS
AWE-STRICKEN AUDITORS.

"Twingeless Twitchell" and His Tantalizing Tweezers

Shakespeare, whittler of epigrams, no doubt said something in some of his plays about teeth. If the truth were known beyond question, it would be found that an aching tooth in many cases has had far greater effect on the world's history than the rainfall on the eve of Waterloo (which, besides annihilating Napoleon's army, gave that dear Victor Hugo an excuse for several chapters of guerrilla philosophy in *Les Miserables*). This is a modern version of the Hugo tale.

A tooth! Its first appearance is hailed with frantic delight by the young mother and the assembled relatives; but how different its end! A book might well be written on the pathos of forgotten teeth. But after all, the purpose of this simple tale is to tell how not to suffer and not to disturb an otherwise quiet Sunday by bringing back memories of hours of dental inquisition.

But before we go any further, you must be told, just as you are always told at the beginning of every short story, that Reginald Delancey—whom you may remember meeting a few weeks ago at the Arcadia Dance Hall—was very much interested in a certain young woman whose name was Ikrima, as she was born in Turkey of a Mohammedan father who with all the wisdom inspired of a twenty-four-inch beard sent her to America to be educated. (The poor little perfumery girl with whom Reggie fell in love at the Arcadia had been abruptly deserted once Reginald discovered that she used a certain cologne, which he decided was a trifle too "racy.")

On Wednesday evening Reginald and Ikrima were strolling languidly down a street on the Heights.

"How slow the city is in summer," said Ikrima in that pretty, poutish way which always appeals to the biggest sort of men.

"Do I understand that you are seeking excitement?" asked Reginald, who always spoke in complete sentences as the result of four years at Harvard. "If I am correct in divining your intent, let us proceed at once to the next street crossing, where a somewhat large assemblage of persons leads me to believe that the unusual is either happening or about to happen."

So Reggie and Ikrima walked with stately tread to the corner.

A good-natured-looking man clad in white flannels was standing on a platform built upon the back of an ordinary touring-type automobile. At his side was a white enamel dentist chair, with all the necessary appurtenances; close by stood a table with medicine bottles and instruments that shone wickedly in the light of a flickering acetylene torch that sputtered vain protests at the darkness.

"My name is Twingeless Twitchell," the little man was saying with mighty dignity. "My business is pulling teeth, and I am frank to confess I am in it for the money I can make. There are two hundred thousand paid persons in this country to tell you how to take care of your souls, but as far as I know, I am the only man who tells you how to take care of your teeth. Yet there is as much brimstone contained in an aching tooth as there is in all the hereafter put together."

Groans rise from the crowd as each one remembers a sleepless night and a swollen face. But "Twingeless Twitchell" gives them no time to think. He holds them with his glittering instruments.

"No doubt you are wondering," he thunders forth, with a splendid gesture of deprecation, "just why I stand here upon this platform tonight discussing teeth. Well, I'll tell you."

He leans forward with the air of him who is about to tell the secret of the Sphinx.

"I'm here to collar the dollars," says Twingeless Twitchell. "I don't like the tooth-carpentering business." (Shudders run through the crowd at the expression.) "I don't believe in art for art's sake, not I. I'm the man that put the *dent* in *dentist* and the e's in *teeth*. And now I'm here to prove it. I invite anyone in this vast audience to step upon the platform and have a tooth extracted without knowing it. I know how to do it, believe me. I started to study teeth at the age of ten, and I've been at it ever since."

And Twingeless Twitchell, with a modest bow, stepped back and awaited all comers. A thrill of anticipation ran through the crowd. People in the el trains twenty feet above leaned out of the windows, entranced at the sight. A taxi went chugging by and then suddenly stopped, and a fat man alighted and joined the throng. Up above on a balcony of a beer garden, a lugubrious-looking German pointed out the enthralling sight to his stolid companion.

A chic French maid came tumbling forth from a nearby millinery shop, chattering volubly in her native tongue.

"It is the spirit of the arena," said Reginald learnedly. "They all want to see a human being suffer."

"Do you really think it's twingeless?" asked Ikrima, with a memory of a tooth she left in Constantinople when a little girl.

Then, on a sudden, a hush fell over the crowd. A man, collarless, red of beard and bald of hair, mounted the steps to the platform with his eyes fixed on the glaring lights, like a rabbit that has been charmed by the bead in the python's eye.

Twingeless Twitchell placed him gently in the chair and raised the torches a little higher. The unknown folded his hands resignedly over his stomach. Then the dentist took a formidable hypodermic in his hand.

"You see, ladies and gentlemen," he explained glibly, "I take this glittering instrument, filled with my specially prepared anesthetic, and do thus," and he injected a quantity into the unknown's gum. Then he grabbed the tweezers, and with all the finesse of a skilled surgeon performing for an academy of the world's best physicians, he eliminated the aching tooth.

The unknown arose with a dazed look in his eyes. Twingeless Twitchell handed him a card with his name and address printed thereon.

"Good evening," said Twitchell, escorting his first victim to the stairway. "Next!"

But Reginald and Ikrima waited to see no more. With hurried steps they left the crowd, wondering if they had actually witnessed a painless extraction.

"I say," said Reginald, after a little, "that's—that's not a bit nice. Just like washing one's linen in public and all that sort of thing."

"That may be true," said Ikrima, "but after all it reminds one that they ought to watch out and never let such a thing be necessary. I could never marry a man who didn't have a perfect set of teeth."

The following evening, Ikrima telephoned to Reginald. The butler answered the call.

"I want to speak to Mr. Delancey," said Ikrima.

"He's not at home," said the butler.

"Where did he go?"

"To the dentist," answered the butler, who was no diplomat.

But Ikrima, with very rosy cheeks, kissed the telephone mouthpiece at the other end.

Sad Scenes on Sentence Day in the Kings County Court

Casual students of Americana, who sit in their armchairs and read in their Bryce or Bagehot that the United States is the greatest respecter of law among the family of nations, should spend a morning in the Kings County Court. Their views on this question, of whatever nature, will be both confirmed and denied by the procession of shifty-eyed criminals who shuffle up to the bar. The great majority are American citizens, and therefore, their legal disrespect casts discredit on their citizenship. But they are also natives of Italy, Russia, and other countries beyond the seas, and therefore, the stigma is cast still further back to the land of their birth.

The County Court of Kings County in Part I is not a cheerful place. Once you have pushed back the green baize door, you are assailed with a sense of distress and disquietude. One involuntarily feels like gasping for breath. There is a musty odor, due partly to bad ventilation and partly to the very nature of the room itself. What sunlight filters through the windows is cut into strips by the heavy bars that grate the openings. The scene vividly foreshadows the noisome cell that awaits many who enter, and its atmosphere is as dismal as death.

There are jacks of all trades, and just as newspaper fiction has taught us unconsciously to think of long-haired actors and short-skirted chorus girls on the mere mention of the name of the street of the white lights, so this story will show, perhaps only too plainly, that the courtroom has its types. However exotic and picturesque they may be outside, immediately they enter the judgment hall, they sink at once to the norm of average insignificance.

The courtroom is always crowded with persons who have no business with the court. It is the great gathering place of loitering humanity. If a woman is tried for stealing a loaf of bread to feed her starving children, the back seats will be filled by strange nondescripts, who hover about like vultures to be in at the end. Let a sensational murder case be called, and the room is packed with restless bodies and inquisitive faces over craning necks. There will be the shuffle of feet in the corridors and a sordid undertone of suppressed excitement.

All these manifestations—and it needs no expert to say it—are merely the expression of a certain aspect and strain of the psychology of the average man. The Roman plebeian who threw his soiled toga over his shoulder and and leaned breathlessly to watch a horrible something transpiring in the dusty arena, was moved by no more cruel and inhuman passion than are many of the black-coated slinking figures that frequent our courthouses. Old attendants will tell you calmly that many of these persons attend every trial of importance without missing a single session. The incisive questions of the district attorney are to their ears the brisk staccato accompaniment to a dominant strain of harsh and sordid melody that jangles never so sweetly on their ears as when the keynote is one of discord and dissension.

Long before the hour set for the opening of the case, these curiosity mongers are in their places in the best seats the courtroom affords. Later there filters in a never-ending stream of lawyers, large and small, some looking as if they knew their business and others apparently knowing none. Many of them are mere boys scarce out of their teens, while others, seamed with the intricacy of years of legal tangle, enter with slow step and weary mien. And then there are just as many more who seem wide awake and intensely interested in all that transpires.

Suddenly the electric buzzer tells of the arrival of the judge, and spectators, lawyers, idlers, all rise to their feet, until His Honor has taken his place on the bench. Then there is a general settling down and a brief silence before the first case is called.

If you have any interest in the prison problem and wish to view the administration of justice in its essence, go to the County Court on the day the offenders are sentenced. The judge is preternaturally solemn, and yet he speaks to the guilty ones in a quiet, soothing manner, more like a father advising a wayward child than the embodiment of the law wreaking vengeance for disobedience.

During the trial the prisoner is often stimulated to baseless bravado by the attention that is focused on him because of his crime. He who has slunk down dark alleys and byways and hidden in forgotten cellars and almost inaccessible garrets is flattered into bravery when he faces a crowd of good citizens as the representative of what they, in ignorance, think of as the lurid "underworld." Imaginative writers picture him to a hungry public as a desperado of sorts, while in reality he is nothing but a furtive coward. But all this cannot fail to have its subjective effect, and no doubt he soon believes himself to have been and done all the wonderful things that have been so generously attributed to him.

But when the time comes to hear his sentence, each man is left alone to fight the battle himself. Behind the judge he sees the sky pierced by iron bars across the window, and the suggestion is all that is necessary to make him cringe. He forgets all that the newspapers say

PRAYING FOR THE MAN AT THE BAR WHO MAY NOT CROSS.

he has been, he knows his guilt, and he is afraid in his heart.

When the judge calls the case, the doors of the pen swing open and the prisoner enters, flanked on either side by blue-coated attendants who view the whole proceeding as a necessary part of the day's work. The first prisoner happens to be a swarthy Italian who, posing as a nobleman, swindled several society matrons out of large sums at bridge and then capped his career of crime with highway robbery and burglary. He is still dapper and well dressed, but there is a gleam in his eyes that is not pleasant to look upon.

"Have you anything to say why the sentence of this court should not be pronounced on you?" asks the judge.

The prisoner shifts his eyes to the ground and shakes his head.

"I sentence you to ten years in Sing Sing," solemnly intones the judge, and the little Italian with bowed head passes through the swinging doors to begin the long years of his imprisonment.

Most of the offenders are foreigners, but there is a sprinkling of native Americans in the crowd. The offenders are nearly all young, and their crimes consist for the most part of burglary, assault, the use of narcotics, and robbery, and sometimes of more serious lapses. Some have the shifty eyes, loose jaw, and weak chin of the criminal type, while others, clear of face and clean of limb, seem to revel in crime for the pure joy of the thing.

The greater part of them take their medicine stolidly with no sign of emotion; but occasionally a man will break out in a wild storm of weeping and implore the judge for mercy. Nine times out of ten this is nothing but a trick of the trade, and as many times it is unsuccessful. The tenth time it suffers the penalty of the nine false ones.

The external apparatus of the administration of justice in Brooklyn, prominent lawyers will tell you, could be visibly improved by a new courthouse, better police protection, and greater encouragement of the youth of evil sections to lead straight lives. For after all, the criminal, so often the direct result of environment rather than any inherited tendency to wrongdoing, possesses a very human, pitiful side to his warped character, which years at hard labor behind prison bars do not improve. The problem of the prison, brought again vividly to public attention by the recent outbreaks at Sing Sing, is only in its infancy. As the city grows still larger and its evil influences crowd our prisons to a still greater degree, the question will affect the social and in many ways the economic life of our time.

The People and the Sea; How They Get Together

Coney Island at the turn of the century could boast of being the best-known resort in the world. Named by the Dutch for its huge rabbit colony, Coney is a narrow sandbar five miles long on Brooklyn's southern coast.

Long before the amusements became available, Coney Island offered a favorite seashore resort, despite its crowded conditions, to those without the means to travel further out on Long Island. And with thousands of bathing suits for hire, Coney could accommodate a sizable portion of New York's beach-hungry population during New York's hot, muggy summers. Yearround residents of the Island reputedly never patronized the amusement parks.

As the 1920s approached, the character of Coney began to change as permanent homes increasingly replaced the seasonal communities, and Coney has never recaptured the glory of its early "Electric Eden."

Very different is life along the beach of Coney from what you have imagined it. You haven't seen it in pictures, you haven't read about it, it is even doubtful if you have found out for yourself the basic idea of the modern life by the ocean at the people's playground.

A never-ending line of pleasure seekers—extending from the very edge of the sea in which they would bathe—heads down the street and around the corner, intent on the interior of the municipal bathhouse.

The three policemen on duty would be of little use were it not for the nongraft spirit of some of the crowd. When a line breaker or a "double dodger" tries to get on the inside of the line, or when a double line begins to form, the man further down cries out, "Hey, officer, they're breaking in on you!" or "Break away there!"

Heads of families, with their dinners of fruit and impossible chunks of bread, stare about, clutching the hands of impatient children. There are the white-clothed attendants inside, pacing back and forth behind the grating like some dim beasts restless with the crowd's unrest. Ever through it all, the minds of them all are centered on the back door that will set them on the sand. They turn sideways, watching you as you stare back or feeling in their purses for a penny for the man who sells lemonade from a wash-boiler and presides over shining, skewered piles of pretzels.

The human side of it does not need words above two syllables; everyone is in their primer and fast getting down to their *A B C*.

And the dwellers from the wilds of Coney's "interior" who come down free of charge on "Shank's mare," already dressed in undress, clasp their raincoats or other garments of even greater interest about the edge. Others sprawl like flies on flypaper, as immovable, as tired, and twice as hot, or drink slowly and with extreme discomfort from warm bottles. Here and there may be seen tots drinking coffee from clamshells.

In an odd, homemade bathing suit, crouched under an improvised towel-tent, the mother of the crowd watches her Adonis of 1930 sprawl upon his baby back in an aimless, placid ignorance of space limits as with reckless, pawing hands he seems to be flinging defiance at the Milky Way, challenging it to produce better butter than he is now churning. It's the baby, the family's baby, and the world is all before him.

Attired in impossibly hot suits of worsted, with sweaters over their shoulders, the young men walk up and down, picking their way between the shapeless, huddled forms with the morning paper over their faces.

Out by the ropes the people diminish to half, to thirds, to bobbing red rubber with eyes beneath, back again to third, to half, to whole—dripping, happy, searching eagerly with their eyes among the "sandees" for their family, and looking for approval of their antics.

Thousands of souls have dropped their individuality with their clothes; the one man who hasn't, stands among them and covers his face with his hands, but his fingers are like a hay rack. He has taken in the material, it was full of interest; he has held life by the coattail and heard skeleton keys in its pocket.

Harmless pictures have been called bad; now reality is bad but harmless. Harmless is the woman who, walking about, frames everything she stands in front of; it is not her fault that she was allowed to walk too soon and that the sea has chosen her for a passe-partout. It is not bad in the man who sometimes eats his dinner with a band about his waist with the inscription *Won't you put your arms around me*? He's merely trying to find out what it feels like to be a cigar. Nor is it so wicked to lie in the sand and lean your head on a man you have said the eternal yes over and sent to bed two hundred nights running with a scolding. Nor is it wicked for a girl to cover a boy with sand. She's smiling now; and when someone else covers him for her, there will be tears. And harmless is the little scream that tells that someone has a grip on life as she is pushed under the waves.

Today the father of the family seldom comes in physical contact with his children. They don't cling about his neck and climb over his body and take fists full of hair and pull it as they used in the time of the cave man, excepting now of a Sunday morning. Bare of the brand of the avenue, sunless of many clothes, soaked with the sun and glare of the sea, a man lies down on his back and feels at last unembarrassed, when, a leg on either side of him, his two hands above his breast, his "kiddie" utilizes his chest for all the springing power that it is worth.

This is just a kind, glad feeling which is not a vacation; it is an awakening. They don't anticipate it until they are down in it, and when they get home they have lost it. It is only for those few hours that we don't count—when the cry of the policeman is ringing and the merry-go-rounds are singing to the children and the pretzel sticks are bare and your toes are wiggling in the sand or when the water creeps up with that funny, dry feeling just above its circle—that you realize it. And it's time to go home. The key number about your neck begins to feel like a pass to another edict when you're taking it off; there's sand down your back that you hadn't noticed, but you're going home, and your conclusions are coming.

This is the greatest adventure of them all; you hurry, you are pushed, torn, hurled; you are hemmed in by diverse parts of the sphere, at your left a German, at your

right poking you in your ribs a Dane, behind you a whiff
of garlic. Wailing children cling to dripping bathing suits; a
wet towel suddenly clasps you about the neck, and you
feel that you have been taken at a disadvantage, and you
are disconcerted to that degree that you search graphically
for a logical epithet in an unknown tongue while your
own is burning to be out.

Sitting astride all your good resolutions, you stare with
ferocious intent into the level eyes of a Swede who has a
better control than you ever had. Tugging, pulling, pushing, you reach your destination; but it's no use—you are in
the middle of the car, and you can't move. Above, the
stretching of the neck. Down the vista the home is calling
and the lights are low.

"The kid asleep, mother?"

"Yes."

"Are you tired, mother?"

"Very."

"Well, anyway, we had a good time."

And what a motley crowd of speakers go there to harangue the crowd: Socialists, anti-Socialists, Prohibitionists, revivalists, "lower renters," Socialist Labor men, and others of less importance.

Of course, this is not the only spot in all the city where street speakers hold forth. Up at Union Square there are similar meetings but almost exclusively by representatives of the I.W.W.; it is no forum in the true sense. Then, farther downtown, in the heart of the financial district, at the corner of Wall and Broad Streets, the "Bishop of Wall Street" for several years collected great crowds. For some time now the Bishop has not appeared there, but gradually some Socialist speaker has preempted his old place.

All things considered, it must be admitted that under the shadow of the statue of Franklin is the one place the curious mob can on successive days be regaled with talks on almost every subject that claims public attention.

It is only within the past three or four years that this forum has come into being. Before that it was used only just before election time by ardent campaigners. Then, one noon, a Socialist appeared on the scene. He attracted a big crowd. It was a success. Others followed him.

There was a time when a permit from the police was necessary for these street orators. But now one of the rules of the Police Department, issued by Commissioner Waldo a little over a year ago, recognizes the right of free speech in the street, provided that traffic is not interfered with, so that now anyone who wishes to air his views can take the stump by the Franklin statue. That is one of the few places where it is possible for a big crowd to congregate without seriously interfering with traffic, either vehicular or pedestrian.

Seldom is the crowd less than one hundred in number; often it passes the two hundred mark. Yet it is practically never necessary for a traffic policeman to interfere.

For a long time it was customary for but one speaker to hold forth at one time. It was figured that from eleven until two—which are the office hours for the forum—there would be opportunity for all to be heard who so desired.

THE OFFICE BOY PAUSES
BETWEEN BITES OF HOT
DOG AND WISDOM.

But one day a fiery young Socialist came along just at the noon hour—the most desirable time of all—and found a bewhiskered Prohibitionist on the stump. The former then promptly took up his position on the opposite side of the statue, and in a moment there were two rival floods of oratory being poured forth. It took but a minute for another crowd to collect. The rivalry grew more and more intense. The fiery Socialist edged slowly around towards his adversary; soon the two crowds had met, and the two orators stood almost side by side. First, one thundered forth that the stopping of the liquor traffic was the one way to save the world. Then the other told why Socialism is the only cure-all for the evils of the day.

The upshot of that memorable day was that quite frequently nowadays there are two speakers going at once.

One day recently the frequenters of the forum were given a real treat. An automobile drove up, decorated with yellow bunting; in the machine were three pretty girls waving VOTES FOR WOMEN banners. Immediately, there was a stampede. Everyone lost interest in how to secure lower rents; it was "all for the women." The suffragists addressed the crowd right from the machine, and they had the biggest audience of the season.

One of the best drawing cards at the forum is the revivalist who has mustered into service as an assistant a cornet player, who varies the monotony of ministerial admonitions with shrill solos—always hymns.

A few days ago one old revivalist so worked upon the emotions of the crowd that tears welled up into the eyes of all who were gathered there. He asked anyone in the crowd who had a mother at home who was being forgotten to pledge himself to write to her. Over a score of hands were raised in the crowd when the clergyman asked for those who would promise to send a letter back home to the forgotten mother.

Most of the speakers use a soapbox to talk from. The anti-Socialists, however, are more pretentious, and their speaker brings with him an improvised platform. He also brings little pamphlets which he sells.

Among the many religious exhorters, representatives of the American Bible Institute are the chief frequenters of the forum.

And through all these lectures, sermons, orations, exhortations, and elocutionary efforts of every sort, poor old

AMONG THE UNCONVINCED.

Ben Franklin stands helpless, a listener by force of circumstances.

The crowds still come, bigger each day—if possible—and the fame of New York's forum is spreading wider and wider throughout the downtown business section of the metropolis.

The Tingling, Tangling Tango As 'Tis Tripped at Coney Isle

Once, twice, thrice the cup of life has been emptied; once, twice, thrice the wheel has ceased to spin and run down; once, twice, thrice a girl, leaning across a polished table top, has learned that only a strip of wood separates her from the garden of love. And each time the cup has been refilled, and each time the wheel has been set in motion once more, and each time the maid finds that the garden has tears upon its flowers instead of dew; and yet over and over the same scenes are thrown upon the screen that is the heart.

So, at Coney, the night in a fashionable hotel sees the same play out to the end. Beneath the glare of the electric lights, under the seductive charm of the band behind the palms, the straight black eyes of Therese glow; the large, red mouth is smiling; the low-coiled hair gives to those eyes the magic that the undertow gives to the swell of the wave.

With her chin upon her jeweled hand, she watches the gliding, attentive waiters, the sense of the colored goblets, the red and purple and gold, slowly removing her gloves as manifold women remove theirs in the great mirrors. A queen in black, with a hat of a thousand feathers, she scarcely looks at what is laid before her. Her fingers never close over the stem of the wine glass; she holds it easily because she is certain of it, as one holds accustomed affection. Her eyes drift over the vivid red splashes of silent sea crab laid out upon its bed of green—the sea and the land united in their fruitfulness; the color scheme that art with hunger wrought.

But never one step did she lose of the dancers clinging, gliding, twisting, losing grip, coming together, mocking gravity with jeering feet, caressing with slurring slide, the man bowed above the little woman held close, like a butterfly pinned to his breast.

"What a gown," murmurs Therese above her glass, leveling her languid eyes, noting the bright spots among the smoking men, the telltale, high-thrust feather that shows some woman has consented to be someone's partner for the dance.

THIS DANCE LOOKS LIKE WORK.

"See that glide," the man behind the lights advises.

Semiprofessional, the dancers who specialize for the company are matched against the dancers who may have had some experience before the public. They are daring, yet within the bounds of propriety because they are daring with averted head; they make the dip in gowns that are meant for strolling and, because they see nothing, are aware of nothing.

Sometimes the proprietor walks close, and a couple learns that there are limits. So Therese learns, as with scornful steps she masters the wonder of the tango.

"Shan't we order a dinner?" he suggests, to get out of the uncomfortable position of a person who has been stopped in the excess of a wonderful motion; the catch in the music that makes the feet move. Therese nods, puts her hair back with crinkled white fingers, and moves among the drooping figures of women scattered through the room, hardly more substantial, hardly more resistant than the chiffon in which they are gowned. The cloth begins its mission just below the white throat and ends just above the jeweled slipper, the lace peeping out softly in sheltering folds. There are the sounds heard nowhere but at a pleasure resort: the popping of corks and the guarded, high laugh of the bored beauty, touches of vivid lightning striking across a shifting scene to the low thunder of the laugh of a man.

The professional dancers go back to their places and order refreshments. Those four old women admire the man dancer's dark face while he, with conscious eyes, sips sarsaparilla, one black pump just behind the other; trim, self-possessed, aware that adulation is being poured at his feet. The middle-aged women who have motors and painted cheeks are going to spoil him if they can; they lean upon his table, throwing back cloaks that reveal wondrous evening creations, and try to charm. The dancer, becoming bored, arises, walks among them a bit, drops a comforting word in this ear, smiles into that face, passes one white hand over the other, bows and steps out into the open as the band strikes up. Somehow the pink-gowned

HE BECOMES
BORED

girl who dances with him comes to him, as a sunset comes over and claims the mountain, and is borne away upon the shining floor.

"To think that he is a prize," murmurs Therese, who follows him with her eyes. "To think that in a moment the old woman in black and green will be dancing where that lovely young thing is now. Ah, here they come."

And come they do. The man behind the lights smiles, but he is not thinking; few people get a chance to think on such an evening.

"Shall we take a stroll?" inquires he, but she shakes her head. "I think I'm going to order some——" Her voice trails off as she listens to the bit of gossip behind her: "Gone to the mountains, won't be seen here for some time; ran off, you know, with the stenographer or something. . . . They say that she is thirty if she's a day, and yet she comes here. . . . The only man in the place who does not use perfume. . . . He's only here to get life on the wing. . . . Don't drink any more, you'll be sick." Therese shrugs her shoulders and thinks that perhaps her own conversation would make an interesting feature among those others. She throws this out as a starter:

"You have never taken me down the walk, where the spray reaches clear across. I think you are afraid."

"Afraid of what?" he insists.

"Afraid of getting—wet."

"I'm not afraid of anything," he says boldly. "I'm not afraid of spiders or policemen, of gowns with thirty thousand hooks up the back, or of the society notes in the evening papers; why, I'm not afraid of the floor manager."

She shrugs once more. "Give me my wraps," she says languidly and turns her eyes upon the room.

Perhaps the most interesting part of the evening comes in with the tired couples who have done the vulgar end of Coney and have been done by Coney in the end. Tired of the hurly-burly of the amusement parks, tired of the popcorn and the candy, tired of the moving pictures, sated with the sand and the sea, dragging listlessly, they come in, search out a table, languidly, with one hand, pushing the loop over the button of their evening wraps; the man just behind, turning his head from side to side; the child hugging its tiny doll. Utterly played out, they gamely drift across the floor, drop into chairs, and say something about "Oh, my, I'm fagged out!" Fumbling for matches follows. "What will you take, dear?" The light flutters, and smoke issues from a mouth already drooping from fatigue. "I could blow pillows instead of rings," he murmurs, and she orders soup. She is almost too weary to take interest in the gowns on show but not too weary to notice one or two of the most startling ones. The purple crepe with the red sash and the red-heeled

THEY COULD'NT HOLD OUT ANY LONGER

slippers catches her eye; she is being soothed, without knowing it; fashion is reviving her spirits, and his, too. He crosses his legs, leans back, and watches the dancers. It is the logical end of a day that has been too full.

The late arrivals get more out of it than these who are in for the opening notes of the orchestra, because they are conscious only of the contentment that comes after entrance and the worry of ordering the dinner and the removal of wraps; they are in on the dessert, as it were.

Half past twelve comes, and everyone is drifting toward the door: the stout woman on whom pearls are wasted, for they are lost in the folds of her neck; the thin, tall woman, who adds sharpness to her figure by steel buckles and diamonds; the men who are conscious that they paid for it all, aware that they are a part of the changing life at Coney, the Coney which a few years ago tolerated nearly any kind of dance and which now tolerates nothing that borders on the sensational.

"Let us walk in the moonlight upon the sand," Therese suggests, "where the waves look like sheer strips of broken beer bottles."

The old Coney is closing down; not stopping, mind you, but changing. We are tremendously interested to see what the evolution is going to be; we are interested to know how shocking society is going to become when it's proper.

No Turkey or Tango in Drag or Glide Dances

THE HESITATION SMILE BE-
FORE THE HESITATION GLIDE

With the exception of such widely famous dancers as the Vernon Castles, most professional dancing masters found their role changing almost overnight from performer to instructor, as the fall of 1913 brought hungry dance crowds back to New York. All the major hotels had adopted the "dancing tea," and the real dance fanatic could dance through luncheon, tea, dinner, supper, and all night long in the presence of chaperons. To accommodate the eager feet of novitiates, dancing classes were available nearly everywhere, many restaurant owners offering classes during the afternoon in the hope that a loyal public would return after dark. Though many managers continued to hire professionals to dance with partnerless patrons, audiences generally preferred watching skilled amateurs, whose skills they felt sure they could duplicate.

The need for dances to feed the craze created a boom market for choreography *instructors. As the turkey trot went out of style in favor of more dignified steps, a dozen others emerged to take its place, and the clever creations of Vernon Castle were eagerly awaited and immediately imitated.*

World War I inevitably cooled the dance fever, but it experienced a healthy revival even before the cessation of hostilities.

In an exhibition dance given for the benefit of the National Association of Dancers at the Hotel Shelburne, William Pitt Rivers worked out to their satisfaction two new dances, the "hesitation drag" and the "scroll glide."

There was a large crowd awaiting his demonstration. The interest grew as the dance progressed. It was the hesitation drag to begin with, and never before has there been such a gliding, sliding hesitancy; never before such a dreamy drag; never before such a culminating triumph as the whirl, à la pivot. It was supreme; it was new. People began to take notice; diners who had ordered soup were drifting away on a larger sea than a fragile tureen. Gentlemen who had ordered and drunk the sparkling drink were suddenly aware that other things sparkle besides the little leaping bubbles in the glass.

It had not been really so much a demonstration as a triumphant pulling down of the flag—the National Association's flag of protest; it was a jeer, a certain, smiling victory. The dance that had lifted the hands of the teachers in horror was working wonders with their feet; for it was a dance that renounced halos for high jinks, disapproval for complete surrender. They greeted it with open arms; that hesitating drag has roped them all in, and they hesitated no longer.

No less popular was the scroll glide. A dance that took one from side to side in perfect rhythm, a dance that never, in all its shifting steps, turned your partner's eyes from you, in a second was charged with being a conversational glide, for her eyes were always opposite, and the Boston turn was there. It was a new dance served up with an old acquaintance.

Both dances are a graceful rendering of those motions that usually seem to stay about the room after the dance has stopped: those angular thrusts of the foot that we remember after the foot has subsided under a table; those bent arms whose incapacity seems to be with you long after they have let go of a hand for a glass; those mistakes that show the novice or the person in whom grace never grew—these, more than anything else, perhaps, are the secrets of the successfulness of Mr. Rivers's combination dances.

"I do not always produce absolutely new dances," he said. "I watched the dance as society was dancing it yesterday, that I might perfect it today for many tomorrows. That emotion, that something that they all feel but put forth very crudely, I work over till I get grace into the ungraceful—there is the secret.

"Music helps me a lot to get the new steps. I thought of the one-step for the whims in that composition 'Too Much Mustard'—there wasn't any dance that would go to its peculiar time, so I worked out the one-step with that as my inspiration. Sometimes a funny walk matures into a pretty dance. But it is inspiration always that perfects the hours of struggle."

"Is there any particular month in which inspiration flows more limpidly than another?"

"Well, I don't know. Of course, there is a certain impulse in the air, a certain spur to achievement when the dancing season is at its height, but I think a new dance is about as willing to be born in December as June. There are some things that you cannot freeze, and dancing is one of them."

Part Victory, Part Defeat at Suffrage Aviation Meet

There have been a great many meetings of one kind and another to further the cause of woman suffrage, but perhaps there has never been such defeat and such victory all at the same time as that of September 5 and 6 at the suffrage encampment on Hempstead Plains.

For the grandeur of the illuminated monoplane flights, there was an untraversed sky; for the outpouring of the golden flood in Mineola after the suffrage meeting and the speeches by Miss Willis and Miss Craft, only $1.50 was collected; for the demonstration of the growing suffrage fervor, only fifty of the five hundred expected appeared to march; for the spectacular bravery of "the only woman aviator," only a slip of a lass in brown who stood among the flowers and refused to rise to the occasion and to a higher strata of air. In like manner, Miss Willis "backed down" and chose the megaphone rather than the glories of a flying machine.

And yet, who shall say that in two scant days there was not enough going on to live and thrill for?

Early in the afternoon yesterday, the parade was started. It may have been because the rounding up of the members was done hastily that there was such a small number in the line—only fifty in all including Mr. Laidlaw, who, we must admit, kept the only perfect time to the beating of the drum, and Mrs. Sadie McKay Keene, the woman painter, who wore overalls and was proud of it and a straw hat. It was evident from this small number that the polo game and the national golf championship had taken the public attention. There might have been fifty-one in the parade, but the cake could not be left, though the money box could be held under the arm.

And then at 4:00 P.M. came the first exhibition of flying. Heinrich in his own machine made two flights, returning each time within a few feet of the ropes. After him, Lieutenant Wald of the German army made an ascension, and shortly after this the trouble began. Miss Willis with her megaphone announced the start of Mrs. Mary Simms, and everyone waited with bated breath for the start of "the only woman suffrage aviator." Stooping down, she pulled the strap to her puttee a little tighter, jumped the ropes, and paused, a brown, saucy little figure, smiling and shaking her head.

"Not today, I guess," she said, "that machine isn't well yet. Two solid days we have struggled over it, down on my knees to her, but not my hat off to her, for she's no lady who refused to rise to the occasion and make her bow."

This was broken up by the auctioning off of five cakes left over from the sale held in the open parlor, where women drooped in chairs like wilting, ungardened China asters or ate fruit languidly. There was a hot competition between the Colonel and the Corporal, respectively, Kraft and Kaltschken. Miss Kraft won out at $1.50, the hesitant aviator lass got the second cake at fifty cents, and Mr. Laidlaw bought up the remaining three and passed them around.

Miss Ruth Law, who was present and who had been advertised to ascend in her own machine, said that she only flew on contract, and as no money had been put up she was not going. Someone offered her real money, and she accepted, taking a passenger in the person of the private physician to John D. Rockefeller. She made several spectacular dips toward the crowd watching below—such daring dips that antis got mixed with the most ardent pleaders, and there was a small stampede. Miss Law seemed pleased at the fear she could put into the crowd and raised both hands and clapped them, though her feet were straight out before her and taut as the wires of a toasting fork.

The illumined flights were produced with the Christmas-tree electric bulbs draped over the cars. Later there was a bonfire built by the men. In its leaping light, that died down to rise again like the breathing of a sleeping man, those who sat about the fire forgot to reach any farther down into the theories and clasped their knees. Then came laughter and a pan of apples baked to the best suffrage ability.

The members were chosen for the First Assembly District of Nassau County early in the day, the meeting being held upon the "old country road" just without the park gates. Though it was to be strictly private, reporters were in on it, even though Flora Gapen seemed displeased.

It seems that they got more fun than glory, more of a vacation than money, and if the proceeds of the two days are to go for a car for the use of the New York State Association of Women Suffrage Workers, as stated, they will have to change their minds and get a go-cart.

"Our School's Open Again; We're Glad to Get Back"

When autumn shadows throw their patterns across the land, they are not the images of fragile, dying leaves, not the bared arms of lofty elms, not shadows of a fading summer; but swinging shapes as of books upon a strap, of round and square boxes held under an arm, of hurrying little people heading toward the nearest school; imaginary shadows of benches with two folded arms atop; of back-thrust legs that embrace a chair with the fervor of anxiety. Yes, school's in, vacation is over, but there is going to be trouble for rules for a month to come.

We all think we don't love it, our school, and the smell of books, as we do that other odor just at the bend in the steps leading down to mother's kitchen: the smell of cooking meat, of peppermint candy, of gingerbread. We all think that school is a good place for summer to pass over. But what of that look that came up into your eyes as you said, a few days before it opened, "They are cleaning the windows."

Boys who have never been to school and girls, too, are pushed into the outer office with the left maternal hand; always the boy holds his hat by doubling up his fist, hanging the hat upon it, and drops his head to the same angle. The halls are so long and so dark, and the other boys stare so, and the desks are so worn and shiny.

HIS FIRST DAY.

Sometimes it does not seem so bad when the father comes along; but for some reason, as yet undefined, he refuses to come in and up to the desk. He gives the child a little push and melts into the woodwork—or so it seems to the child who, if it be a girl, turns her head from side to side, letting first one long pigtail slide off one shoulder, then the other pigtail off the other shoulder, in her vain endeavor to discover and get comfort from the discovery of that parent who should have been the pillar at this time.

Out of the endless flow of accustomed children, like scrap-drift thrown upon the shore, the little new child is seen, first here, then there, always conspicuous as she comes in on the wave of these old-timers, conspicuous in that she does not know what turns to make or what forms to appropriate. At last the wave subsides. High and dry, like a little house on long, lean spiles, the new child sits, a pencil to its lips—its legs dangling.

The benches are full, and the room is deadly still; the last bee of summer is buzzing in the warm sunshine of the window; blocks of light fall on the printed pages—surely a good excuse for inattentive eyes. All the girls and boys have their chins upon their hands, all the books held open by the elbow. Everyone is profoundly conscious that they are studying hard, and then suddenly that sense of a watching eye upon them is borne to each simultaneously. It is in the room and known to every member as swiftly as scandal is known in a little town. Every pair of eyes leaves the pages, every book, unfettered, slowly drops back its leaves like so many good intentions, the chin comes out of the palm, all at the wrong time.

There is someone watching; the official eye is upon them and has caught them with their minds wandering. In the shadow of the long, cool hall, the officer of order and peace walks up and down, his hands in his pockets. Back and forth, back and forth, now under the picture of fallen Rome, now under the garden scene in Venice, now under the architectural splendor of Notre Dame, before the bust of Lincoln and the head of Washington, and so back again, in order. But his eye, no matter if it is turned away from you, knows just what you are doing and seems able to foretell what you are going to do.

At twelve, the children from the kindergarten and the high school alike leave their benches or chairs and head for the garden, if they bring their own lunch, or to the basement where there is food for all who wish to buy.

At the ringing of the bell, from all parts of the building as in a fire drill, young America comes, under full sail— mostly taffeta four inches wide—hurrying to get into line; and the girl who gets on the wrong side for the hot foods and the sandwiches calls out to her chum, who was wiser, "Grab a tongue sandwich for me, Mary; I've got your frappé."

The line moves slowly, past the counter filled with hot drinks, meats, and salads. Sometimes a girl will try to break in on the line by dodging under the ropes; but the head teacher is there, and a reproof is in order. With their loaded trays they pass out at the door where the cashier is stationed; and she, with appraising eye, says "Thirty cents please—next!" And so on into the hall and the room where the long tables await them, balancing a tray in one hand

and a bowl of soup in the other and a roll between the teeth.

It's a guess that Virgil has their minds at 11:59, but it's a certainty that chicken gumbo has it at 12:00.

The boys, on the other hand, take the lunch hour for a sort of topsy-turvy period, and seldom does a boy eat the lunch his mother has put up for him. Swapping is the pasttime, and a loaf of bread made on the upper terrace at Flatbush may find its consumer six to ten blocks below.

It takes some time to get the school in smooth running order. Classes have to be graded and new children tried out. Vacation has to be conquered, the mind has to learn its daily task. A month from now everything will be going with machinelike precision. There will not be any stopping to powder the nose in the hall just one second before recess is over, there won't be any shuffling with papers, and there won't be any uncertainty as to the right room and the right desk. There may be less excitement, but there's bound to be more order. The older girls will leave enough of the noon-hour to spend in taking a stroll about the grounds or sitting upon the benches within the iron fence looking toward the open street. City flowers caged with city grass.

It is part of that system that brings the children up together in close companionship to the age of fourteen or so to divide them then for the period of high-school life. The boy and girl who were sweethearts at eight look at each other through the bars of a fence; the boy who used to play their turn at marbles, buy them candy, and fight the other boy who was "sassy" is growing into the dignity that comes with long trousers. If sometimes they cross the breach for a few blocks, and he escorts her to the gates, they are both very self-conscious, for the other boys may be looking—especially that kind of young lad who is generally at liberty to give information on any subject.

Happy in their dances, in their reading clubs and sewing circles and the excursions to museum and park, singing, back to the green-paneled wall of the auditorium as pretty jewels undetached from their cards, tall girl and slender girl alike are hovering about the teacher. The boys in line for gymnasium work, the stamp of a hundred feet in drill, the swift "right about-face" order and the swift compliance; the single boy run, and the basketball, the horizontal bar, and the wrestling mat; the yard in which to play at marbles or discuss regulation of politics; the roof garden with its

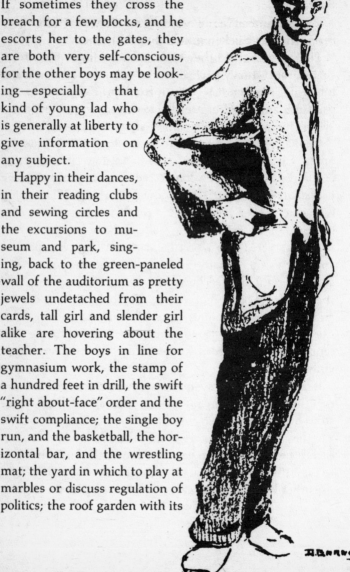

potted flowers and the netted ceiling. The memory of all this—and yet someone says that we don't love our school.

But remember that picture—how it always hung there, from the first day that you decided it was out of drawing—of that bust and that exact same missing tile in the stairs. The school in which you made that friend who, in after life, sent over the jelly and lent you the spoons. The old familiar books, the lockers, the teacher growing a little grayer, the companions a little wiser.

Well, perhaps we don't love it, but somehow we're glad to get back.

Seventy Trained Suffragists Turned Loose on City

As president of the National American Woman Suffrage Association, Carrie Chapman Catt was America's best-known advocate of the American woman's right to vote. Disapproving of the violent tactics used by militant suffragists in Britain led by the Pankhursts, Catt stressed working within the system and traveled all over the country and the world to speak to activist groups. When she opened a two-week school program to work for the 1915 election, when a vote on the suffrage issue was expected, 150 women from seventeen states enrolled in the school at 180 Madison Avenue.

After the passage of the 19th Amendment gave American women the vote, Catt organized the League of Women Voters. Though British women were granted basic suffrage two years earlier, it was at a considerable cost of life and suffering, and they did not receive equal voting rights until 1928. Catt later worked for the peace movement and died in 1947.

And now comes the suffrage school.

In how many ways has education been given us! In elementary schools, in high schools, in business and technical schools and in colleges. We have pored over books and maps; we have spent the daylight and burned the midnight electric light in years of toil, with the hope of becoming good citizens.

Then came along an eminent professor who declared

that books, taken by the yard, would do more for human education than all the colleges in creation. We thought, at the time, that this was (speaking of education) "going some." Here was a chance to become a Solomon in a month or so.

Now even this record is broken; for along comes a suffragist who opens a school for suffragism and promises a presidency in two weeks.

One may be very optimistic and still not care to go to school again at the age of—let us put it mildly and say— thirty, and so the reporter tried to get the information concerning this suffrage course over the phone. The truth was, there was a fear in the reporter's mind that the presidential chair might be thrust upon one who was at that moment unprepared.

A voice from East Thirty-seventh Street said, "Hello?"

"Hello," quivered the reporter.

"Hello!"

"Hello!"

"You have the advantage over me," the reporter said, wearily, and hung up the receiver.

It had to be done at close range!

Among seventy or eighty students there are bound to be some high-minded formulas for life. In fact, the thresholds to some minds are so high that one has to learn to hurdle to get into their rooms of thought. High-mindedness is necessary if in two short weeks you are handed the country; if in two short weeks you learn suffrage from the beginning to the end—the rise of it and what the suffragists call the fall (which came in '53, when a woman was first prevented from voting); if you are capable of governing and controlling history in two weeks. Oh, well—remember that all disasters happen in a very short space of time. Fire overtook Rome, Pompeii became black crape on the door handle of the future in an hour, and it took such a pitifully short time for the *Titanic* to sink beneath the sea.

Mrs. Carrie Chapman Catt, instructor in suffragism, has a fine confidence in individualism. She says that to get your public you must first get yourself. "Organize yourself," she says, "and the country will organize." As she spoke, seventy-odd students developed "that student face," leaning over their notebooks whereon burns the flaming truth of futurism.

"How shall we get the crowd?" inquired a timid student, who had been rounding up an obdurate husband for thirty years.

"That's the simplest question in the world to ask," says the lecturer, "but it's a hard one to answer. But first, never wear a dress that shows your feet in front. Never let the audience carry away a mental picture of a pair of silhouetted pedal extremities.

"Second, never hold a militant pose; don't strike out at your audience with a fist that has done duty as a biscuit molder. People may like to have their minds molded but not their anatomy.

"Third, do not dress in spots; yes, I mean spots. If you look 'giggery' to the audience in front of you, they are liable to go wobbling home down the middle of the street. You can get just as intoxicated over a dizzy dress pattern as over a pint of Twelve Star. Fourth, don't wear hat or gloves; the hat shadows your face, and the gloves veil your soul."

"But what," queried another anxiously, "is there left to say to the public? Everything for suffrage has been said."

"Not so," declared Mrs. Catt and Miss Hay in one breath. "To demonstrate it, come over here, stand upon this platform, and address—well, let us call this an audience from the factory world. Proceed!"

Trembling, and white of face, the unfortunate victim stepped upon the platform. Terra firma had never been less firm, stars and stripes had never occupied so much of her mind. Ideas had never thinned out to such a wraithlike simplicity.

"We want the vote—because we no longer want to be the clinging vine. You know the tighter the vine clings the deader is the oak. You see, the best thing to do is to attend to your garden. . . . If I should die before I wake—I couldn't possibly be more frightened—oh," a swift hand to the breast, and a would-be future ruler dodged to her seat.

"Very good," Mrs. Catt approved, "but, students, what should you say in criticism of her method of delivery?"

"Perfectly dear," said the students.

"Not the right answer. The voice was thrown into the air too much. Speak out, my dear, and you'll gain confidence."

Not only has this suffrage school taken up the question of getting the crowd, but it has laid out a few rules to pursue after the crowd has been rounded up. The alpha and omega of the suffrage creed is: Never hold a meeting, no matter how small, without taking up a collection!

This was carried into effect when the "tryout" speeches, in all the Brooklyn parks, were indulged in by the timid students; and though at some points the scheduled speakers were absent, there was a regular from the district to make up for the disappointment the public felt when there was no one to smile over.

The suffragists meant to do it up brown in the short time that they set for the term. There was first the daily morning session. In the afternoon there was voice culture and, in the evening, lectures at the Hotel McAlpin.

Mrs. Catt said that men would be welcome at these lectures and would be admitted to the school. The men did not seem to think so. At least, there was a marked reticence on their part, only one man being seen, on the horizon, in the entire two weeks.

When asked if the school had come up to her expectations, Mrs. Catt paused. She took up the little silver hammer with which she proclaims golden silence. At last she said, hesitatingly, "We don't know what we expect."

So what is the public to expect? Remember, there are seventy-odd perfectly good suffragists, trained to the hilt, loose in our city.

Arbuckle "Floating Hotel" to Be Closed

When millionaire John Arbuckle died in 1912, he left no will and the fate of his favorite enterprise, the Jacob A. Stamler *floating hotel for girls, in the hands of his next of kin. Barnes's article in September 1913 may have helped the hotel's impoverished residents convince Arbuckle's sisters not to close the hotel. However, the identical controversy arose the following August. The* Stamler *was finally closed for good by the Fire Prevention Bureau in November 1915, influenced by memories of the* Slocum *disaster in 1904, one of the worst maritime tragedies in U.S. history. Over 930 persons died, most of them German women and children headed for a day's outing on the Sound, when their excursion steamer, the* General Slocum, *exploded and burned on the East River. Within view of Manhattan residents, the captain lost his head, steering for North Brother Island when a quick landing nearby would have saved hundreds of lives. Many of the victims were found to have drowned because the life preservers they clutched had rotted aboard ship.*

There is a poem tacked up on the bulletin board in the *Jacob A. Stamler*—the floating hotel moored at the foot of East Twenty-third Street, Manhattan—which was a few days ago a sincere tribute and today stands as a pretty good bit of irony:

We honor the man who lends a hand
  To those you seldom heed:

The city's toilers, whose lives are crushed
  By Capital's selfish greed.

John Arbuckle was the man who lent the hand, while he was living, and intended that the helping hand should still continue to give hope when he was gone. The irony comes in the withdrawing of that hope.

The sisters of Mr. Arbuckle are drawing the curtain on his dream, closing the hotel that for seven years has been a refuge for hardworking, poorly paid boys and girls.

Is it any great wonder that instead of spending their evenings over the piano or the game table, this family of about a hundred should gather together and talk over this, to them awful, change? The sudden withdrawing of support has left them so dazed that they cannot even plan a winter home.

"If Mr. Arbuckle's sisters had been coming down here twice a week," said Mr. Sheeley, the manager, "and mixing with the girls and the boys, it would never have come to this. If they had shown the interest that their brother did, that little bulletin would never have put fear into human hearts.

"Mr. Arbuckle came down here twice a week and took his Sunday dinner with the crowd. His sisters may be acting under the impression that there is a better form of social work, but there is not as far as I can see. Above all, Mr. Arbuckle had the right idea of helping the poor, not by giving them charity but by giving them a chance. He bought this ship just after returning from a sea trip; he paid around $160,000 for it and spent to maintain it $15,000 a year. Originally, he had it moored down by the

Battery, in pretty deep water, moving from one spot to another; but on the day of the *Slocum* disaster he made a change, and since then the ship has been kept in dock. From the first there were plenty to make a large family. At $2.80 per week there was no vacant room, and while this does not pay the total cost of maintenance, it keeps the self-respect alive in the poorest. Self-respect meant more to Mr. Arbuckle than anything else.

"If he had known that a day would come when the old ship would be sold and his plans for helping the laborer— well, he would never have said, as he did say many times, 'If I should die today, this hotel would go on just the same.' Thinking that, he left no provision.

"The boys and the girls are not asking, nor expecting, that the hotel will be kept open for another seven years; they are only asking that it be kept open till next June. All the best cheap boarding houses are filled at this late date, and they are panic-stricken at the idea of leaving now that the winter is coming on."

When asked how he himself took the change, Mr. Sheeley shook his head. "I don't like it at all. In the beginning, I was not very enthusiastic, but it makes a lot of difference when first one girl, then another, comes to you and gives you her pay envelope to mind; and when they come to you and ask your advice about buying a new dress. My wife never cared for it, and she will be glad to go. She is the only one who welcomes the change; it's been kind of severe on her. We've been a pretty big family and a mighty happy one. If a girl came here really down and out, without a cent but with a good story, she got her room and her meals cheerfully and was treated just like the other boarders; but she was not allowed to rest on charity for a minute. She had to keep moving and find a job, and sometimes it was remarkable to see the difference in a girl in two or three days. From a dejected, ambitionless person, she became as spirited and as fully aware that there was a world to conquer as the next one.

"You should have been here the first night they heard of this. They all stared at the bulletin for a few minutes, then the girls started crying—some of them—and the boys tried to cheer them up. But through it all the only words you heard were, 'Where shall we go?'"

F. A. Higgins of Brooklyn, the Arbuckles' attorney, said in answer to questions: "Mr. Arbuckle's sisters, Mrs. Catherine Jamieson and Miss Marie Arbuckle, have not made public their reasons for discontinuing the hotel started by their brother; however, the main reason can be found in their different views on charitable work. They never approved of the floating hotel, and they do not approve of the present conditions. They do not like the idea of young girls having to walk through that district at night coming home from their work. It is a rough, dirty section of the city, and they think no girl should be forced to walk through it. The sisters, however, will not cease their charitable work."

"Have they made any answer to the petition of the hotel guests?"

"No, not as yet."

"Do they intend to?"

"That I could not say."

As a farewell event, the guests of the floating hotel have set apart October 4 for a barn dance aboard the *Jacob A. Stamler.*

The Home Club:
For Servants Only

Perhaps there's nothing new under the sun, but this new thing deals with a club anchored in ether and drowned in the shine of the Milky Way. There may be nothing new under the sun, but some people are capable of putting speed to stardust and perspective to our planet. It's not what's under the sun that counts but what's under the skin, and, well——

Mrs. Ransom S. Hooker has put a railing around comfort and kept it all on her side of the fence. She has opened a club called the Home Club at 203 East Seventy-second Street, "for servants only."

We don't know just what this is going to mean. At present it means a parlor where friends may come, a diningroom for members, and room for some few to sleep. At present it means that, of a winter evening, dancing will be in order and singing and other entertainments will liven the jaded worker. What it may eventually develop into, we dare not speculate on.

At least, even now young men may call and sit on the parlor lounge with a club member, all under the sympathetic gaze from the back of a sympathetic chaperon's head. Then, there is an ever-widening knowledge of the mistress. Each servant discusses what her mistress has left undone on the day. Around the employment world there goes a chain of your weaknesses, madam mistress: what you are goes on before you, for now the story of your character is in the hands of club members, who discuss your life as you live it day by day.

Why a servant's club? Why a peanut gallery at the opera is equally pertinent. The answer: Because as a paste diamond needs some kind of a setting to make it a brooch, so a servant must have a club to be a progressive.

We are beginning to wonder whether a servant girl hasn't the best of it after all. She knows how the salad tastes without the dressing, and she knows how life's lived before it gets to the parlor floor.

Number 203 East Seventy-second Street means dancing and singing and rest for an hour and a phonograph and pictures to look at. If she's out of work, it means a room for two dollars a week and board optional and, best of all, the chance to get acquainted with fifty other members. This number, though it sounds quite large, is 200 short of the paying mark—or in other words, 200 more members are needed to put the club on a paying basis. It never has paid; that is one reason why it has moved from Lexington Avenue, where from last November it has been run along the present lines.

Mrs. E. B. Hall admitted that anyone desiring to donate linen to the club would be considered a patron saint. Also, bric-a-brac and books are requested from interested persons who have more than they want. Mrs. Hall only made two or three specifications: no Shakespeare and no Darwin. The most urgent need seemed to be pictures, with frames, of an uplifting character. Art students in their first year are requested kindly not to submit specimens, as some of the inmates are of a delicate and nervous temperament. A good suggestion would be a study in cabbages or a panel of peas.

There are a few rules that members have to conform to, and one among them is that no late hours are to be kept unless Mrs. Hall, the chaperon, knows where the member in question is. If she is out to the theatre with her young man, all well and good; but if she is found anywhere other than the place she said she would be, that member discovers that there is one bell in East Seventy-second Street that she may not ring.

Five dollars a year, the membership fee, does not seem to be felt as too much by the girls. Mrs. Hall says many of them have paid the five down at once without waiting a month between the installments; then, too, she says the girls that become members are the kind that always seek companionship of a better sort. If they were not a better class, they would never enter a club, preferring to spend their days off outside and their evenings in some cheap amusement house.

Mrs. Hooker intends to enlarge the establishment just according to the demand. In the beginning the club grew out of a belief she had that here was something needed, a demand that had not been answered, not properly and competently supplied. It was the working girl's chance, a chance for her growth, a chance for her to feel the responsibilities of a club life, for the many responsibilities she has.

To enter the club there have to be references of the best kind offered, and a girl has to look right as well.

This life makes a woman kinder to her kind, for she has a chance to learn her sister worker, not from a doorstep capacity but that close companionship that comes from a cup of tea and a dance together or out of an evening over a magazine or a chat in a dusky corner.

Mrs. Hall was asked how she liked the responsibility that was put upon her shoulders at the opening of the club.

"I don't mind it because they are no trouble to me, and so I haven't anything to mind. A servant girl has learned, before she comes here, not to be a care; that's part of her job. Of course, I am worried sometimes over some situation that arises, but after all, the members are as capable of looking after themselves as any other adults. Being servants had merely made them a little less troublesome, a little less self-conscious, and so a little less liable to take offense than ordinary young women."

We do not regret, we who have never been able to have servants, we who have to get down silently on our knees and scrub the floors behind drawn curtains. We do not regret, we who cook and darn and sew alone for our family, small or large. We do not regret when, as we say, this happens and the Home Club has called and been answered and there is no maid to serve tea.

We do not regret that sometimes actions go against aprons and that a fire is forsaken for a flame.

Veterans in Harness

In the fall of 1913 Barnes conducted this series of nine interviews for the Brooklyn Daily Eagle with elderly men still at their jobs. Most had arrived in this country in the great wave of immigration during the late nineteenth century; most avowed a work ethic seldom heard today; only one would find no employment today in his chosen profession—"engineer" Tom Baird, fire-stoker on a ferry line.

For these men, many of the great events in the life of the city were within recall. New Yorkers universally felt a great pride in the construction of the Brooklyn Bridge from 1869 to 1883, the first steel-wire suspension bridge in the world and the longest suspension bridge at the time of its completion. Designed by a father and son named Roebling, the Bridge stood as a landmark in time against which other events took their perspective. It was frequently eulogized; critic James Huneker described it as "a huge harp ready for the fingers of some monstrous musician."

Many also remembered the well-publicized trial of Brooklyn clergyman Henry Ward Beecher for adultery in 1875. Called the Shakespeare of the pulpit, Beecher had a distinguished reputation as a reformer—fighting for woman suffrage and abolition—and when a hung jury yielded no verdict, the public decided with remarkable unanimity that Beecher had been wrongly accused.

The building of the elevated trains had brought more noise, more bustle, and for some more business; economic "panics," arriving every twenty years or so, had ruined livelihoods and shaped lives. Many great men had shared their histories with the city, including Seth Low, mayor first of Brooklyn, then of New York, and president of Columbia University for eleven years.

Postman Joseph H. Dowling
Forty-two Years in Service

Scene: The post office on the corner of Washington and Johnson Streets. The lights are low and burn a steady blue. In the dun, the forms of moving mail carriers talking in low tones together among the great bulk of the mailbags. Upon tall stools the clerks nod over the ink bottles and the stamps, the grated window throwing patterns on the wall, the gentle murmur of a great city putting on its nightcap outside.

Enter Joseph H. Dowling, the oldest mail carrier in service, seventy-seven in April; short and gray, his official cap pulled over his head, the empty mail pouch over his shoulder. He looks around and slowly sits down, taking his cap into his hands, the mailbag—wherein an hour before a world lay undistributed—slipping down. He speaks.

"Forty-two years in service and never a sweetheart in all the blocks I've walked. Married fifty-four years, twelve years ahead of the mails," he laughs. "It spoiled a good deal of the romance of the road, but thank the mercies that she's been spared to me along with the children—the children, and the oldest is fifty-three.

"And the changes that I've seen," he goes on. "Why, I helped build the Brooklyn Bridge. I stood under the bed of the East River and bossed men—foreman with human lives under me—and Lord, how the city grew when she started. I'd go down it seemed between tea and dinner, and when I came up they had built a block."

He passes his hand over his eyes. Back in a darkened corner a letter slides noiselessly down upon the pile of the uncollected.

"I remember the time when there were no stages in Brooklyn, and no cars, and it seemed to me as though at the reckoning there would be very little complication with nothing more intricate to record than the birth and the death of a few people who never dreamed of competition. And then the cars came and the elevated went up, and then I was satisfied that there was going to be a reckoning hereafter that would involve a lot of rapid calculating.

"In the beginning I used to listen to the wheels running overhead, and I said, 'At last the world has a second floor.'

"In 1871, the year I came into service, there were only forty carriers to cover Brooklyn, running routes from the East River to Stone Avenue, from Flushing Avenue to City Line, and only two deliveries a day. At this time there were not over seventy-five men in the office—officials, carriers, and all. The post office was then a wood frame building just below the Eagle Building. Out of them all only two are left who started with me, and they are still serving as clerks.

"I served alone a route that eight men cover now; my usual delivery was about twenty-five hundred pieces. I served under nine postmasters—Samuel Booth was the first. Those were hard days, and we got fourteen hours a day, till the eight-hour day came along and gave us a second excuse for going down on our knees. Still there were some blocks to the route that we would not have taken away from us about Christmas time.

"I'm a Yankee through and through, as my folks for five generations were born, as my father before me was born, in Brooklyn, and I've lived here all my life. I used to go to school back in Adams Street, studied a map that hadn't any Brooklyn on it above a few blocks. Where the fountain now stands in front of the Borough Hall, they were building a prison, and as children we used to play hide-and-seek among the incomplete cages."

He looks about him. In the dim, blue light the mail carriers, still young, are preparing to go home. He does not see them; he has gone back to the years in which their fathers lived.

"You talk of temperamental people; there's nothing so temperamental as the mailbag. You people who know nothing of it do not understand." He touches it with reverent fingers. "Here, in this, have laid letters that spoke of love and letters that held broken hearts. When I was five minutes late in my rounds, five hundred lovers held their breath and five hundred sorrows waited to be born." He shifts in his chair.

"I wonder just how many people realize how short a time it takes to see a street full of new faces. Some blocks keep the families for generations, and then again in six months you are taking mail to strangers. It seems a bit funny when you miss the photograph that used to hang just inside the hall, the photograph of the mother in the old country. You get to connecting numbers to people—like convicts it seems—and then suddenly you realize that the number that you have seen upon the ceiling as you lie awake in bed has another family attached to it, and you have to reconstruct all your thoughts to fit it.

"Well, I have just three interests in life now: the health of my family, the coming of the pension, and continuance of the widow and orphans fund. I'm president of it, and I think about that more than anything else."

The room is empty of life, but still the blue lights burn on, and the mailbags throw shadows across the floor.

He rises, his hat in his hand. "The saddest thing in life is the bringing of the black-bordered envelope." He nods. "Aye, the black envelope. And the brightest thing is my home."

He steps out into the night.

Conductor "Kid" Connors
Forty Years Ringing Up Fares

Scene: The tracks along Meeker Avenue. Year: 1913. Time: 3:30, any day. (Incidental remark: It was some job getting Connors on the run.)

John Kelley, "Kid" Connors's motorman, comes along on the front deck of a trolley car, power and brake handle in hand; old, too, and "wise in his craft."

Swinging upon a strap, as his ancestors swung a thousand years ago when a wind swept through the jungle, pitched with the mincing step of his trade, the unsteady floor of a running car, is "Kid" Connors, Brooklyn's veteran conductor.

"I'm ringing up the fares," he says, "and it's many a character I've rung up on my memory. It's the cars that have made America. The swaying, swinging, six-wheel cars, the jumping, rolling, rock-a-bye, four-wheel cars, the yellow-nosed cars that poke their noses through the fog over the Brooklyn Bridge, little flaunting cars creeping along like glowworms upon a terrace vine. The cars give you humanity; in a way, you get it on the jump.

"Born in 1847, I came from County Wexford. I was young and timid then. My friends got me a place on the railroad. I did not think I would stay; that was forty-one years ago," he laughs, passing his hand across his chin. "The tracks that run around the world bind us tight; there's many a man who can thank the car for his business career. The car takes your self-consciousness out of you, it makes you unafraid, you meet everyone; the car is the universal doorstep."

The chink of coins is followed by the ring of the register; it is pacifying, this murmur of money, amid the din of heavily laden trucks and the sounds of a noisy city from streets full of color. Out of the speeding car's windows are streets full of red petticoats that bring the crimson to the puddles among the cobbles; full of drab shawls and nearly bare feet, of pleading brown hands tense with the lust of barter.

Above this the ancient land mariner hears the question: "Have you ever rung up any hearts?"

"No, there's no time for the registry of love on the cars; the cars mean work and the game of beating the clock."

The car slows up across the city in a winding line of black, carriage on carriage, following the nodding plumes of slow-stepping horses. The conductor nods toward the cortege. "He used to ride on this car every morning and evening. He got to his home in five minutes, the way I used to run. He's going home today, but he won't make the run in schedule time."

MICHAEL CONNORS

The car moves once more.

"When we started—that was in the panic of '72—we worked fourteen hours a day with twelve minutes for dinner and only made about $2.50 at that. The first car ran on Myrtle Avenue one sunny afternoon in '54. As the city grows, so the railroad grows.

"The first route I served regularly was Graham Avenue. I served nearly thirty-three years on that. For eight years now I've run Meeker." Kid Connors paused upon his strap, a heavy man with a good hold upon optimism. If no world trembled at the touch of his hand, his hand has not trembled at the knocks of the world.

"When I first started, they had some very hard rules. Oh, you had to be on time in those days. If I reported a minute late for duty, I lost my run and went to the bottom of the list, had to wait for the promotion of the man ahead, or for death or some other incident that would gradually bring me back into the order of the list. We had shorter swings, too; now we get from an hour-and-a-half to three hours swing. A swing, you know, is time off for lunch between runs. Everything changed with the coming of the transfer system, about ten years ago. Now we get paid by the hour; we get longer swings, and we can be late four times before we get dropped to the bottom of the list.

"Does life change with the years? Of course it does. Everything changes in quantity, not in quality. The people are about the same; I'm carrying a former patron's son now on the cars that I know is his son from his likeness. Nothing changes but the growth in population and the younger strata that comes in.

"Am I content? Of course I am. I'm so happy that I don't feel that I need my picture taken; in fact, I have not had one taken in over forty years. When a man is fearless of time, he does not heed to preserve his looks against discontent."

He looks out, a smile upon his face. "I never made a night run, though that's the easiest—fewer people riding, and the dark in the city makes it seem less like a job.

"And what have I to say for the people? The people that ride on the cars are not the gruff, disagreeable-mannered beings they are reported to be. Nearly always the man will give up his seat for a woman, and if she has children and he wants to compromise on comfort of mind along with comfort of body, he takes the kid or kids upon his knee.

"Some men that railroaded with me ride in their autos now, but all I have is experience and an arm full of stars." He extends his left arm, on which gleam five golden emblems of service: the first represents twenty-five years, the others five years apiece.

"When shall I retire? Not until I cannot see, or until I lose the power in my legs. While I'm here, the cars are Kid Connors's and Kid Connors belongs to the cars."

Waiter Patrick Dunne
Forty Years Carrying a Tray

Scene: The sitting room of a Brooklyn hotel. The evening is advancing, and the twilight creeps about the pink candle shades upon little tables. The dull brown of oak and the gloom of dark corners are broken where the light sparkles on the rounded sides of a cut-glass punch bowl, little sharp-edged tumblers, and groups of silver. The smoke of myriad cigars, the household cloud of civilization, blots out the ceiling.

Waiters are hurrying about with the napkins of their trade upon their arms, balancing polished trays the shape of half-circles, endeavoring to carry all the edibles on one journey.

Enter Patrick Dunne, tall, cleanshaven, well preserved, well groomed, well satisfied—welcome. He speaks.

"Oh, this is the season for business. The sense of cold outside, and then the lights burning behind lace, the odor of the roast and bay leaves and flowers can't be resisted. Summer is all very well, but winter is the time for prosperity. Tips! That's when the tips come in."

Patrick smiles and shifts his napkin along his arm.

"When did I start? Forty years ago. Born in '52, in Kings County, Ireland; stopped there twenty years, and now I have been in Kings County, New York, forty more years.

"I began as a railroad man; and winter, my delight now, was my misery then. I was too cold. So I broke into the waiter job, served six years in a private family, and since then, excepting for a short time, I have held one position.

"When a chap applies for a waiter's job, he has to start at the bottom, just like any other man, by carrying away the dirty dishes, bringing in the water and butter, and setting the tables. The waiter apprentice is known as the 'bus.' I never had to begin this way because I was in the wine business in the old country, and I had a way with me that they liked.

"I used to have very long hours, but since an illness of three or four years back, I have had beautiful hours." He nods. The word "beautiful" expresses his sense of complete satisfaction. "And," he adds, "I get the same pay. Just come up from twelve to two and from four to six. The rest of the day is mine."

"How have you kept so young?"

"By going home at six."

"What do you do from two to four?"

"Keep in good company; take an interest in someone else's opinion of things—and laugh."

He moves away, coming back presently with a contented air. "There have been two or three great days in my life. If a person has to live a great day, let him live it in a dining room—a public, popular dining room. If he wants to know what a real big day is like, let him be a waiter. That's the way to realize it all.

"I remember when the Brooklyn Bridge opened. All New York came over, just to say they had ridden the rails, and they were hungry, of course. I'd hate to try to convince you how many people I served that day. It was grand. I can only think what it would have been like if there had been two bridges opened instead of one.

"I've served some very interesting people in my time—men like Henry Ward Beecher, Judge Fullerton, J. J. Hill, and all the Beecher lawyers. They were a jolly bunch, even though there was a great trial in progress.

"Dinner has a strange effect upon the world—a leveling, humanizing effect. The spirit of the dining room is one of cheerfulness, and if they are not exactly happy, the diners smile that way because everyone else is smiling. The evening is the best part of the day. A different class comes in at twelve—mostly businessmen, who are almost too busy to think and too busy to be content. But in the evening everyone laughs. Those people appreciate you better, think more of your service, are pleased with themselves, and let a little of that satisfaction run out to you. Of course, they are the hardest to please because their women are with them, and they are particular. At twelve they grab at the menu and order anything, nearly, and eat it with their mind on the stock market or on the political tangle. But in the evening their minds are on their companions, and these companions must be well fed. So they are particular; they linger longer, for they know that a whole evening is between them and the next day's work."

"Don't you ever get hungry, serving so many nice and tempting things?"

"No; I don't get a chance to get hungry. You see, I'm on good terms with the cook; that is——" Patrick hastily puts a crease down the center of the white napkin.

"And do you intend to go on serving all your life? Are you not going to retire?"

"What should I retire for? Does a man retire from his skin or his hearth? I like the job. I think it would be wise if more young men took it up as a profession and tried to do well by it as a profession and did not consider it lowering. It has many a big problem in it, and it can be done ill or well, according to the way the waiter feels about it.

"I like it. The only place I am not waiter is at home. My wife is head waiter there. I would not give up my job to anyone but my wife."

Fireman Michael Quinn
Forty Years a Flame Fighter

Scene: Superintendent's office of the fire station house in Bay Ridge. Behind the superintendent's chair is a long row of photographs of officers who served before his time, and a glimpse of white cots through the half-open door, all in a row and very still, waiting for the rotundity that night brings. There is a glistening, polished bar of brass running from the first floor through to the dormitory.

Seated in a position denoting extreme comfort, and with a look in his eyes as though green and pleasant meadows were before him and the bell of the fire wagon far off, is Michael Quinn, forty years in the service.

If one has spent one's morning in the battle of life and flame, and one's afternoon, surely the evening can be given up to supervising the rising of the asbestos curtain on the last act of life wherein there are ballet girls and nights at home.

"I'm going to retire soon," he says. "I could have done so twenty years ago and have received my pension; but I wanted to fight right up to the limit. Now I want a rest. I haven't slept in my bed at home for forty years. I'm kinder longing to feel what it seems like to blow the light out of the candle on my own table. I'm kinder anxious to listen to the breathing of my own kin. I'm kinder anxious to lie abed once in a while and make faces at the rafters.

"This is my day now; I've worked forty years for this. It was the pension attached to the job that made me take it.

In other trades they turn you out like an old horse to die
when you have done everything you could. It will be like
getting out of prison to me.

"I was first assigned to Engine Number One located at
Fourth Avenue. From there I was promoted to the hook-
and-ladder company in Van Brunt and Seabring Streets—
you see I'm a great fellow for sticking to a job when I get
it. Oh, I haven't told you where I was born! It was in
County Clare, Ireland, 1853.

"In the old days the Fire Department was one funny
affair. I remember how a man came to us one morning,
looking mournful and chewing a straw. He said that he
had bought a stove, but he could not carry it home as he
did not have any horse. Our chief said amiably, 'Well, you
can have the tender horse for the afternoon if that will
help you out any.'"

He leans back and laughs in his gleeful Celtic style and
pulls his mustache. "And in those days," he said, "we did
not get any credit marks for saving lives. Not that we
worked for that, but now we cannot calculate just how
many lives we have saved because of the absence of files.
Personally I've only saved one life, received but two scars,
and I'm contented with humanity at large, if it's not given
too much freedom.

"I'm contented with myself in particular. I've always
tried to do my duty, and I have never been reported.
That's some record. I hope they took some notes about
that in heaven.

"Before the electric alarm system came in, we used to
have lookout towers for the discovery of fires. That way
we knew when a house was on fire only when the flames

MICHAEL QUINN.

came through the roof. This may have been spectacular and lent some warmth and color to the scenery, but it was not very comfortable for the occupants of the house. Days have changed and things with them; a man can get a credit mark now if he stops a horse from running away at a slow walk, and if a man saves a life, he gets a bushel of medals so that he has to charter a clothes basket to get them home.

"I've studied human beings a bit in the clarifying that flame brings; and in spite of all that has been said, women are not as courageous as men in a case of fire. Women are not naturally strong in composition, and they melt into incapacity, like lead, when a fire starts licking the crayon portraits off the parlor wall.

"In my time I have served all through the department. Always was attracted by fire as a kid, and I served six years as a volunteer fireman without pay—that seems like a pretty big achievement.

"I'm a member of the Society of Old Brooklynites. I've been fifty-seven years here; married, too, and have ten children. I'm a member of nearly a dozen clubs. I like to meet society people, because the more refined people are, the madder you can get them, in a real red-hot way. A slum dweller will throw a rolling pin at you, but a society woman will drop slices of mental ice down your back, and you feel pretty chilly when she gets started. I've had a lot of pretty good arguments with them, and I always enjoyed them.

"I hate to think of the fires I've been in. The biggest was the Brooklyn Theatre disaster. Three hundred lives were lost, and I carried out a score of bodies.

"Most people lose their heads in a fire and don't know what to do. One rule is always good: keep near the floor. If the smoke is so dense that you lose your bearings, get close to the wall and go around it till you put your hand on the best thing in creation at that time—the hole the mason left. If you lose your way, there's always the hose to guide you back to the door or window. If all these things fail, there's nothing left but to get down on your knees and pray; you know you don't do that first merely because while life can be kept any other way you don't like your neighbor to think you are going to ask for what you could take."

"Were you ever afraid?" asks the visitor.

"No, not that I can remember, though it's as silly to say that all firemen are brave as it is to say all men are courageous. There's a difference in all men; some are afraid and some are not. Only, if one shows the white feather he is branded for good. The boys point the mocking finger at him, and he might just as well go back to nature and pick out his plot of daisies.

"There's not much in a fireman's life that is pleasant. We may not lie at home, and we only get our meals by luck. There's nothing very exciting in the fireman's life, because in the end he gets accustomed to death and the sight of fire and smoke, and the sound of the hissing steam is to him what the cake is to the surfeited child. But there's one thing that makes up for it all: the sense that you have saved someone for somebody.

"Contentment among the boys is another pleasant thing to me. I like to sit up here and listen to the drone of the voices below coming up to me, telling me that there are men beside an engine who are alive at the sound of the alarm. I like to sit up here and know that there's nothing so swift to action as the Fire Department.

"And yet," he finished, "I'm going to rest now."

John F. Maguire, Elevator Man Twenty-four Years in a Cage

Scene: Hall of Records, in particular the second elevator to the left. A hurrying crowd of people who have wills to look over and who rejoice or regret the making of them; who weep over deaths, yet are mindful of the spoil left when the tide went out; men and women alike, with the serious faces that speed puts on humanity. Smiling from the midst of it all, like a genial brother to them, stands little John F. Maguire, formerly of the city of Dublin, a royal Dublin Jackeen. Twenty-four years he has been in the elevator. He speaks:

"The battle of Chancellorsville put me here in this dumb car. I was wounded and turned five toes up to the daisies—or in other words, I lost my leg. After that, instead of having sense, which it should have put into me, and sobered me for a long time—instead, I say (and me only nineteen), I went and got married, the most foolish thing I ever did. She was the first; the second has followed her, and now," he adds, "I'm looking for another.

"I got the appointment for the elevator running after I had struck home and spent all the money I had in the bank. I ran the elevator in the Municipal Building for sixteen years, and those elevators are only matchboxes. In spite of that fact I never injured myself nor any passenger; not so much as a scratched finger; not so much as a pinched foot; not so much as had a narrow escape to make things lively. Under my handling that car remained sober, which is the only way to be. From there I went and served a month in the Borough Hall. The Municipal was, at the time I started, the only building in Brooklyn with an elevator.

"Instead of talking altogether about my trade, I'd like to say a word about my beliefs, and my strongest has to do with suicide. There's only one way to commit it—and that is to remain single. You may get into a heap of hot water, but it's better to be soused in the warmth of the Indies than it is to sit on an iceberg and look into the distance cluttered up with icicles with never a kid to welcome you home or make a nuisance out of his little self. This is a theory that all the businessmen hold.

"I remember once a fellow told me that he wouldn't have a woman in his employ. When I asked him why, he said because, with $900 per annum, a girl will settle down and become an old maid. With the same cash a man will look about and marry some nice girl. The way to populate the world with spinsters is to give the girls good-paying jobs. They nearly always shun love and end up with as much softness and milk of human kindness in them as a box of herbs.

"Now, if it's agreeable, I'll get back to my elevator job. Well, I carry up as many as 4,000 people a day, a load every

JOHN F. MAGUIRE

minute. Multiply that, and you will see how many people I carry a year. They all go up; the trouble is, I have to bring them all down.

"You might think that being in a cage all day would leave an impression of bars and prisons on my mind; but the fact is, I'm so used to it that it is like riding in a feather bed. I'm as contented as if I were sitting at home in an old rocking chair with my pipe in my mouth, dreaming of the old peat bog of Ireland—dear old sunny Ireland. And the city of Dublin in particular, where all the real Irish come from, the good, merry Irishmen, like—like—" (he looks about the ceiling with the dawn of a smile) "—well, like me!

"You wouldn't think," he finished, leaning forward and breaking the stern lines of a face in repose into mirth, "you wouldn't think that I had put in a lot of my time thinking up pretty names, like Daisy, Rose, and Morning Glory, to call the lassies when they need cheering—the other poor lassies that work over the typewriter in the court, or who hurry about in the darkened corners of this building like poor doves caught and pining away for the air. Not but what they are happy, too, sometimes; but I think they like to be reminded of the fields now and then by someone thinking enough of them to call them flowers. Flowers they are, too, bless them all.

"I never hear the cases, it being a sort of mute court. No one talks excepting the judge. So I have to be interested in the reading of faces. Every new face—and there are many in a day—brings me a new problem, and so I don't get a chance to be tired. The day is gone before I am aware of it, just by being interested in my kind.

"People generally count time from the year they started working in that city by the changes in the streets. I don't; I haven't time to see the changes in the street—or rather, I don't get the opportunity, because I'm in here from eight to five o'clock. So I count time in the change of dress or the manner of the people.

"Listen, then, and little Johnny Maguire will tell you what kind of a city he would think there was outside from the people who ride in his car.

"I think that, to begin with, the weather in the summer was somewhere around five hundred degrees in the shade and in winter five hundred degrees in the sun. Something must make the ladies partial to chiffon and lace. There must have been a great increase in the height of the buildings, because while the ladies walk as though something was awing them, they always have their noses tilted as from watching bricks going up in the clouds. I should think there must be a monstrous fellow with a tail and horns who wields a stinging lash, for they hurry so in their little red boots and their black and tan pumps and their always-high heels. I should say that the city was very magnificent and that men had built it, because they are so pompous and proud, and they have such mighty gestures, and they talk so loud. I should sum it up by saying that it is some city, but that people are conceiving things which, when they cease to be dreams, become sometimes nightmares; for instead of bringing calm and the glory of having produced something, people hurry and hurry to get it, and the long shadow of the tallest skyscraper points a finger at them and says, 'Are you not thinking too much of your walls and too little of your gardens?'"

He turns sober eyes to the shining sun that comes in through the door. "And yet without tall buildings, where would Dublin Jackeen be, and where would come the necessity for finding names like Lily and Rose and Daisy to give to the tired little lassies who hurry about the corridors? What would become of the Blarney stone if there were no Irish kisses to fall upon it?"

"Uncle Tom" Baird, Engineer
Sixty-five Years Running Machines

Scene: Docks at the foot of Atlantic Avenue. The water is rolling rather unevenly, and the ferryboats pitch slightly, like men who dream of trouble in their sleep. The yard, as it is in all ports where the world comes across to sip our tea, is an uneven-cobbled stretch with scarred, sea-bitten timbers thrown down to lie a year untouched, and an office door somewhere that swings in the wind.

Way out at the end of nowhere comes the sound of the after-dinner laugh, stealing down the alleys with their pools of shining water, where among the many doors and the many high stools that lean against the walls like sad and world-wise herons stands Thomas Baird, known as "Uncle Tom." Eighty-nine years old, sixty-five years in the service as engineer to the Union Ferry Company; running from the foot of Atlantic Avenue to South Ferry for fifty-five years, in charge of the dock engine for ten.

Tall once, Uncle Tom is bowed now, his hands curved with the endless gripping of the shovel, his body curved with his long grip on life; old and white haired but with the young eyes of a man who has shed none too many tears.

"What can a man of my age tell you about the world? I've lived too long and grown tired and lost my power to know what the world is like to the younger generation. I'm tired of living it, though I want to live as long as I can." A self-contradictory speech, but there was no hint of a smile on his face. "No, I don't think much of the way the world treats one, but then, I should not kick. I have perhaps as many friends as any man living and perhaps less enemies, and I've had the privilege, so far, of keeping my job."

This time he smiles.

"I've been in this position since '48. I ran away from home when I was fourteen. I thought I'd like the sea, and I went to the sea, and I've had my fill. My family wanted me to learn a trade, and I didn't want to, and so I went away. My first boat was the packet ship of England, running to Liverpool. I signed for a term on board the sloop of war *Vincennes*, a term being three years; but she got ashore, and I was discharged after only a year-and-a-half of the specified time. I wanted the sea, and I got what I wanted and a good deal more, too. It may seem strange," he nodded to himself, "to believe that I do not like the water; but if there's one thing I will be glad to see the last of, it's the stretch of blue from here to South Ferry. I'm tired of it, and I would like more than anything else to finish my days among the green fields of Jersey, where I was born."

"Were you not of Irish descent, then?"

"Oh, yes, my family comes from the north of Ireland. But I was born here in Jersey, and I have lived forty-eight years in Brooklyn, and I want to live another forty-eight."

He looked about him and finally dropped his hands in his lap. "Yes, another forty-eight, but the boss says, 'No, Tom, you will never get another loving cup.' You see," he leaned forward confidentially, "you see, I had a banquet in my honor at which a loving cup was presented to me, when I had been in the service sixty years, and I am looking forward to another, but I suppose that I will never get it.

"I am a great-great-grandfather as it is, and I can't expect to see many more generations before my own makes the last voyage. I'm a widower; been married twice and have my eye on a nice little house just in my street. Her husband died a while back, and I told her somebody would marry the house. She only laughed, so I guess I'll say that I don't want to be married again. On the whole, I'm sure I don't want to; it's too much responsibility when one gets to be my age. I'd rather watch the affairs of the young."

He seemed content to say no more. He had lived so much, seen so many things, felt as all must feel, that at last he had come down to just the elemental things, the few facts that remained out of a life sifted fine, the few fundamentals that would go to make up his life before the end.

"But what has been the happiest thing in your life? What do you like to think back to most?" he was asked.

His eyes twinkled as he answered without hesitation. "I like most to look back to payday—I like to think that there has been good money earned by me in the last eighty-nine years. The happiest thing in the future is the day that we call payday. For all the pains that you suffer, for all the

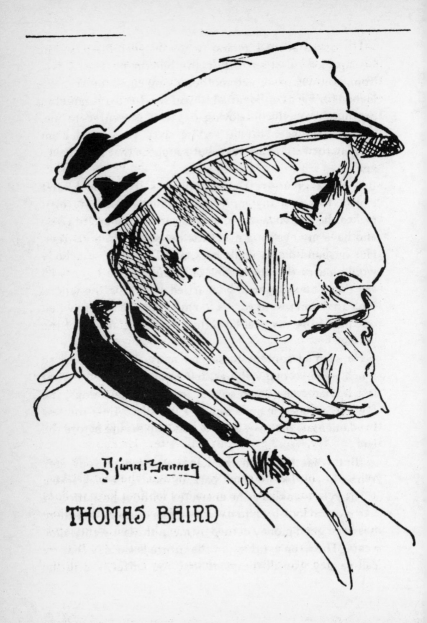

THOMAS BAIRD

heartbreaks that you get and give, for all the emotions that a soul is born to and must bear before the pass-over, the only thing that you get in return is money. That sounds terrible, perhaps, but think back, and you will see that money was the only thing that came to you without a price for further holding."

He laughed suddenly. "I'm not really pessimistic, as they say, only I want to get back a knock at the world for the knocks it's given me. That's not right, though; I've held my job sixty-five years, and there are hundreds of men out of work—men that fill this city. There's one class that breaks my heart, because I can understand it better; it is composed of those engineers that come here and lean awhile on the doorjamb and never say a word. They just watch me feeding the fire like I would my children, just watch, and I know what they're thinking: 'He's served his time under the deck and now in his old age is still feeding the fire and oiling the wheels and watching the whole machine.'

"I will die at the trade that I chose, happy and content with a job well done, while the watcher is out of work. Often we never say a word; but oftener he asks me if there is any chance for an engineer here, and I have to stop and say, 'No, I guess not, pal—later.' He knows what 'later' means: the oldest and best of us must give the younger man the job some day; though," he said briskly, "there will not be anyone in for my job in a long while."

He turned in the doorway. "I'm going back to my engine now, but when you refer to me in the mental book of accounts, remember that for sixty-one years I've been a Mason, and after that remember that I've made all my runs without a slip, that I never had a call-down, and that Uncle Tom still remembers the ferryboat *Brooklyn*, the first he ever ran."

Daniel Sheen, Newsdealer
Fifty-five Years Selling Papers

Scene: The basement of building number 35 Rockwell Place. On the wall seven pictures of seven springs of the year fading into fall; three papers upon the red tablecloth, spread in its turn upon a table; a coal fire and a pungent cloud of pepper and onions and steam from a wash-boiler. In the corner, a red cushion behind him, looking at a dirt pile in the front of the house where workmen still labor, his hands folded in his lap, sits Dan Sheen, eighty years old and, as he expresses it, at the end of his summer. A newsdealer since '58 and still a newsdealer, a good lover, a good husband, and a good mourner.

"I came from England in 1857 and started here as a carver in a restaurant. My means were pretty limited, and I thought often while I was working how it would improve matters for my girl and me if we could get a shop, she being always handy as a good English wife should be. I feel the loss of her more now, I think, than I ever did before. I'm growing old; I want her now that I shall soon be giving up my job altogether and stopping indoors, with nothing to look at because I can't even read the papers that have been my livelihood for so many years. No, I'm not even able to read the headlines. So I sit here with nothing to do and only the memory of my girl for company." He looks sadly out of the window and shakes his head.

"And yet it's all worth going through the pain and all—if," he turns around and looks at the crayon portrait upon the wall, "if you have enough sense to marry but once, having got the only little girl in the world the first time. I did, and I'd rather keep the memory of one such as she than have it marred and make me speculate with the bitterness of one or more sharp-tempered ones in after life.

"Well, as I was saying, I thought it would be a mighty good thing if I could start a shop on my own account, and so I rented a shop front in Hudson Place, still keeping my job as carver. My wife attended to the customers—it was a candy, cigar, and notion store—and at night we would reckon how much we were progressing. Then it was that I thought of adding papers to the shop, so the first stock I got I carried on my back to save expense. This is the way that you must do if you are going to make any profit: make yourself serve the place of machinery. Make of yourself a ledger, an adding machine, a cart, a horse, and a good patent handcart all your own, out of courage and hope. You will in the end own a little piece of mother earth, if it's only a patch. That's me. I own number 35, and though it's nothing to look at, it will keep me from depending on the state, I guess." He smiled for the first time, and there was a hint of the tenderness of many thaws after the frost in his eyes. "With the help of my wife long dead, God bless her," he said.

After a pause he went on:

"Well, then, the boss, Mr. Collins, puts off his baker, and I take it up myself along with my other work to help

DAN SHEEN

him out—expecting, as a man might, that my pay would be increased. But no, he walks up and down the dining room like a man gone mad in the fall, and I wonder silently over my pan of biscuits what has him, and I guess pretty straight: that it's the custom that's beginning to fall off that's worrying him. His patronage was a southern one, and as the cold set in the people went south. That left Collins high and dry, and he was pacing his cage. At last he breaks it to us all that he's going to dock our wages a dollar apiece. I've been astonished in my life, but that was the time when I was more than astonished. I wouldn't stand for it, of course, and left.

"Then began a chain of various experiments. I started a stand where they are now digging a subway. There was a newsdealer in ahead of me; he had a big business and had, besides this, a permit to sell papers on the horse cars. But he was given to drink, and I knew that he would end where all drinkers end. He hired boys to catch the flow of people down Fulton Street. When I came in, his wife used to shake her fist at me and call me an infernal Englishman. He was worried to death. I got a boy, too. In the end we each had six, and we were having a pretty silent but nevertheless effective war. Then one day he died; we needn't ask how. I knew that my day had come and that I need not worry; it would only be a short time before his wife would go the same way—and she went.

"I had a big business and loved it as I would a child. I could tell by looking at a person what kind of paper he was going to buy. I've sold as many as six hundred papers a day. The *Brooklyn Eagle* was my favorite from the time I went into the business. From there I opened a place on

Fulton Street, and from there to Myrtle Avenue, where I
soon found that there was nothing doing. If one person
indulged in a paper, sixteen people clustered around him
and read it over his shoulder.

"The next stand faced the present subway; that stand I
had twenty-eight years. I had a large route, too, that went
to smash when they put the cars through Livingston
Street and furnished rooms and apartments went up. It
was a risk to serve papers to them if they had wanted
them. Why? Because people in lodgings often don't pay.
Anyhow, things and people have changed from the old
times when I first came over. Honesty could be found
then.

"When the newspapers started in to build their kiosks,
or newsstands, under the elevated stairs, we came before
Seth Low—a committee of three—and put our case before
him, explained that it would be our finish. He said in that
grand, gentlemanly way of his, 'No kiosks will be built
under any el stairs if it means trouble for the newsdealers
of Brooklyn'; and that was the end of it.

"It was the building up of Brooklyn that ruined my
trade; the coming of the cars was a boon to civilization but
not to old man Sheen. I had to keep moving my stand to
catch the people. In the end you see me now on Hudson
Place, with only a little movable box and the necessity of
my standing there only three hours a day, from 6:30 to
9:30; shows you that it's about time I quit. The people get
their papers on the elevated before they get to me, and the
subway takes the trade away, too. People don't drift down
here any more, and perhaps I don't make a dollar a day—

though I'm not doing it for the money that's in it now. I do
it because I get so tired of looking at four walls all day."

He leans back and closes his eyes in a back room, and his
sister can be seen moving about in the dim light of a
darkened room, through a burst of steam from the clothes
boiler, to disappear in it again. Old and bent and tired, but
serving still, she comes into view and is swallowed by the
steam from the pot that boils upon a hot coal fire.

Robert Merchant, Court Clerk
Forty-seven Years Keeping a
Book of Fate

Scene: The County Court House. The light is dim in
the corner where the jury sits, and the gloom is thick
behind the rows of chairs. Little, furtive men in black, and
tall, omnipotent officials move about on feet of justice;
severe, silent, watching the clock and not appearing to,
watching the door and seeming only to listen to the murmur on the other side of it; passing from the dim gleam of
the tall windows into the obscurity of dark woodwork,
emerging again as beacons in the upright lives of men.

Seated in the corner, bent low over his desk, is Robert
Merchant, clerk of the court forty-seven years, writing in
the Book of Fate some other man's name. Some of them
say, who have seen him bending over his desk for the last
forty years, that Robert Merchant is a very nervous man

and yet seldom speaks. Many of them have talked to him; all of them have seen him and could draw his face from memory if gifted with the magic of line; yet none of them could tell what he was, whence he came, or what he stood for.

"In the beginning," he says, "I was just a baby like other boys; in 1835 that was, in Prussia—Germany. I was the tenth of eleven youngsters, and I was a German. By that I mean that I inherited all the faults and some of the virtues of the German race. I loved beyond anything my family. After that I loved life.

"Because I used to see ships building, I grew to love them, too, and then when one day a particular beauty was finished, I thought I would try a trip with her. I was ten-and-a-half years on the sea, ten-and-a-half years backed against forty-seven in court and, oh!" The timeworn face broke into a smile which, even though a smile of reminiscence, was guarded and only a shadow of one. "When I see the water I want to go back. I can't bear to go to Coney Island and look out at the sea, for I know that it's calling me and I want to go. I have to turn straight around and look hard at the land, or God knows, I'd do something foolish.

"That would seem as if the life on the sea had been for me at least a happy and contented one." He looks about the court at the moving figures, at the figures multiplying in the row of seats, at the clock. "Yet I received more pain there than anywhere else; more injustice, for one of my captains was cruel. There I learned what it meant to obey, whether it meant death or not. There I learned what it means to hold one's tongue and be misrepresented. There

I learned to hear and not repeat. There I learned the sting of the lash, and there I learned to be commanded and to command. I became second and then first officer and should probably have ended my days in the merchant service if it had not been for the panic of '56, which altered the seaman's life, as all others. Though one could prior to the panic get a ship, one had to put up money after the panic, and not having the money to put up I knew that I was due to look for something else. I was a bonny lad, too: wore my hair to my shoulders in black curls, and the crew used to pinch my cheeks and call them pink, and me cute. Finally I went ashore for good.

"While looking around for something to do, I drove a grocer cart and clerked in the business; yet I felt that I was born to serve a nobler purpose, and I was not at ease. Then I was in the Navy for two years, aboard the frigate *St. Lawrence* as acting ensign. I resigned and came back to Brooklyn and have been here ever since. I started in here as clerk; there were only six judges for nine counties in that day, with only two courts running—one for jury and one for special term.

"Court life is a terrible education. You learn to doubt yourself; you learn to speculate on life, which is in itself a danger; you learn to be bitterly pessimistic, if you don't guard against it; and you learn to be afraid to sin. If people could serve in court life for a while—if they could seem to take it seriously, this increase in crime—I think there would be a sudden improvement for the better.

"Do I intend to retire? Sometime, but not yet. I'm still a young man; anyway, that's the way I feel about it. Yes, in the beginning I had some vague notion about becoming a

ROBERT MERCHANT

judge; but then I never had much ability at speechmaking, and I never cared for politics and so there you are—and sentencing a person is a grave responsibility. There used to be about two thousand cases in a jury calendar; now there are fifteen thousand cases in the same length of time, and the figures are still doubling up, with seven different parts in which to try them. Life's getting complicated. The saddest thing is the size of the code now and the size of it when I first came to America. The people have all changed, too. To what do I attribute it? I dare not think to what it should be attributed. I try not to think."

He slowly traces the last name in the book with a dry pen. "I always wanted a law office, but I never saw my way to it. I have been getting in love and marrying so frequently: three times, and four children of my own. Yes, the brightest, blessedest thing in my life is my family. That's a German trait and one of the best, the love for the family. That's what made me marry three times, and that's why the race is such a virile one."

Robert Merchant once more sets to tracing the names upon the paper in front of him. He lets his eyes wander about the room in search of something in the past. "It's funny," he says at last, "that the things you remember the best occurred in your early life. The things you love best are the things that you lived then, and the things that you return to in your thoughts are always the things of the long ago. So when you ask me to tell you my story, I relate the story of my life at sea. When you ask me what I wanted to be, I remember not all the things I have wanted to be for the last few years but that one thing that stood out as all to me in my childhood. And when you ask me what is the happiest thing in my life, I go back to the inheritance of my fathers. So when you ask me what has been my saddest moment, I remember the death of my first daughter. And when in closing I strive to tell you what has meant most to me, all that I can say is that I dare not look at the sea."

Avon C. Burnham, Physical Culturist Seventy-seven Years Training His Army

Scene: The parlor of 176 Quincy Street. Nothing moves across the surface of the many tall mirrors; nothing stirs the feathery plumes of the dead goldenrod; nothing living puts its hand forth to claim its music from the keys of the silent, black piano; nothing speaks in the voice of the people. There is desolation in the corner where rise tier on tier of departed actors. Fading glory it is in a fading room; and yet between the screen of painted silk and the great double china plates of a time gone by, a single ray of sunlight shines, dancing briskly in arrogant, dwarfed, irregular intervals, breaking the somber black jug into a golden glory, patting the fronds of the golden-rod with fertile fingers—a touch of agility among the immovable.

Enter Avon C. Burnham: small like the sun ray; brisk, too; stepping with the swift movements of the agile old man, proud of his carriage, and proud of his aim. He speaks:

"This is where I live. Yes, this is where I live with you, my lady." He stoops and pats the sharp nose of the collie beside him; then he straightens up and says, looking at the ceiling with a head so well back that only a crown of white hair can be seen, like snow upon the unlearned mountain:

"I lost my wife, God bless her, over a year ago; and I won't go home to my boys. I have to keep my life young, though half of it lies asleep. And I have to keep this parlor and the gym downstairs if I'm going to remain in the army—the army that I've trained to sit up and breathe right, the army that from animal became man. That army is almost seventy-seven years old, too."

He comes around in front of the fireplace with skipping step.

"Life! Life! Life! Humanity! Humanity! What is it all, after all? Watch it on the street, watch it in the cars, watch it in the homes, watch it in the mirrors. Men used to fight like men in the jungle. They stood up straight, and they hit like men at the upper part of the body. What do they do now?" He threw his eyebrows into the argument here, crouching down into a comic little heap. "They crawl upon their adversary, they come to victory or defeat crumpled up like soiled napkins. They grope for the anatomy of their partner behind the ropes. With baffling, crooked steps, they creep and crawl and dodge, always hunched up; they are animals. Our people are animals—we are all animals now. We don't stand straight, we droop from the shoulders. When we are forty-nine, or less, we have a head in the middle of our bodies. Did it ever occur to you that a head was not intended to be in the middle of a body but a continuation of the spine? Did it ever occur to you that we were meant to use our lungs and not our cunning in getting things? Ha, ha!" He laughed a sharp mocking laugh and folded his energetic little arms.

"It makes me laugh to hear people talk to me. They say, 'Well, well, well,' when they see me; and I reply that of course I'm well. I keep well—why shouldn't I be well? I'm young yet. There's no chance to go to your grave head first. Straighten up, and put your head in the air; that's what air's for.

"I suppose by now you will be wondering what my business is. Well, for fifty-five years I've been teaching physical culture. I was physical culture teacher in the Polytechnic Institute for twenty-one years, and for ten in Adelphi, and then I ran a gym all my own for a while. And now? Well, now I exercise for my own good. I always wanted to be well formed, and ever since the time I used to watch the boys doing stunts in the windows of Dr. Jones's gym on Cranberry Street I have been active in my desire. Why—" he ejaculated once more, cutting himself short with his own vigor,"—why should we decay at the age that we now do? Why should we be so afraid to walk as we were intended to walk? Why are we afraid of what some-one in the street will say to or of us if we don't wear just what they do? Why don't girls come out of their wobble and walk? You don't see graceful Amazonian women walking about. You see paint and powder and a yard of some kind of confining cloth and a slope in the middle; you see round shoulders and the death of the body already set-ting in.

"The only thing to fear," and here he drew himself up to his full height, about three feet below the chandelier, "is the excess of physical culture. The boy or girl starts in, gets the mania as we get the mania for drink, and kills himself at the bells, swings himself into the other world on a horizontal bar. Basketball is all right for boys, but now our girls are going in for it. They jump for the flying thing, they strain and injure themselves, and they are invalids for the rest of their lives. Men are not a bit more sensible."

Here he sat down, not one whit tired from his exertion. He had been making the room rock with his demonstrations.

"The gym practice that has been so largely introduced in the Christian associations is all very pretty, but it is of no use. They work at too high a rate of speed. In fact, speed seems to be about all they strive for. Then they have cute little dances which are of no value to the muscles. Oh, well." He lapses into silence—not to last long, however. He jumps up and runs to the other side of the room.

"I do a lot of acting and elocution. Downstairs in the basement I have a regular little gym that I fitted up for individual work." Here he turns to the family album, and looking upon his wife's picture he shakes his head. "We would have been married fifty years if she had held out a little longer," he said and smiled, while the tears rose slowly to the blue eyes.

"Fifty years! Were we happy? Well, what do you count happiness? I don't think there is such a thing in this world. We were always together, always together. That may or may not be called happiness. We raised our children, and we made the children obey. The modern children are, oh, unspeakable! They are without dignity. This is the fault of

the apartment house: they are cramped and see too much
of each other. They are pushed into the street to get the
inevitable street education. They are rude, as rude as
children can be, and they get away with it. They are
uncivil; they are selfish; they are overbearing. And with it
all, they are only animals—they walk like animals, they
spar like animals. In business life they are prey; in home
life they are brutes. I've lived in Brooklyn since '45, and
now I don't care when I go. That's what I think of life."

The withered goldenrod was stirring softly under the
breeze that stole in at the window.

"Why don't you go home?"

"Why don't I admit that I am an old man and be done
with it? No, I am going to keep right on kicking until I
turn my last gavotte, until I swing my last club. I'm made
to go, and I'm going until the wheels stop. Oh, glory, it's
grand to be nimble on your feet! That's the way I taught
the little girl up there, the third from the left, to do the
dance—so!" He whirled about the room on pointed toe, his
hands raised, grace and youth dancing in the shadow on
the floor. Dancing so, he turned the corner of the open
arch and disappeared in a triumphant whirl with coattails
waltzing; disappeared into the realm of bottles and glasses
of disorder that is a lone man's, and the gallery of silent
faces looking down upon him from their tiers and tiers of
prominence on the wall; disappeared in a whirl of exulta-
tion to the dust and ashes of a broken heart.

Who's the Last Squatter?

Riding up toward Coney, between Park Place and Ebbets Field, up on an embankment is a line of shacks. A year or so ago they were squatters, and now—they are not! But——

Get off at Consumers Park, go up Washington Avenue, and you come upon a stretch of uneven ground divided by a cut down to the railroad tracks; black loam on which grow rank bushes, between the branches of which is thrust the white, drooping beard of an old goat, sage and seer, blinking in the noonday sun, content with the color of the coming autumn.

On the other side of the divide, from chimneys that loll from the little thatched roofs as a seasick mariner lolls upon the deck, smoke rises, drifting slowly up, covering the heap of whitewashed wood with a mystic cloth of haze.

This is "Pigtown," and here are—or, rather, were—the squatters whose existence is deplored by society. It was quite out of the question to sympathize with them, for they got what we did not: something for nothing. And yet, go out to them, stand beside the hut, and watch the line of cars twisting along, watch the hurry of people who work for their rent, and somehow there creeps into your heart a mad desire to place your foot on earth and claim it as yours by the inalienable right of birth.

Thus they stand, watching the city crowd these lean-tos, with their broken panes stuffed with rags, their doors sagging at the lock, their patches of tin like the patches on

119

a beggar's knee; the little cracks through which they seem to gasp with the filter of smoke from a badly drafted fire; drab, rusty white, leaning over the embankment to watch the city crowd in their purple and fine linen. Surely one who undertook this expedition would think that at last the real Brooklyn squatter had been found, especially when the said visitor's oxford got entangled in a goat rope and the pigs went gruntling into the parlor, while hens and hares scuttled behind the grapevine and a buxom woman came out upon the scene with a clothes stick and arms akimbo.

And yet it is said that the last of the squatters resides here in one lone hut. Which of the two was it? The house across the divide—the house where the goat peered from behind scrub oak?

Ask the buxom woman, and she says, "Aye, that I can, there is but one of them left in the whole of the country around, and that one is over there." She points ruthlessly to the shack that is breathing laboriously with its heart full of smoke.

"But," she adds, "what should you be lookin' for the last of the squatters for?" And suspiciously she adds, "If you be takin' me for one, you're right mistaken, as it's me as can show you the papers to prove it. Me payin' forty dollars the year and ownin' the house as it stands, and the big irony of it: that if I owned no part and paid no rent I'd call it mine in twenty years, and me livin' here eight already.

"But squattin' or no squattin', it's a sad place to be, when the vegetables won't grow and money not goin' no distance at all; me takin' out a quarter only last week and comin' back wid no change at all and buying soup meat, seven cents worth, and it lastin' only two days, and Johnny not able to eat at all, and then me man coming home from the stone crusher wid his finger smashed.

"No, there ain't no squatters here since they were cleared off last winter, exceptin' one." She pointed across the divide. "She's the only one left, her and her brother and her brother's kid."

'SURE THAT BE THE
ONLY SQUATTER'.

Across the divide a girl was swinging the gate.

Get to the bottom of this mystery: slide down the embankment and cross over—looking out for the third rail—and speak to the only squatter left.

"Been talking to Winnie McGraw, have you? She told you we were squatters, didn't she, and I'm the only person who ever came in here with a face cloth. No, I'm not payin' rent, but I'm no squatter. The lady as owns this land put me in as caretaker, and no easy job it is, with the likes of her across there, making trouble for us.

"There's only one squatter left, you're right; and that," she said, pointing across the embankment, "is her. All the rest of them was cleared off. There used to be an inn here called the Dew Drop Inn, and there the squatters used to congregate and cook chickens around the fire—chickens that weren't rightly come by. On the New Year's Eve, when the old year was a-skippin' out and the new one came in, they caught them with forty-eight hens. That was the end of the land grabber, exceptin', as I say, her. Aye, she be the last of the squatters."

And you leave the hills with their feuds, and you know not if you have found a squatter or not. You look back, and the little whitewashed shack is groaning under its load of smoke, and the weather vane in the garden is revolving slowly. A girl sits opposite her man at one of the tables, and the music box is playing "Oh You Little Devil."

You give the ticket man your nickel and jump for the Park Row local, for you are due to get back to civilization.

Chinatown's Old Glories Crumbled to Dust

As Chinese immigrants to the U.S. in the western states ran out of railroad and land reclamation jobs, racial tensions drove many of them to the east coast, where beginning around 1850 many of them settled in New York City, around the intersection of Mott and Pell Streets on Manhattan's Lower East Side. By the turn of the century around twelve thousand Chinese lived in Chinatown and had only just begun to encourage outsiders to dine in its many restaurants. At the time Barnes wrote this article, in November 1913, Chinatown had for years been torn apart by the bloody feuding of rival underground societies called tongs. Though the six major tongs served many legal functions to their members, New Yorkers associated tongs only with news of gambling raids, opium smuggling, tong-related murders, prostitution and white slavery rings.

Chinatown's white "mayor," Chuck Connors, died in May 1913.

We are just about prepared to give up looking for Bohemia.

Three of us set out the other night to discover Chinatown. We were brave and faltered not; we were courageous and questioned not the other. But fear tagged behind and goaded us on with a sense of danger and of pitifully wicked things, which we must see and might not enter into: a crooked street lit with blood-red lanterns; balconies where China lolled; high, slim boards lettered in tea-packet alphabets; a shot fired in the night; narrow alleys that led into darkest China; getaways, and heavy-curtained rooms where half-dead little bundles of yellow bone and skin sucked the pipe; the dance halls and the tea tables; the queer wire-manufactured music, or the tom-tomlike teakwood shell and the stretched-skin drum; girls who grew old in a year and men who laughed at death. We expected, the three of us, to eat chop suey as the mildest thing we could do, and we expected to taper it off with a tong war.

As from Park Row we picked our way toward Mott Street, did a hissing ball of fire shoot out? No! Did elemental, pigtailed Chinamen grasp our throats with six-inch manicured nails? Did the Chinese script suddenly break loose at us and impale our courage upon a sandalwood, scarlet-ink-dipped brush? No.

"I want," murmured the sporting editor loyally, "I want to see a lantern. Above all, I want to hear the war whoop of a Chinaman, and after that I want a rice cake."

There is no Chinatown.

There are a few stacks of tea at a quarter a packet; there are a few grocery stores wherein no human can move, with odd edibles piled high. There are a few weather-beaten signs banging in the wind. There are a few Chinamen—but not one carried a dangerous weapon; not one wore a pigtail; hardly one wore the Oriental costume. In the entire evening only one woman was seen besides Miss Florence, the mission worker. And from the hundred dark windows not one face peered.

Where was Kelly's, Jimmy Kelly's, the dance hall with the tin curtains? A broken basement, a litter of bull pups, a growl from the dark, a stumbling crew ascending, a light in the gloom; tables piled in a corner, rusting away; little alleys that led into another house and out into the get-away streets; lightless chandeliers; a crooked tobacco sign; and in the middle of the floor, an inch of dust upon its glory, an opium lounge with a capacity for four, inlaid with pearl and dropping into decay. That was Kelly's: immutable dust—nothing more.

What of the Mandarin Club? What of the Chinese theatre with their plays of a hundred acts? The latter is a mission, wherein men swelter and become Christians.

Oh for the departed glory! But what can one expect when the sidewalk spills people into the middle of the street? China is walking the straight and narrow path of necessity. Only now and again does one realize that Chinatown is inhabited, on such silent feet the residents walk; they live in the realm of their own mind and pass nothing out to their neighbor. Perhaps because of this monotony of their life, their art failed to be pitched in a higher key and was satisfied with flat tone and flat surface.

There were just two Chinese lanterns in the whole of the section as far as we could discover. They were used as decorations in the kitchen of a restaurant where the Chinamen cooked for the betterment of the appetite—a spotless, wonderful kitchen, heaped with spotless, wonderful, shredded vegetables and shredded meats.

China has given up serving the devil and is serving America. And in spite of the fact that there is no Chinatown, it is hard to attempt to describe the place which has lost its dance halls, its opium joints, its dens and its ter-

WHEN
CHINA
BENDS
LOW

rors, its color and its revelry, its riot and its Chuck Connors; for in death it is appalling.

Out of the winding end of Doyers Street comes the only beggar that the street knows—bent low, pleading aloud—for iron has to run to water, and the hills have to move and walk, and the sky has to break and miracles must happen before a Chinaman feels the leaden bands parting from the walls of the heart and asks for alms. There he was, begging with wide, lamenting gestures, with no hope of success, a bitter, staggering, broken, crooked body wending its way through a broken, crooked street.

For leagues the sky runs in dark blue, dotted by the stars, until it reaches that space that looks down upon Mott and Pell Streets. Here the sky goes out and the stars die, and there is only a black, impenetrable, overhead abyss, a black, gaping hole up in eternity—prophetic because of the Chinamen that hurry furtively beneath it, who get neither sorrow nor pleasure from the sound of their family indoors nor any delight or sorrow from the sound of their neighbors outdoors.

When the three of us succeeded at last in tiptoeing our way out of the singsong oracle embrace of the joss house custodian, who leaned with inimical eyes upon the counter of dolls "that would grow up"; after the endless and indistinguishable murmur to fallen gods and after penetrating clouds of incense, we backed down a dirty, gray staircase and through a hallway, and crept, gliding like monster shadows, by door after door, watching with our eyes wide open for a Chinaman and sniffing with our noses for the pungent smell of the poppy that lays down its life that it may conquer man.

The sporting editor opened a door suddenly, and the three of us shot into a room. Waterloo may have been lost grandly but not as grandly as the Chinaman inside was lost. There he stood defiantly at bay, pipe in hand, startled and shaken out of a dream, playing a swift game with a chance that he would not be discovered. He toyed with a bottle of amber-colored oil, and we smiled. "Hit the pipe, old man," the sporting editor said, and in the dim, smoke-choked room, the Chinaman, with little almond eyes that grew slowly smaller, relapsed again into his dream.

A RARE
BIRD
IN CHINATOWN.

And then passed in parade the chop suey and the tea, inimitable tea which never tastes the same out of its element: the blue, handleless cup, the surroundings of beads, and the tables wherefrom all the pearl inlay has been pried by tourists who think that the essence of Chinatown might be carried in the pocket; the funny, black, noiseless waiters, who have mastered Webster enough to write the bill of fare in English—the Orient meddled with by Americans who were fools enough to break the calm of a foreign element with a sudden scarlet smile, accompanied with a word in slang.

Then there was music, muddled out of all proportion, when a tango was twisted from the keys of a jangling piano in short, spasmodic thumps. It was a wail produced by foreign hands—hands that brought forth the only music that the old instrument could produce—verily, a heathen god singing English ditties.

And upon the floor with the loose, swinging motion of the tango, like some pasture gate gone wild on its hinges, the Yankees danced, snapping their fingers, humming, twirling. From the silken draperies we watched as we drank our tea, and the sporting editor realized his rice cake dream, and the little Chinaman looked on with half-shut, untroubled eyes, for he was getting paid for having let the bars down.

For this we had entered, and because of that entrance we were due to see, and we saw and were disappointed to find that no nation can so run the gamut of evil; no race can live so swiftly that in the end redemption does not put out a claiming hand. We were disappointed, but not sadly; we had hopes but were not left with a sense of an evening spent uselessly. We had the memory of tea, and we knew that we had brushed the hem of the blackest crape.

We turned back. Behind us, leaning round the forbidden

corner, were the lights of Park Row. At our elbow a
Chinaman cut sections of sugar cane, and inside in a dim-
lit room sat an Oriental doctor musing over his scales and
herbs, and the restaurants wafted their warm, pleasant
aromas upon the heavy air. And so we left here the room
in which the idols lay wondering and the New Year cake
fallen away in dust and the tin blinds of Kelly's as sightless
as the everlasting dead, and the house where Chuck gave
up the ghost and where the prayers were entangled in the
edges of a spiked language but the heart truly mourned.
And as we passed into the lights of the Row that beckoned
and beckoned, the sporting editor said slowly:

"Well, I've had the rice cakes, and I've seen the lanterns,
but there's nothing now that could make a Chinaman cry
aloud, because all the dust and decay of a glorious funeral
would sift down upon him and bury him in ashes. Let us
hit Forty-second Street and see a dance."

Chinatown is a period over which the alphabet of our
city has to step.

There is no Chinatown.

Why Go Abroad?—
See Europe in Brooklyn!

Three thousand miles away, on a foreign shore, pictured to us in the graphic language of men who went and saw and, seeing, wrote; painted for us by dreamers who unite conception with oil; dwelt on by us as something yet to realize—of its sorrow, its charm, its serenity, its splendor of color united with splendor of line, the splendor of little things and the splendor of great—that is the land of our hearts. We are going to it when we have saved enough, someday when the teapot bank can hold no more, or someday when our uncles decide to rent a seat in ether, when we are grown. That is the land that is swarming with incidents and is profligate with gasps. We are even now in the throes of the mental shiver of expectancy.

And yet we have opportunity, we stay-at-homes, to go down to it and see it for ourselves. How many of us have discovered it? Just how many know that Europe is in Brooklyn?

Wallabout! Wallabout! Wallabout! Why in the world haven't you sensed it? Here you can see the colored quilt that covers a spavined horse, the tambourine that receives the proceeds of a soul in that soul's metal—music which brings forth a dime or an onion from the listeners in the shops.

Why, oh why, my feet, have you not dodged the pun-

gent, omnipotent pepper, the crescendo of screaming pea-
nuts roasting, the howl of the hucksters, and the background of tired, silent horses ruminating in the sunset?

GIUSEPPI AND HIS BANANAS

Over this presides the genius of time represented by the clock in the market square, in
the tower house where sits the market clerk
over his ledger count-ing up the quarters he
has collected from the farmer for standing
rent in the aisles of the square. As the clock's
hands come around to-ward five, you know
that the few who are widest awake are due. Between the
clock and the restaurant abutting, with tall glasses of
spaghetti and crushed brown figs, hangs a low-swinging,
lax line of clothes beating a flapping tattoo upon the blue
of an awakening sky. Giuseppi grew up to its tune. The
clock and the stores and the streets and the very city itself
he has learned to sense by smell, as he handles his bananas. Giuseppi, soaked in it, no longer knows that his very
coattails spell Florida, that his floating tie and his rakish,
bagging shirt all are weaved with the flax of fruit.

Life is changing, but Wallabout goes on, stark calm in
the gray of a winter dawn. Night is pierced by an upward-

thrust chimney which smokes in great lazy gasps. Low boats purr in the harbor, and the wet canvas flaps upon a wet dock, and there is the spray and the rime and the tumult of the sea. Then the dusk lifts, and the houses become buildings and the windows and doors take form and the cobbles come into existence. Slowly stealing in from the forty roads of produce, the horses come: carts piled to the point of satisfaction with cabbages and turnips and beets, and upon the seats, their heads upon their breasts, the Long Island farmers sleep as they bring our dinner in.

From the holds of the dusky boats that murmured in the dawn come the imports, the grapes, the nuts, the figs, up from the sheltering decks, hauled and cursed over by men in open shirts and dirt-colored trousers. So comes our dessert.

And then we must sing of the "mulligan" that brews in the pot of our little Italy, that pot of soup that simmers upon the hob in some humble home; that lyrical, street-gathered mulligan, gleaned by women in monstrously tucked skirts and enveloping shawls caught at with furtive eyes; for even though it is not forbidden, the getting makes it sweet.

THE ULTIMATE SOUP

By twelve the market must be clear of carts;

and rubbish men and women make room for the street cleaners, who gather up anything that may have been overlooked. The square has to be cleaned for the night renting when the six o'clock loads come in. The commission merchant has got through handling the beets and the cauliflower and the beans and the celery. He has put his price on the load as it stands, and he has already by twelve

SOMETIMES IT'S A WOMAN WHO PEDDLES

disposed of it all to the merchants of the market. He folds his hands and loiters about waiting for the next line, and the marketeers handle the goods and smell of the fruits and count up their profit and their loss and never seem to know that they have been done out of so many cents to the pound by a few yards; for these Long Island farmers stand within a block of their markets, and yet they wait for the commission merchant to buy first.

Every bit of broken box is reduced to kindling and run off with by barelegged boys with their soapbox carts. Every hoop and every nail and every scrap of paper is likewise collected, and the busy mother stands behind and goads with little hissing foreign curses and menacing circles of the arm.

Life, bustle, color, Europe, barter, gain, loss, Wallabout, Wallabout, Wallabout, somebody, anybody—something is here to be learned. No trip to the foreign land is needed if it's atmosphere you want. No need is there to stifle in the body of a ship for six or seven days if it's accent you want. No need to count the money in the teapot if it's movement and music that you seek. The organ grinder with his tambourine-beating wife wedges between the crowds and receives in the soul's metal a dime or an onion.

Navy Yard Teems with Work Undone

In late 1913, as Europe awaited war, the U.S. Navy built battleships. The New York was its largest ever and the world's first battleship with fourteen-inch guns.

Termed a "super-dreadnought" for its design similarities to the Dreadnought built in Britain in 1906, the New York was commissioned the following spring.

WHAT THEY WOULD WITH 6 MILLION

How many sides has a battleship? Two?

No, three; for there's an aesthetic side.

How many interpretations can one put to the intention of a battleship? Only one, it would seem: the intent to kill. And yet the shell that now lies in the brickbound Hoodoo Dock Number 4, thrusting its bow to the sun with the name *New York* in gray, can be interpreted in many ways. She is built to take life if it is necessary, and yet in her build, in the whole stately line of her, there is the sense that life is precious, for she protects her cargo with 575 feet of proud iron.

Ask the sailors who stand about her, who smile in the sunshine or in the mist of an early morning, who take their hands into their arms or who sit upon iron piles and swing their legs—ask them what the battleship *New York* means, and they will reply: "Six millions of dollars."

Six millions of dollars; and yet, does she look it? This thing of gray in her battle colors, this leaning, almost human thing which rears up two masts triumphant in its incompleteness, as a man who loves and has no arms. Swinging from her on ropes, men walk the tipsy platform, staggering under a load of fresh paint, dabbing her leaden cheeks with a slapping, reeking brush—dropping glory and honor and souvenirs upon their ragged clothes. At each splash of the bristles, they put the war clothes straight. The grim, leveled guns point out like menacing fingers. Beneath, men bow down, dodging a red volley of bolts that are riveted in with a million staccato raps. Everywhere sailors slop water and wield the mop, scouring away the trail left by pots of tar.

Yes, six million dollars, and two years building, and she'll be out in March. And why does she lie in the hoodoo dock? Because she needs painting, and Dock No. 4—once quicksand and greedy for its toll of life, bricks and cement and woodwork—now holds her safe.

There is nothing about the surroundings of the ship that would make one dwell on her import. Ashore, groups of men huddle about a hot tar and log fire, warming their hands. Sailors walk about and talk of foreign lands, walk about and talk about foreign skies, walk about and talk of

war, while their white caps flare out in the light. They call
them "little caps of woe" at times, because they have to be
washed so often. To go to war one has to wear white caps,
if one is a deckhand; and to wear white caps one has to
wash often, and so the men wash. Someday they are going
to pop the question and secure a life laundress; but in the
meantime they tip their caps lazily to one side and forget
all except the sun glare that rests upon their brows.

BOWED DOWN BY THE WEIGHT OF THE GUNS.

At quitting time the significance of the ship is felt. Glancing along its decks, one hardly realizes that the capacity for giving men employment is so great. Six hundred of them pour off at twelve, seeking their lunch; some of them merely "come ashore" for the change and eat their lunch upon piles of lumber; some sit at the dock edge and throw crumbs to their hungry reflections; others gather, gossip, and tell what they would do with six million dollars if they had it.

And then, take the Navy Yard as a whole—the background to the building of our war vessels; two stone pillars, two immovable marble eagles atop; a short incline inward from the street, the ordinary waterfront street, with its corner saloon—and you are cut off from 1913 just as though Father Time had used the scythe the other way for once. You find yourself turning pink in the glow of the red, square, brick-paved court of the yard. You see green grass walled in with brick, low houses built of brick; endless signs that keep repeating NO TRESPASSING, and NO THOROUGHFARE; doors half-open, giving the eye entrance; low-bending forms and a leaping flame, steam, and dust, and hum of machinery, and the low throbbing of controlled power growling at the leash; rafters that cuff the smoke until it bends, and bending, shudders out at the doors and windows to thin away in the air and disappear before it reaches the bay. You cross streets with twisting tracks and horrifying, swift-moving, invincible cars, baby-size yet menacing as they round corners, darting past and scurrying like gray mice through the passages of the red-paved town.

And the sailors in all their arrogance swagger down the street arm in arm and talkative, mincing up life's highway with flapping collars and pantlegs and the swing that the sea gives them. Civilians who can never feel at home there lean over the edge of their chins and look with curiosity at the bricks they stand upon. They never become wholly accustomed to the neat, colonial, old-time world of the Yard; for though no hoops ever move across the lawn, though no gallant's leg in silk stocking ever wends slowly about, still there is a stillness, a hush, a reclusiveness about it that seems the guardianship of the guns. To the four corners of the earth they point—to east, to west, to north, to south they guard the grass of a silent city; with wide-open, iron mouths they rout the spirit of hustle that is in America, and nothing disturbs the peace above the murmur that is at the heart of all things.

Forlornly, though huge, the "intelligent whale" greets the visitor. They put holes in her for eyes, and she could not see. They put a mouth in her, and she could not breathe. They put motion into her, and she did not respond. They carved her out in the image of the monster of the sea; but though the whale has but enough soul to keep her alive, with eyes no more intelligent than the sea flowers at which they stare, still man could not make her and keep her as competent.

This is the only failure of the Yard. All other things are breathing deep breaths that make for importance. The Yard bristles with importance; the sailors bristle with it; the soldiers will bristle with it. All the ships, large and small, come in on tiptoe. The docks sense it; the air is still with it. The men feel it, and the battleship is power personified. And still, with it all, there is a sense of the incomplete: there is power but unutilized, there is grandeur but uncrowned, there is hope of conquest and yet uncertainty. What fate will this new ship *New York* meet? What will her record be? What has she been building for these years if not for victory, and yet who can say what her ultimate end will be?

Yet they are putting her war coat on, these tiny men way down below there; a bucket to this plate, and fling it on with haste, for this is peace work; dip and swing and splash, and know that you are putting the epaulets upon the shoulder of a Navy captain; slap it on and know that you are embroidering the coat of the master of the sea, the latest in the eyes of men. This is the sight that we all stare at. Yet the pity of it is that, as the man upon the crane said, just before it hoisted the last load of coal, "In six months the world will have forgotten her and fall to admiring something new."

If Noise Were Forbidden at Coney Island, a Lot of People Would Lose Their Jobs

Coney Island, a five-mile strip of beach and amusement parks, could accommodate a third of a million people on a good day. Its three major amusement complexes—Luna Park, Steeplechase Park, and Dreamland—offered customers a myriad ways to experience the new technological wonders which were changing the country's lifestyle in an atmosphere of craziness and fun that released the tension caused by those changes. The Steeplechase Pavilion of Fun, one of Coney's most outrageous attractions, offered the paying customer a variety of opportunities to be made a fool of. In order to exit the pavilion, one had to walk through a rolling barrel, crawl through a dog kennel, maintain composure when a blast of hot air lifted a skirt or carried off a hat, or receive a spanking from a clown—all within plain view of an audience of several hundred amused patrons who had just endured the same ordeals. Elsewhere at Coney, one could throw china, climb a fake Pike's Peak astride a real burro, throw baseballs at the head of a black youth good at ducking, witness hourly an electrical model of the Titanic sinking, and eat and drink oneself into unconsciousness.

When the dance craze reached Coney Island, the proprietors of dance halls at Luna Park were forced to ban the vulgarities associated with the tango and turkey trot in order not to alienate their family clientele. Hiring professional dancers partially solved the problem, encouraging *an audience to watch the dances as they should be done. Nearly all Coney's vaudeville houses headlined dance acts.*

By far the most popular of New York's dancing professionals were Vernon and Irene Castle, who began their dancing career while broke in Paris in 1911. As Vernon told a newspaper interviewer, he had been asked to demonstrate the turkey trot and, not knowing the step, had invented the Castle Walk on the spot, with immediate success. Returning to New York in 1912, the Castles galvanized the dance craze already underway, with Vernon's sleek grace and clever improvisations perfectly complementing Irene's innovative wardrobe and elfin prettiness.

For the summer season of 1914, Luna Park constructed a dancing pavilion dubbed the Castle Summer House, which Vernon and Irene briefly initiated before returning to their exhausting schedule of classes and performances in the city; for future patrons, the Castles posted a letter stating that they would dance there regularly if they had the time. Barnes described the Castles' hectic lifestyle in an interview with them in 1914.

I have seen a good many sad people at Coney Island, but none so sad as the man who carried a twenty-inch, red plush bear by the right foreleg about with him all of one day last week and tried to forget that he had made a lucky throw.

I've seen a lot of symmetry at Coney, but no symmetry ever ran through a family with the perfect perfection of a bevy of frankfurters.

To say that Coney is bright and glad and shining and new and full of paint and prospects would give me the rarest pleasure; yet to see what there is in the other end of a nickel is in the blood of all of us. And so, though Coney is cringing in the glare of a broad day with the furtive eyes that a woman wears when she's lost a hook, and though the awnings have lost their paint and the streets their beauty, and the sense of perspective is gone—still we will continue to spend that nickel, that dime, that quarter, trying to see where was the glory of yesterday.

As one breaks through the crowd at the station and dodges the little man in red who tries to take you somewhere free, you catch the terrible, high-pitched, feline wail, growing louder as you listen to the indrawn, corset-hampered wail of sensation that a woman lets loose as the dip of death is taken.

It is not a beautiful thing to hear, and yet if Kipling were to lean against the traffic a moment and hear this cry, he would go away and write something about "the wail of a wincing woman."

The sound of articulate Coney is the voice of the female; the body of Coney is the man. Endless men in twos, threes, and fours walk the streets with never a sign of a girl for miles, it seems. Once more it is the times speaking. When a girl is seen she is usually alone or with another girl, and when she is not and does embellish the side of some young, barefaced man, there is not a picture studio that is not bartering for her future place in the family album. Not a picture man but tries to reproduce ancestors. "Have your picture taken with your wife," he shouts and smirks beside his dummy automobile. And if she gets by him with the young man who is obviously not her husband, a fat man opens an abyss of portent and literally tries to throw nourishment into her system.

If an embargo were placed on noise at Coney, if silence were required, there would be a lot of people who would lose their jobs. If the transactions of the mongers were carried on in the sign language, there would be money in manicuring.

Perhaps the best of Coney is not its showy side after all—not the part that has a nigger thrusting his head through a canvas loop to taunt the money out of place, not the sudden wild dashes that the photographer makes upon the wayfarer, not the garish-colored Japanese lanterns and the sideshow with its fat lady and its human enigma, not the stands of penny cones and three-penny ice-cream sandwiches, not the merry-go-rounds with their ring-grabbing, fully elated, abruptly consequential society of riders—but that little dim, ivy-grown beer garden with its sedate squares of cheese set rigidly in the center of the little green table and the papa and mama eating a quiet lunch from an egg basket while the voice of another country speaks. "Das iss goot!" is heard.

At a table at the left, two long-haired bourgeois sit and draw their future in little sad trailings of forefinger and thumb upon the dust. A girl feeds chunks of weird Italian bakery stuff to a wailing baby. All this you caught between an ivy leaf that curved up and an ivy leaf that curved down.

"Yah, das iss goot!" wafts over to you again.

Then the bent-over fortuneteller appears with her two moth-eaten birds and her table of cards and her bleared eyes and the tap of her stick reaching in a thin staccato down the street to a doorway within which they have motion pictures with fried potatoes and roast beef for nothing extra.

A man stands there swinging a cane. He is dwarfed and

somewhat stout and cheerful, and his trousers bag at the knees. "Step right in! Stay as long as you please; it doesn't cost you a cent"; another revolution of the bright, toffee-hued cane. "R-r-r-r-ig-g-ght in—step right in!"

Up Surf Avenue, looming six feet seven, in gigantic suit of serge, steps the giant jauntily. He lifts the testing hammer; he hits the rubber cushion; the block ascends, runs up and up, hitting with scorning swiftness two hundred, three hundred, four; the bell rings; the block descends, a little regretfully. The giant takes his hat off; he wipes his forehead; he smiles and displays enough teeth to furnish two ordinary men, it seems.

The goad is effective; lesser men pay their nickel and try to put themselves in a class with the man who is six feet seven. It is ridiculously easy—the bell rings at once, the lesser men's muscles have answered the call. They cannot understand their strength; they are stronger than they thought; they try their arms in a few palm-up motions in the air—they look at the bulging, animallike, gorilla muscles of the giant; they go away and either get vastly drunk or propose to marry. The giant smiles.

I said, "Why do you do this?" and he said, "Five dollars does it." Advertisers please take notice.

And that's merely Coney's hip of fate.

I don't suppose anyone has rightly estimated the number of little businesses in Coney, and yet I'll wager that there are more businessmen per inch in Coney than in New York. The streets are broken up with seemingly a million little booths with a thousand-and-one different things, and yet each booth is stocked with about the same things that the others have. Hot-dog stands come one in every three. Of the other stands, the shooting galleries are too numerous to count. There are, in fact, more shooting galleries than anything else at Coney, excepting sand.

The municipal bathhouse stands on long, white legs knee-deep in the sand, like a patient, colorless woman. A really very good person can lose his character out there. There's nothing to prevent him from getting down to his basic impulses. I've seen a lot of nice people who didn't look it. Like the best chairs in the parlor, they are better under linen.

Then another thing—people should be careful about going into the water; some can just about stand going in half-mast.

The Steeplechase looked nice from the outside, but I didn't go in.

Well, after I had stood about Surf Avenue long enough to catch any runaways or any fainting fit or anything like that, and after I had made those mental notes about the bathhouse, I turned around again and started back.

I heard emanating from one of the sideshows a noise that was half between a melody and a regret. There were also inside some torrid-zone war cries and a glimpse of some turbans.

I went in.

A fat sucking pig (dead) lay with his nose in the folds of a Somali Islander. The Somali orator started beating up bad incentives on a stretched goat skin or something and about fifteen chocolate-colored savages started whooping and dancing—not our kind of dancing. It was a dance between an Indian war dance, like the ones you see in a motion picture, and a movement all their own. They had a lot of sheeting wound around them and a good many spears, which they occasionally threw at one another or at the crowd, or sometimes at a target which, in spite of the fact that they never do anything else, they never hit in the right place. Then they showed us how they cleaned their teeth, how they nursed their babies, and how they chewed gum. The last exhibit was rather the best of all.

I told my companion that I did not think much of this. But he said he did; he said it explained a lot of things.

After this we drank two of those abominable things that a white-clothed attendant passed off as sodas, frothing about a large, lassitudinous lump of badly frozen cream which took considerable willpower to swallow. The after-effects are also no impetus to a dervish. A few hundred people per day bring sedate, weekend dregs of ambition here merely to dose them with cheerful chemicals in chiffon.

We strolled through Luna and could have been weighed fifteen different times for fifteen cents. The crazy village and the Castle house are somewhat close together—we hope there isn't any significance in this. The Castle house itself is white and green and attractive and brittle-looking and somewhat Venetian and prosperous. It's going to give a lot of people a definite excuse for idling more time away inside the city of the crescent moon.

What's the use of going into details about the things that are new about Coney, anyway? Everyone knows that each season brings its surprises. The only thing to do is to hold your faith in some part of humanity while testing the depraved inventions that some mean person has contrived to play upon you.

It's not much use trying to tell the number of things that are likely to make you ashamed (for the first time) of the shape of your beloved's calves. If you insist on trying a hazardous-looking spectacle and end up on your back several minutes later with all the beauty of perspective on you, you should at least take it good-naturedly.

There is one nice thing about Coney, one perfectly happy element—its policemen. They are the most unconcerned uniformed individuals I ever saw. They are perpetually upon a holiday, or so it seems. They never hurry—that would be losing caste; they never worry—that would be losing prestige; they never find anything wrong, for that would be absurd. They move about upon timed legs, and they smile endlessly a placid, comprehending, wooden smile.

It's all right, anyway. Every place hasn't a joyful reputation, and those that go to it find that they are welcome and that they might indeed have spent the day in worse fashion.

There are things here that hide the obvious—the sun that touches cheap linen lightly, the wind that shares its caresses equally, the waters that engulf gently the awkward tyro, and last but not least, the kindly sands of Coney, that cover many feet of clay.

"Come Into the Roof Garden, Maud"

Long before the invention of air conditioning, the coming of hot weather to New York lay like a hot blanket on the busy dance-hall trade. Roof gardens had been popular dining spaces for some time, and when a hotel introduced dancing on the roof to take advantage of the breezes, New Yorkers thankfully thronged to it. Whether the breeze entered through a dome netted to keep out bugs or through the windows of a top-floor "roof" garden it allowed die-hard dancers to keep on stepping through the summer of 1914. Even the best hotels, including the Waldorf and the Ritz-Carlton, offered rooftop dancing, though the Plaza managed to keep its garden on the ground floor.

Among the most popular entertainers at rooftop cabarets was a dancing duo, the Dolly Sisters, whose glamorous production numbers outdid their competitors, the Vernon Castles. Born in Hungary, Jenny and Rosie—as they were called in America—attained fame as dancers but also sang and acted. A movie of their lives appeared in the 1940s, starring Betty Grable and June Haver.

First of all, enter the atmosphere. And this, the atmosphere of a roof garden, is ten percent soft June air and ten percent gold June twilight, and a goodly percent of high-hung lanterns and the music of hidden mechanical birds swinging under the tangle of paper wisteria fifty feet above where, between guarding panes of glass, shine the electric signs, plus a few stars, of Broadway.

A good deal of the grace of God is there, too. It is a majestic something that keeps a distance east of the champagne bucket and goes out upon the dancing space not at all.

The thing that is really lacking is a sense of humor. There are not ten people with a really good laugh in their systems in a whole evening on a roof garden. A sense of humor, of course, is never well fed. Here people scan the menu too often and too long to allow the humor to get upon its basic legs. A woman is a terribly good sport and wants to enjoy herself; her escort is growing old in the attempt to make it an evening of evenings.

"That," she says in the very first appeal of the thing, "is the most hideous gown I ever saw: all sliced up where she should be careful and all bunched around where she should be coming out; no arm at all, no arm."

"What's wrong?"

"Everything!" she said with high-held glasses. "Everything. Why don't women get a sense of the decorative when they dress?"

"But you know," he soothes, "they are really fearfully and terribly magnetic; they make an appeal."

And therefore he has gone into history as a blind innocent, with no sense of order or the law that stands next to the things that are right.

And yet he is right. They make an appeal. Everything on, in, and about a roof garden, from the little white and green matchstands to the wide-spanning arches of red light, is an appeal. Sometimes it is an appeal for silence; sometimes it is an appeal for laughter; often it is an appeal for help.

Terribly appealing is the soft mélange of the French
sisters, wound about in their yard or so of silk, their wide,
comprehending eyes, their wider, less comprehending
mouths with a generous space for rouge. Appealing the
little foot that awaits the tango; appealing, too, the dumb,
rigid silences of the chaperon, who feels that there is
nothing here for her but to maintain her sense of right.

A typical roof garden is the Jardin de Danse. It is at least
the best in the sense of its fullness of spectacular dancing,
the dancing of both the professionals and those who go up
to do likewise—if they can.

The fifty-mile look is here, too. Let me explain.

People from out of town can't hide it. Even people no
further away from home than the Bronx hide it very
badly. The born-in-the blood persons, those who seem a
part of the place, are those who live in the hotel opposite,
or in the apartment just around the corner, or at most, no
more than five blocks away.

This doesn't include Judy O'Grady, who dances upstairs
upon the roof in the garden of children's and husbands'
clothing swinging in the breeze off a back alley. It is those
places about Broadway where the sound of a taxi is personal.

And now the band begins to play.

The conductor, a great, towering figure in white flannels, stands knee-deep in green foliage, which may or may
not be false but which looks extremely like asparagus
gone to seed—fine and green and feathery, a soft accompaniment to a fearsome pair of legs.

Up and down and sideways goes the little conducting
stick; and up and down and sideways go the head and the

bow of the violinist and up and out goes the laboring chest of the cornetist; and the Chalmerses and the De Vans from Yonkers drift out upon the floor, while the aesthetic four hundred (who are aware only of that part of their body where rests money in stock and bond value—the breastbone where hangs the string of pearls, the waist girded tight with priceless stones, the buckled shoe, and the fingers holding the brittle champagne glass with Tiffany-encircled fingers) wait a second before they arise, for to be late is to be fashionable, to be hesitant is to be haughty.

"Some day I shall put in such a floor. I don't think the floors along the avenue have received their proper share of attention. Why not have a dancing space like this in the Blue Room?"

"What's the matter?" someone says at a table adjoining, and a voice comes back over your shoulder, high and feminine:

"I am suffering; I am unhappy."

"And why so?"

"Ah," the voice goes on, dramatically broken, clinging softly to its feminine cadences, "I left the pudding in the oven, and the canary hasn't been fed." Then the snip-snip of pistachio nuts being cracked at the table to the left, and the dancers are coming back.

"I felt like a perfect fool," giggles the youngest Miss Van Allen, "when the music stopped, and they just threw about a sort of noise like rice in a sieve, and that silly Negro with a grin on his face kept batting that poor old drum."

"I always feel like a nut, anyway," returns the young

man with the hair thrust back as though he has just been reverently handled by an archdeacon.

"Oh, well, we're having an awfully good time, aren't we?" they say in chorus, and decide that they are.

Taken from an artistic point of view, the best moment to catch the atmosphere of a roof garden is when everyone is just about to sit down. The colors rise and fall and scintillate and surge, crouch, scream, and cry and grope and cough and are bold and are clever and are witty and are wise. And every tone is so very apparent in his or her temperament, and taste is so good and so foolish, and all taste is worth its modicum of moments.

Around comes the white-coated attendant thrusting a dog with a musical inside at you.

"I just love those little joyous animals," gush the Van Allens, and the white attendant passes on, the basket of furry folk held out in front of him.

Someone says something about the types of women that find their way into the atmosphere. Each hour has its particular type: those who come in the beginning and care so much; those who come behind and care less; and those who come in almost too late to have made it seem worthwhile. There is the couple that comes in at eight-thirty sharp, intent upon getting all that's to be got, like a boy at a circus; those who come at ten-thirty and dawdle with a glass of something; those who come in from eleven to twelve, not even deceptive in their careless ease.

The real element knows its garden so well that if blindness found them suddenly they could walk with their hands behind them up to a particular table—could, still with their hands behind them, pick out a particular chair, and in the end could find the floor. These men may range from banker to mere journalist; but the woman who comes with them is languid, impressive, wears long, lassitudinous side curls, and strings the contour of her face to the sharp-pitched key of a large expanse of white forehead and a sudden, downward wave of well-ordered hair. She is essentially crepe; she moves in long, pathetic lines; she is boldly conscious of large hands and ample feet—she has even made them fashionable by endlessly displaying them with a studied simplicity. A lot of anything can become fashionable if one gets used to it—even the Rossetti neck.

She is called the "dangerous woman." She likes the name, and she has made the most of it. The pillar of fame is her background; the best possibilities in an ordinary future are hers to do with as the small woman may not. One expects to see Juno pluck grapes.

She doesn't make a good talker, but he does not wish to talk. She makes few attempts because she knows that what looked good in Shakespeare's eyes as a quality to be desired in woman is still good.

"You mustn't take any more of that curry," she tells him, her chin in her palm. "It's too late at night." Thus, she has even his dreams in mind.

"It won't hurt me."

She shrugs and, chin still in hand, turns away. He shouldn't feel rebuked, but he does. He knows that the things that may be in an ordinary mind about the effects of curry are doubly full of import in the mind of the dangerous woman. He takes the fork out and lays it across the plate from rim to rim. He has not given up. He's given in.

He could find it in his heart to love her if she would
yearn, but she won't. He could become eloquent if she
were roguish, but she isn't.

We have all seen her trimphant, sitting high over the
tide of lesser beings, a passage to the deeper sea, brooding
over the moonlight, queen in her nautical learning, smiling still.

The Miss Van Allens have spotted her long since. They
have taken in the shape of her head, the way she does her
hair—the exact whole, separately and collectively. They
turn to each other and feign horror, and in their mental
notes they don't forget.

Women are supreme when it comes to getting back to—
shall we say?—supper. If she does nothing else well, this at
least she does magnificently. She will leave—thereby making it necessary for the man in the case to leave also—the
most picturesque little order of a salad, even if it is lobster
in its most excruciating intimacy. She will arise and walk
slowly away from the most ravishing pastries and the most
vitally tempting glasses of something; she will abandon the
best of a bird delayed in its flight—leave it all languidly to
go through the mazes of some new step, and finally come
back to it coldly, as though she had never known that it
existed, or rather, as if it did not matter whether it existed
or not.

And yet, of a certainty, she is the hungriest thing in the
whole of creation!

And then, too, she is as illogical as usual.

"Where is the roof?" she says, stepping out of the elevator and casting her eyes up toward the perfectly substantial roof of lights and twining flowers.

"We're on it now," he assures her, leading her by the elbow to a seat near the red ropes leading from the Dollys' dressing room. She can see the inimitable Sebastian rush on with the whole of a girl in his arms and dance like a Spaniard of old, with the burden material of his love.

"But I don't see the sky," she insists, puffing her three rows of silk girdle about her hips and breaking the paper around the tip of her fan. "I don't see a single piece of sky."

"The sky hasn't come out yet," he returns, beckoning the waiter, who has already insinuated them into place around the symmetry of one of the thousand little green tables. "You see, this is a place where people come to enjoy themselves."

"Well?"

"Well, you can't if the sky and mosquitoes get in."

"Yes, but this is a roof garden."

"Well, a roof garden can have a roof, can't it?"

Subsiding, she looks at him as though it were all his fault, which it is partly; for ten to one, if only women visited roof gardens there would be no roof to the garden. Even if it rained buckets, they would prefer to sit under individual umbrellas and soak themselves in the truth of the thing to the very letter.

Therefore, having talked about the dresses, which never seem to please two people alike, and having remarked on some hat and upon some coiffure, and having left the champagne bucket unnoticed upon the floor, and having taken their fair share of the dances—she accepts it in its good and its bad points and is humanly sweet about it to him who has disappointed her. She is loyal ever after, as a fact, and brings huddles of other women to see it and

explains nonchalantly all the things she could not understand and is one more of them who can come in without
looking interested—the very essence of refinement.

But there's someone who has got them all beaten for
love of life: little, dark-faced, handsome-eyed, lithe Don
Carlos Sebastian with palpitating Dolly in his arms.
Breaking through the roses of the flowering arch,
stampeding onto the floor, round and round he whirls,
laughing, exuberant, bursting with life, throwing all of a
passionate race's feeling into a passionate dance. The morsel of French in the morsel of silk clings to him and springs
away and laughs, too, and grows reckless in his reckless-
ness and is thrown from foot to foot and balance to balance in a wild, movement-loving whirl.

And there they sit, by love, the onlookers, and are
commonplacedly interested and say they wonder what the
man is saying who gets up to announce the prize winners;
and finally the woman glides off in front, coaxing a tired
man into just one more step.

Oh, well, it's an awfully jolly thing to be able to dance
and to watch others dance, and the roof could come off if
you wanted it to, and you loyally don't.

Broadway Thinks It Is Only Street in Only City in the World, Says Atteridge

When Barnes interviewed Hal Atteridge and Harry Carroll in July 1914, their stars were rising not so much upon the show they had written with Sigmund Romberg but upon a single song—"By the Beautiful Sea"—which was fast becoming the most stepped-to song in Coney Island's dance halls.

Harold Atteridge, who wrote its lyrics on the subway going home, was born in Illinois and wrote his first lyrics for a college show at the University of Chicago. While working for a music publisher, he penned the lyrics for two songs in Madame Sherry, a successful operetta, and decided to head for New York where, in 1910, he got a job with the Folies Bergère. He topped that with a job offer from Broadway mogul J. J. Shubert and became the primary librettist for the Passing Show series of revues, each of which burlesqued the events of the previous year. Though the productions that preceded and followed the successful 1914 edition did not always receive favorable reviews, they continued until well into the 1920s. As Atteridge told an interviewer, he generally wrote thirty-five songs for each revue, of which twenty-five were performed; he spent only thirty to sixty minutes writing each song's lyrics.

After several other shows with Carroll, he worked with a number of other composers, including Al Jolson; his best-known lyrics include

"Fascination" and "Bagdad." He later wrote for radio and film productions and died in 1938.

Harry Carroll came to New York from his native Atlantic City to work as an accompanist in theatres and vaudeville houses. He composed almost exclusively for Broadway shows, with an early hit called "The Trail of the Lonesome Pine." Aside from "By the Beautiful Sea," he is best remembered for "I'm Always Chasing Rainbows," which he based on a Chopin melody, with words by Joseph McCarthy. He died in 1962.

To say that they are young, very young, hardly expresses it. One is young at thirty-nine, they say; but here were Carroll, not yet twenty-three, and Atteridge, not quite twenty-seven. Success, coming to them before their pinfeather state, might easily have spoiled and tarnished any natural greatness that either possessed; and yet, they are as cleanly, as simple, as unaffected as somebody who is really somebody and as intelligent as a person who isn't.

Rarely did they speak in those numbing sentences that are the sentences of power; rather, their speech was the languid flow of well-bred direction. To be bitter, one has to have sat out more than one night of pain; to speak with secret power, one must naturally have grown bitter inwardly. Perhaps this is all wrong, and they have lived too much and rounded out too conspicuously for the eye to catch, but on the surface at least they are boys—fine, direct, unspoiled boys, with at least seven ideals between them.

Harry Carroll, who wrote the music of *The Passing Show*, does not come up to the Bible. I don't mean the standard of that book, but literally: he does not stand much higher than a letter box along an RFD route or a hollyhock that has been restrained. His rather large head sits like temporary judgment upon a pair of small, swaying shoulders.

Hal Atteridge, who wrote the dialogue and lyrics, is tall, slender, and neat. He looks directly at you out of eyes that make you forget the crooked nose and the slanting, twisted smile.

Carroll ate ice cream like a child, and Atteridge chewed a perfect point off a perfect pencil. In the background rose the solid chest of some prima donna, and rank on rank the lesser hits came and went, extending no thanks to providence, giving no thanks to good fortune.

Some of them leaned upon the battered piano and ordered music to order, and Carroll gently promised them a song as fast as they asked for one and promptly forgot it. One girl who had lost her job in the *Follies* snapped her fingers at the memory of a sad moment and flung the tomahawk of a woman's bitterness into the ample foliage of Miss Kelly's family tree.

A kindly halberdier who had stood long moments in the perfect sunlight of a buxom scene, where paper oranges hung low for a hungry lover, tried to discover which of the throng he hated least.

While Carroll played the piano with one hand, he chased up illusion with the other, the ice cream melting upon the "Lonesome Pine."

"To create a piece like that running at the Winter Garden," began Atteridge, "you have to creep upon your public. Now I was born in Chicago, but I don't dare admit it. A Broadway crowd—and by that I mean the theatre crowd—thinks that Broadway is the only street in the

only city in the only world. If you were not born in New
York, you necessarily must have been born and bred and
reared or rather nudged up among the elephants or buffa-
loes.

"Michigan is a place out of which an Indian once stuck
his head and let somebody in Macdougal Alley make a
copy of him to put on the cent, and Boston holds only
beans. To a Broadwayite humor is provincial if it was
thought of across the line.

"They are terrible, they are unworthy—they really are!
Ask Harry."

Harry nods. "Positively—not an ideal, not a sacred thing
among them. They never think of tomorrow, and they
never think of yesterday, and yet some yesterdays would
be worth raking up."

"Yes," goes on Atteridge, "the thing that Broadway likes
is, after all, the thing that a little town likes. Those notes
in the local paper about Sarah Ann's visit to her Aunt
Jemima are only Broadway in a small way. In an opening
night performance of a Winter Garden show there must
be a reference to Diamond Jim Brady and the Dolly sisters,
or your play dies. The reason is that they are sitting right
out front, and they have come to see death.

"Death at the play is a very terrible thing; it's as sad as a
lantern on a wreck. I guarantee that a man with a nice
disposition will come away from a first night and be willing to leave the prussic acid in the almonds. And it's the
most critical crowd in creation."

"Broadway has for sale anything that you will buy, you
know," Harry wandered on. "All of us have a lot of house-

hold goods that we cannot put upon the market, but even these have their price on Broadway."

"When I first struck this town," Atteridge broke in, "I crept into Ziegfeld's office one morning and offered him a song and a set of words that should have set laughter at a premium. He rose to his feet in that majestic way that only Ziegfeld knows, and he said 'Yes' under compression—that he would see me the next day and that I was to bring the song along.

"I came back, of course, and waited at least three hours for him, and what did he say when at last I was admitted to his presence:

"'What it is, young man—what do you want?'

"I waved the song at him.

"'You accepted it, you know,' I said.

"'For what?'

"'For your *Follies*.'

"'Ah.' He turned around and crossed his hands. I spoke to him again and, after a few moments, repeated my questioning reminder. He never turned around. My song never came out.

"I had crept upon a producer only to find that I should creep out again as absolutely unknown, as thoroughly forgotten, and as easily as the fog that hung upon the chimney pots."

"When I first struck this town," Carroll said, twirling the piano stool around, "I stumbled into it on a New Year's Eve. There was a low haze over the dock, but the streets higher up were full of confetti and gay women, and I didn't know whether I had struck paradise or hell; afterward I found it was paradise. I have had one long song, my life has been comparatively easy, and success has come soon but not satisfaction. I am not what I want to be."

Hal Atteridge smiled softly. "Tell her what you want to be, then, boy," he said.

"I want to be the father of another such operetta as *Madame Sherry*. I want to live, I want to be remembered. I like to be liked. I think honest approval is the most desirable and wonderful thing in the world.

"Writing popular songs is merely setting your heart upon a blotter. Words sink in, never to come back. The other night I was on the roof and the band struck up 'By the Sea.' I tell you, I never felt so proud and glad and happy in my life. I felt almost sick with a nausea of delight. I wanted to loosen my belt. I wanted to sing, and most of all, I wanted to cry. I was as perfect as the lady who received the apple in the shape of my soul, and I was marching on."

His eyes were full of laughter, but the narrow chest beneath the best of a tailor's art was unsteady, ample proof of an organic upheaval.

"But," I said, "does it not spoil your pleasure some to have to write music to order?"

"No, I'm used to it. I can write a song with one hand, hook up a dress (just got married—I'll tell you about it in a minute) with the other, and all the while my mind can be occupied with the meanest things. Oh, well, it's lots better to make music to order than it is to steal a piece—a lot of so-called composers just naturally swipe anything that hits them as catchy.

"Now, the other night the automatic piano in the corner

had been started by someone's penny, and I sent over a pencil and pad with my compliments to Hirsch and told him to get busy."

"Tell me," I interrupted, "what the public is looking for."

Atteridge laid down his pencil (I have it now). "Catchy words, a little soiled, something that can shock them into laughter; and dancing—a lot of that—but sensationalism and scenic effects most of all. What they are going to like later on, nobody knows, but that's what they want now."

"How do you feel the public pulse?"

"By mixing. You have got to be a good mixer, and you've got to mix. If I stayed up in my room all day and went to bed at 8:30, I would be out of the world, because the world does not go to war until twelve or thereabouts. All the causes for future divorce are born then, and all the hearts are broken then, and all the deals planned and all the romance and life lived then. You know your public by keeping beside it, by eating with it, by smoking and drinking and laughing with it.

"I have to write my stuff just by sheer determination. I can't get my ideas by wandering into the subway or going down into the streets, as one wild journalist had me get my inspiration. I don't get inspired. I can't wait for inspiration. I get my orders, and I obey like a soldier, and if there's a noise going on like a boiler factory I have to go on just the same.

"First nights are the things that make me earn my pay. It's then that I really suffer. As I said, they have come to see a funeral—Diamond Jim and the others—and they are prepared, they have their crape and their flowers with them. Well, when I see that arctic circle, I just can't stand it, and I go away and have someone pat my wrists with cold water and feed me strengthening things and talk strong and kind withal; for then it is that I am laboring with my soul. Most of all, the public wants speed."

"You bet they do. Listen to this." Carroll swung around once more and put that piano into such action as it never had known before. "And if Miss Collins isn't satisfied with a song, you have to write it over again, and some singer says she will not appear unless she has at least four songs to sing, and another won't sing at all if somebody else in the cast sings first, and so on. Oh, it's the life!"

"Well, are you happy now?" I inquired, turning to Hal.

"Quite, thanks. The play is a success, and I hope that I'll have as good a success next season and for many seasons. Wish me luck," he added, extending his hand with a delightfully frank movement. After this, Carroll shut the piano and finished the ice cream.

"Well, ma'am, before you go," he said, "I'd like to tell you about my wife. I promised I would. She's small, like me—twice as nice, four times as pretty."

"More than that," broke in Atteridge. "I ought to know. You got me out of bed at the horrible hour of eight in the morning to help get you married."

"Well, lots and lots prettier. I have known her two weeks—and am perfectly satisfied."

"That's what gets me," Hal said. "She's only a part of herself—she's twins." Comically he looked down at the blushing Carroll.

"Yes, ma'am, she's twins, but she's worth it, even then."

"Worth what?"

"The risk and getting up so early."

"But I don't see——" began Atteridge.

"Don't see what, old boy?"

"I don't see how you're going to tell 'em apart."

Carroll turned in the doorway and surveyed the stars of the past and the present and smiled.

"I'm not going to try to," he said.

My Sisters and I at a New York Prizefight

Racial enmity accounted for much of the popularity of prizefighting among the middle class in 1914, when Barnes wrote this article, as whites searched for the champion who could defeat the great black heavyweight Jack Johnson. Their unlikely Great White Hope turned out to be "Cowboy Jess" Willard from Kansas, who actually disliked the sport. After taking the title from Johnson in 1915, Willard studiously avoided nearly every opportunity to defend it and finally relinquished the championship in a disappointing bout with Jack Dempsey in 1919. Barnes interviewed both men, in 1915 and 1921, respectively.

"A large percentage of the spectators were women."

This bald statement of fact had repeatedly caught my eye and attention from the sporting pages of many newspapers.

Friends had several times asked me, "Have you noticed that, of late, women have taken to attending boxing matches?" I had not noticed it, but I wished to if it were fact.

Therefore, one night I found myself at Far Rockaway and in Brown's Athletic Club. Far Rockaway, which lies some fourteen to sixteen miles up Long Island, is scarcely more than half-an-hour's journey from the homes of Manhattan. It is within the boundaries of the city of New

168

York and has many beautiful summer residences occupied by New York families. The clubhouse stands a few feet from the railroad, inconspicuous, dun colored, crouching.

A man leans at the ticket window with its admission prices painted in red. Women stop before him, hesitate for the fraction of a second, then, putting down the two dollars required for a ringside ticket, pass on slowly, their faces set in a smile. The man at the window does not even raise his eyebrows.

Out in a beer garden, empty chairs are leaning across tabletops on which brown pools, now run dry, trace fantastic memorials of past feasts. Beyond, through a blue mist of tobacco smoke, gleam rows of human faces, and feminine laughter rings out in a shrill, piercing scale. I, a woman, join the others and watch the women come.

They do not appear self-conscious, nor is there anything in their behavior to indicate that the situation is unusual. They look indifferently upon the raised square with its shivering, taut ropes, its limp towels and scarred brown pails, the stools in the corner, the sponge in its pool of water that widens ever and drips to the floor below. And they finger their chatelaines and speak of the boxers' build.

The men who make up the audience are opulent and portly; they smoke cigars; their hands, gesticulating, gleam with a flash of diamonds. The women are frail, slender-throated, swathed in the dainty trickery of silk and crepe.

This was the first set of three four-round bouts, with "Black" Lahn and Mike Rosen to lead off; two ten-round bouts to follow; and the last and star feature to be between Phil Bloom and "Young" Gradwell.

Across the bare ground walks the referee, the turn of his head indicating expectancy and importance. Life for him, at its most exciting, lies within the space encompassed by the ropes. Men have trodden greater fields than this but never did chest expand with more conscious pride.

And now the scene, enveloped in still-denser haze, seems to grow more and more remote. The lights appear dim, further off. You sense a long, low line of heads—those of the men hatted or with rumpled hair, those of the women elaborately coiffured, oddly incongruous. At intervals through the blue-gray of the smoke the red of a cigar tip glows brilliantly, smolders, and glows again. And from within the enclosure of the ropes a white arm flashes as its owner thrusts out one hand for the glove or submits to the scurrying rubs of zealous, eager seconds.

"A fine, clean-cut fellow," says one man behind me; and another, "Look at the muscles of his back!" But a woman says, softly, "He has fine eyes."

Then these two, whose names are scarcely heard—for their fight is a mere episode preceding an event—stand out to play their part, the simplest and most human that the evening is to see. As they grip hands, eyes measure carefully, muscle for muscle. Then, with a sudden squaring of the jaws, they start the game.

After a sudden, uneasy stir, the crowd settles down to watch. Some lean forward with hands, palms outward, thrust between their knees. Others lean back, with arm extended over another's chair. But the women who dared the ringside and the girls further back sit rigidly upright, balanced between wonder and apprehension, their faces still set in a fixed smile, as of a man beheaded while a joke still hovered in his throat.

As the worst part of death is not the dead but those that mourn, so it is not the boxer that is horrifying but the crowd that knows no mercy and seeks but sensation. Through the cry that goes up the boxers close on each other, chins thrust out, wary, watching, alert. They come to a lock, where head meets breast. They move stiffly, jerkily. Then the slap of the referee's bare hand resounds on naked flesh; they are thrust apart; then they meet again.

And each one of us, meanwhile, sits motionless, scarce permitting a breath to pass our lips.

Then, like a bird thrown helpless against the bars of a cage, one of them is hurled against the ropes. With wet, shaking limbs he strives to regain his footing. He strikes out, but his fists feel no shock of contact. His antagonist becomes a blank; his arm muscles seem numbed. But he still fights on, and to the audience his arms, moving ceaselessly and ineffectually, seem like the branches of a tree caught in the fury of the blast. A low groan escapes him as he vainly endeavors to combat this overwhelming force. Then comes an abrupt stillness. He hears the taunts of the crowd, but they do not affect him. Only a great loneliness, a sense of complete isolation, fills him as he slowly sinks to the floor.

And there stands the victor, looking around with dulled eyes. In the last few seconds he has lost touch with his surroundings; they merged for him into a swaying, struggling figure on whom he was expanding all the might of his muscles. He runs his fingers along the top of his belt and taps it gravely, as if to assure himself that he is not in a dream.

The referee is bending close to the man who is down but who still, seemingly, refuses to accept his fate. Sprawling on his knees, head bent on supporting hands, he strives for breath. The referee stoops lower, his mouth now close to the boxer's ear. He begins to count—"One, two, three"—in a voice loud and full of command, as if he would like to tell the boy to get up and try again. But the figure on the ground only sways to and fro; he is no longer a fighter but a great and bewildered pain.

"Seven, eight, nine."—the referee straightens up, and feet first, they carry the lad through the ropes to the oblivion beyond the ring. He has failed.

"God!" says one woman softly. Another, sitting wedged between brother and husband, argues hotly upon the relative merits of the fighters. A third, just behind her, who has never ceased to smile picks up the ribs of a broken fan.

You realize presently that a man dressed in white is selling ginger beer and ice-cream cones. Then there are some who can even now wish to eat!

The star bout comes at last. The glove is laced into place once more; another arm is rubbed with alcohol. Gradwell bends back for the douse of the sponge; Bloom thrusts his face out to receive the forward swish of water thrown from an adept hand. Drops of it fall on our faces like drops of rain—a boxer's baptism.

They shake hands.

All the men are aware from the beginning that Bloom has the best of it; somehow they know the things that count in the game, and their interest is proportionate to their knowledge. But the woman's interest lies not in strength but in beauty. She is on the side of the boxer who has a certain trick of the head, a certain curve of the chin, a certain line from throat to brow.

Why try to describe it? The star bout was not the one in which the human game was played. The first round was the same as the last—a listless, apathetic battling of two who seemed very tired, very weary, who climbed over the ropes in the end only a trifle more tired than they had come.

For them the battle had lost its zest. The shock of clashing bodies no longer roused the blood. It was a business, not a sport, and the human element of the first amateur bout was lacking in this more finished contest.

In the blank pause that followed the finish, a man suddenly struck a match. It illumined a face drawn, paler than it had been, with eyes more heavily lidded. The match went out, and I was left to puzzle and question.

Was it, after all, the men in the audience who had been careless and indifferent to pain? Was it the sound of a snapping fan that I had heard? Was it a woman's voice that had murmured, "He has fine eyes?" A woman's hand that had gripped my arm in the dark? A woman's breath that had ceased so suddenly?

And whose voice was it that had cried out just before the finish—"Go to it, and show us that you're men?"

How It Feels to Be Forcibly Fed

In their effort to get the vote, British women committed acts of civil disobedience by the hundreds. Finding, however, that their imprisonment had little effect upon government policy, they adopted the tactic of hunger striking while in prison. Many became ill, and the Home Office, unwilling to allow prisoners the popularity of martyrdom, ordered that hunger strikers be forcibly fed by prison officials.

How many of these women died from the effects of forced feeding is difficult to say, as the usual effect was a general deterioration of health; when a Miss Lillian Lenton, charged with burning down the teahouse at Kew Gardens, contracted pleurisy and pneumonia, her doctor attributed her illness directly to her feeding experience. As the effects of forced feeding began to defeat its lifesaving purpose, the government hit upon the policy of releasing weakened prisoners, allowing them to recover at home, and rearresting them for further incarceration.

The feeding method used in Britain differed somewhat from Barnes's description, employing a steel gag to allow a tube between the teeth, thus damaging the teeth and jaws as well as the throat. Some women, unable to withstand the torment for long, ate their meals and paced themselves into exhaustion or threw themselves at their cell walls until they lost consciousness.

I have been forcibly fed!

In just what relation to the other incidents in my life does this one stand? For me it was an experiment. It was only tragic in my imagination. But it offered sensations sufficiently poignant to compel comprehension of certain of the day's phenomena.

The hall they took me down was long and faintly lighted. I could hear the doctor walking ahead of me, stepping as all doctors step, with that little confiding gait that horses must have returning from funerals. It is not a sad or mournful step; perhaps it suggests suppressed satisfaction.

Every now and then one of the four men that followed turned his head to look at me; a woman by the stairs gazed wonderingly—or was it contemptuously—as I passed.

They brought me into a great room. A table loomed before me; my mind sensed it pregnant with the pains of the future—it was the table whereon I must lie.

The doctor opened his bag, took out a heavy, white gown, a small white cap, a sheet, and laid them all upon the table.

Out across the city, in a flat, frail, coherent yet incoherent monotone, resounded the song of a million machines doing their bit in the universal whole. And the murmur was vital and confounding, for what was before me knew no song.

I shall be strictly professional, I assured myself. If it be an ordeal, it is familiar to my sex at this time; other women have suffered it in acute reality. Surely I have as much nerve as my English sisters? Then I held myself steady. I thought so, and I caught sight of my face in the glass. It was quite white; and I was swallowing convulsively.

And then I knew my soul stood terrified before a little yard of red rubber tubing.

The doctor was saying, "Help her upon the table."

He was tying thin, twisted tapes about his arm; he was testing his instruments. He took the loose end of the sheet and began to bind me: he wrapped it round and round me, my arms tight to my sides, wrapped it up to my throat so that I could not move. I lay in as long and unbroken lines as any corpse—unbroken, definite lines that stretched away beyond my vision, for I saw only the skylight. My eyes wandered, outcasts in a world they knew.

It was the most concentrated moment of my life.

Three of the men approached me. The fourth stood at a distance, looking at the slow, crawling hands of a watch. The three took me not unkindly, but quite without compassion, one by the head, one by the feet; one sprawled above me, holding my hands down at my hips.

All life's problems had now been reduced to one simple act—to swallow or to choke. As I lay in passive revolt, a quizzical thought wandered across my beleaguered mind: This, at least, is one picture that will never go into the family album.

Oh, this ridiculous perturbation!—I reassured myself. Yet how imagination can obsess! It is the truth that the lights of the windows—pictures of a city's skyline—the walls, the men, all went out into a great blank as the doctor leaned down. Then suddenly the dark broke into a blotch of light, as he trailed the electric bulb up and down and across my face, stopping to examine my throat to make sure I was fully capable of swallowing.

He sprayed both nostrils with a mixture of cocaine and disinfectant. As it reached my throat, it burned and burned.

There was no progress on this pilgrimage. Now I abandoned myself. I was in the valley, and it seemed years that I lay there watching the pitcher as it rose in the hand of the doctor and hung, a devilish, inhuman menace. In it was the liquid food I was to have. It was milk, but I could not tell what it was, for all things are alike when they reach the stomach by a rubber tube.

He had inserted the red tubing, with the funnel at the end, through my nose into the passages of the throat. It is utterly impossible to describe the anguish of it.

The hands above my head tightened into a vise, and like answering vises the hands at my hips and those at my feet grew rigid and secure.

Unbidden visions of remote horrors danced madly through my mind. There arose the hideous thought of being gripped in the tentacles of some monster devil fish in the depths of a tropic sea, as the liquid slowly sensed its way along innumerable endless passages that seemed to traverse my nose, my ears, the inner interstices of my throbbing head. Unsuspected nerves thrilled pain tidings that racked the area of my face and bosom. They seared along my spine. They set my heart at catapultic plunging.

An instant that was an hour, and the liquid had reached my throat. It was ice cold, and sweat as cold broke out upon my forehead.

Still my heart plunged on with the irregular, meaningless motion that sunlight reflected from a mirror casts upon a wall. A dull ache grew and spread from my shoulders into the whole area of my back and through my chest.

The pit of my stomach had lapsed long ago, had gone out into absolute vacancy. Things around began to move

lethargically; the electric light to my left took a hazy step
or two toward the clock, which lurched forward to meet it;
the windows could not keep still. I, too, was detached and
moved as the room moved. The doctor's eyes were always
just before me. And I knew then that I was fainting. I
struggled against surrender. It was the futile defiance of
nightmare. My utter hopelessness was a pain. I was conscious only of head and feet and that spot where someone
was holding me by the hips.

Still the liquid trickled irresistibly down the tubing into
my throat; every drop seemed a quart, and every quart slid
over and down into space. I had lapsed into a physical
mechanism without power to oppose or resent the outrage to my will.

The spirit was betrayed by the body's weakness. There
it is—the outraged will. If I, playacting, felt my being
burning with revolt at this brutal usurpation of my own
functions, how they who actually suffered the ordeal in its
acutest horror must have flamed at the violation of the
sanctuaries of their spirits.

I saw in my hysteria a vision of a hundred women in grim
prison hospitals, bound and shrouded on tables just like
this, held in the rough grip of callous warders while white-
robed doctors thrust rubber tubing into the delicate interstices of their nostrils and forced into their helpless bodies
the crude fuel to sustain the life they longed to sacrifice.

Science had at last, then, deprived us of the right to die.

Still the liquid trickled irresistibly down the tubing into
my throat.

Was my body so inept, I asked myself, as to be incapable
of further struggle? Was the will powerless to so constrict

that narrow passage to the life reservoir as to dam the hated flow? The thought flashed a defiant command to supine muscles. They gripped my throat with strangling bonds. Ominous shivers shook my body.

"Be careful—you'll choke," shouted the doctor in my ear.

One could still choke, then. At least one could if the nerves did not betray.

And if one insisted on choking—what then? Would they—the callous warders and the servile doctors—ruthlessly persist, even with grim death at their elbow?

Think of the paradox: those white robes assumed for the work of prolonging life would then be no better than shrouds; the linen envelope encasing the defiant victim a winding sheet.

Limits surely there are to the subservience even of those who must sternly execute the law. At least I have never heard of a militant choking herself into eternity.

It was over. I stood up, swaying in the returning light; I had shared the greatest experience of the bravest of my sex. The torture and outrage of it burned in my mind; a dull, shapeless, wordless anger arose to my lips, but I only smiled. The doctor had removed the towel about his face. The little, red mustache upon his upper lip was drawn out in a line of pleasant understanding. He had forgotten all but the play. The four men, having finished their minor roles in one minor tragedy, were already filing out at the door.

"Isn't there any other way of tying a person up?" I asked. "That thing looks like——"

"Yes, I know," he said, gently.

The Girl and the Gorilla

When Dinah the gorilla's captors, from the New York Zoological Society, found her in the spring of 1913, they kept her in Africa for eighteen months to accustom her to captivity before bringing her to the U.S. in the fall of 1914, when Barnes wrote this "interview." By Christmas, Dinah had outlived any other gorilla in captivity but was suffering from paralysis. She eventually stopped eating and died of malnutrition the following August.

A new species has come to town!

We thought we had a line on all the different kinds of femininity in the world, their fads, fancies, and fashions, their virtues and their indiscretions—when suddenly enters Dinah, the bushgirl.

She is neither very feminine nor very fragile, to look at. She has fashion's wide shoulder-cape of hair, but this is as far as the semblance goes, as she stands before us leaning upon bowed forearms, taut as suspense, looking out of faraway eyes upon a life called civilized.

Such is the gorilla woman, the only living captive of her race.

Looking in at her from the public's side of the bars, I perceived only a vague, gray thing with head sunk between shoulders—a bundle of unfathomable apprehensions. But when I stepped into the cage, with the keeper Engelholm on one side and Professor Robert L. Garner on the other, she stood abruptly upright and, putting out a crinkly, black, glacé-kid hand, demanded something—something to eat. Her appetite is astounding.

Keeper Fred Engelholm was a little doubtful as to the way that Dinah would receive me, I being the first woman who had come within caressing or battling distance. But Professor Garner seemed confident that Dinah would find something, however trifling, in me that would meet with her approval.

She ambled toward me with her knuckles doubled under her, a slanting bulk of body that shut out what little light the cage permitted, until she reached the chair they had set for her.

There is a queer sort of drawing-room caution about her. She has a cold sort of appraising stare that holds neither envy nor malice. The crowd that collects outside her cage she does not see, or if she does, it might as well be a row of cabbages. Apparently she does not object to cerise or black stitching upon a pair of dress gloves.

I found—for I had come to study her—that the largest and most splendidly satisfying thing in Dinah's life is herself. She would rather stand well in her own estimation than upon a social footing.

The professor, who surely ought to know, told me that she had her own way of talking. So I said to her, "Look here, Dinah, what conclusions have you come to regarding our United States?"

She took her knees into her arms with an air of long-studied calculation that would have given an analytical novelist infinite pleasure. Rocking from side to side on hairy haunches, she began to laugh—an extraordinary laughter, that disturbed the virile hair upon her breast.

Her mind was as a blank of well-arranged ignorance!

Three feet of the newest womankind in the world was making me feel—well, awkward, to say the least.

She did not trouble to answer for a while. Looked down upon, she is merely a little gray blur. Reviewed upon her own level, she is a small wildcat elevated wrecking train. If your dignity permits a competition in faces, you will be left three miles behind at the first loop of the jeering mouth; for believe me, Dinah has the most perfectly ordered set of unbalanced jokes on view of anybody in the world. Her face is the jumping-off place for humor.

Having crawled after her for some twenty minutes, I sat up and argued. I said to myself: Now we will see if, after all, the advantages of civilization do not enable me to dominate this rather unique situation.

Once again I lit out upon her with "Now then, Dinah, answer my question. What do you think of our United States? You have been here a month."

She paused, her head poised sidewise.

"Let me see"—she cupped her hand about her ear and dusted a piece of lint from her shoulders. (I freely interpret according to Professor Garner's rules.) "The first thing that really attracted my attention was the meter upon the taxi that the professor hired to bring me here to the zoo. That thing climbed exactly three-and-a-fourth times faster than a chimpanzee, four times faster than an ordinary monkey, and six times faster than a gorilla. I hated to see anything get away from control so.

"Also, I was quite grieved," she continued plaintively, "to observe that the sun has no chance in New York and that the moon is only a past memory. I couldn't make out whether it was daylight or electricity."

She took a stroll about the cage, ducking between Engelholm's legs and looking very much like the other side of a funny camera. She paused abruptly and smiled.

"There is one thing that I haven't tried yet."

"And what is that?"

"Chewing gum. Gee whiz! I would like to find out what it is in that little delicacy that keeps so many people rotatory beneath their hats. But I have been getting the most weird and winsome feed here at the zoo that ever passed my understanding: bananas, oranges, meat, and French rolls in particular."

Certainly a bushwoman has come to us who is little and quaint and gray; and you who go up to the Bronx to see her will discover that there is something terribly old about her, and yet not old at all. Her eyes alone will make you seem to remember something that has gone before. She weighs less than fifty pounds and stands about three feet high. She is immature yet and will grow as time passes. I am only wondering if I will then be as willing to hug her and have her embrace me in return as I am now.

When she puts her arms about you, it feels something like a garden hose. It is at once impersonal and condescending, and yet rather agreeable. And when she laid her head upon my knees, I was not embarrassed but only pleased that she had found something in me, as representative of the women she had come among, to make her trustful.

Of course, she had to spoil it all by gravely putting an orange peel upon her head.

She moved off at the same time, Engelholm after her, she disrespectfully making faces at him—faces so mean and comprehensive that Engelholm got riled on the instant with a kindly sort of scorn.

Outside, the crowd roared in delight as she ran easily out of reach in a side-swinging, ungainly, loping movement, Engelholm catching up a little at each turn—Germany gaining upon Africa with difficulty.

She growled ominously when, lunging forward, he caught her by the scruff of the neck and paused in full view of the crowd, wiping his forehead, holding her off like luggage from back home.

"She's so darned cussed," he remarked illuminatingly, as she tinkered with her ear. "As nice a little girl when she wants to be, and then as mean—as mean——" He searched in vain for something that would symbolize Dinah's soul and personality.

Failing, he stood and shook his head. It had just been borne in upon him that even here Kipling's remark about the female of the species holds true.

My Adventures Being Rescued

The business of being saved was brought to my attention one day this week when few people were occupied with the all-engrossing thought of salvation.

The business of saving and being saved, like the Brooklyn Bridge, is an institution. We save money, time, breath, and occasionally words, all of which are easy and comforting compared to the saving of one's body.

It is nicer to have the city pray over you than it is to swing above a city yourself and say a few prayers on your own account in midair. It is a fearful, almost a terrible thing, to climb onto a level with the sparrows' nests.

Three times that morning I was saved, and each time I had wished it onto myself. When you get into a fix by the act and workings of providence, you are looking for salvation in the natural course of events. It is a different matter to get into danger for the express purpose of making providence practical.

Up at Sixty-seventh Street the School for Recruits was alive with its merit pupils. With exact precaution and skill, each recruit went through his morning task. The hose shot a long, heavy stream dripping and sliding down the bricks and across the windows. One man gasped as a copious and undesired bath was thrust upon him.

The blue shirts, blue trousers, belts, and caps, the for-

185

midable yet kindly faces, and kindliest of all, Chief Larkin smiling at me comfortingly—these were my stage settings and surroundings.

I had watched the man padding across the shed roof and seen him stretch out stiffly and taut, to land comfortably in a man-encircled net. I looked past the ladders, over the heads of many men and into the faces of many more, as my eyes ran along the buildings. In every window they were watching us—me—in the court below. It was the first time in my knowledge that I had earnestly desired to be sure of living ninety-nine years.

Through it all, I caught Chief Larkin's order, "Fetch the belt." I felt like the man who hears the hangman's words, "Fetch the rope."

One of the boys brought a wide belt of canvas and leather and strapped it about my waist. I followed him up a winding flight of stairs to the topmost window.

At my belt hung a full pound weight of steel loop. It swung and swayed and pulled me down. For even the iron that saves and the hands that succor have their inconveniences.

I climbed out upon the sill. I looked down.

Recruits who had been men dwindled to funny, grotesque shapes, futuristic patterns without purpose. The faces at the windows were blurred masks.

I reached across the crimson sill and swung against the sky some hundred feet or so above the city pavement.

Out on the other side of the wall the world had stopped to look on. An auto slowed down. A flock of school children and a couple of "white wings" all stood with heads upturned skyward. A man with a screaming white apron tied about a conscienceless girth, who had been cutting perishable merchandise, grinned in the glare of light shining and dancing upon his cleaver. A drowsy expectancy lay along Sixty-Eighth Street and touched the spectators with a sort of awesome wonder.

I was a "movie," flashing transient pictures upon a receptive sky.

As I dangled and sprawled against the horizon, I realized that it was no family inheritance of courage nor yet any individual bravery of the soul that kept me from becoming horribly sick. What prevented it was the perhaps ridiculous sentence that I kept repeating to myself: "There is one act that must be committed beautifully—suicide!"

Needless to state, I reached the ground quite safely.

The method of descent that I had just demonstrated to my own satisfaction and to that of others was the method used when a fire has reached such a point that a fireman cannot hope to make a safe and sane rescue. The rope is shot up to the window—a thin, strong rope—onto which is tied the thicker, stronger one on which I had descended.

Now I retraced my steps once more to try the second method, the one more commonly in use.

This time, I climbed out on the sill as before but sat and awaited the fireman coming down from the roof.

Revolving like a great undecided bird he came, crying out an order which I was prompt to obey—a command that I should put my arms about him under his own and hold tight.

I reached out, I felt myself sliding, the sill was jerked suddenly away from me. I felt his body take the wrench, felt his breath as he grunted softly. Then slowly, very slowly, we swung onward and down.

Space is a good thing into which to hurl epithets, but it's not so agreeable to swing in.

The rescuer kept whispering "Golly, golly" and making funny noises in his throat, little self-approving noises, agreeably confident. Our hearts beat as closely as those of escaping lovers in a melodrama.

Once more I reached a foothold. We swayed apart, walking tipsily upon the slack net, and then slid to the ground.

The third adventure was with the ladders, a shaky proceeding with slippery spindles underfoot. I hoisted the ladder to the window above, and I jammed its spikes into the ledge.

In this wise I went all through the business of being saved.

The world's machinery moved again as I touched the ground to stay.

The belt was unstrapped. My dress was brushed. The Chief felt my pulse and pronounced me "Game, all right!" The boys made remarks about my weight and the good old hemp, suggesting that I do the stunt every morning for exercise, also for the benefit of the free-amusement-loving public.

Wild sky-tangoing had been mine, and the memory of it I shall cherish doubly because it was the first time in my life that I knew what a coward I was.

After this I asked the Chief what was the best fire escape so far devised, and he said:

"These newfangled, fire-escaping things that have been invented from time's beginning have not proved practicable, that's why we have not adopted them. We are still awaiting the inventor who will really invent something that will not take fifteen to twenty minutes to excuse itself in. All so-far-discovered methods have proved inadequate because they operate too slowly. Therefore, we returned to the old method—the rope, the fireman, and the girl."

Djuna Barnes Probes the Souls of Jungle Folk at the Hippodrome Circus

Jungle Jargon

A monkey with a dreadful past
  And sprawling bigotry of mind
  Kept pinching all the cats behind
The scenery—it could not last.

It was a juggernaughty thing
  Of jungles and of peasantry;
  It laughed a little pleasantly,
It sang a song—it could not sing.

And down below where blind bears walk
  Or lurch in tears upon a rug—
  It is because they cannot hug,
It is because they cannot talk.

They are denied all things but weight
  And rug value in days to come;
  No wonder they are stricken dumb,
For this was never Dante's fate.

And, too, what lion has no wish
  Napoleonlike to fold its hands
  Upon its breast, to brew dread plans,
Or to receive a Judas kiss?

And in dim stalls, both huge and high,
  Soft elephants still undulate
  Like old duennas out of date—
Like widows who may writhe and cry.

And out of corners soft with light
  A thousand little puppy-wails—
  They shake a thousand funny tails
Upon the other side of night.

A circus, if of pleasant kind,
  Doth give the animals a chance
  To note the foolishness of pants,
And so it brings content of mind.

And so, having established the fact that there is something to be said for both sides of the bars, let us pass on.

Once more it was the old tent ground again. Once it had been beneath the real tent, and once I had dangled my legs from those tiers and tiers of seats, which seem always to collapse at some other performance than the one you attended, thereby leaving you sedately out of history. Once, too, I had crawled beneath these same seats after the end of the last act, after the exit of the convict-coated zebras, and had hunted for pearl pins. I distinctly remember that it was pearl pins; no other sort of loot seemed worth crawling upon hands and knees among the popcorn and sawdust for. I crawled, and I found—not a pin but one solitary cuff link, for which later our military friend conceived a passion; it seemed to reconcile him to one arm.

And here again it was the "top" above, the "kinkers" all about, and the "circurious" about to wake into action.

For every ton of earth that is thrown upon the floor, a yard of childhood comes skipping back. They may talk of the cost of the earth, but it's only the kid who really can appraise it properly. Animals and children: this is the state of creation; after that it is civilization.

However, let us plunge into a state of chaos.

Where many times with mincing step and shapely poise the dancing form of chorus girls had minced before the public, now with languorous length and Bismarckian mirth the great peanut-eaters stepped out. These gay, giggling chorus girls of the jungle, devoid of ballet skirt or tights (for what would Porthos do with chiffon and lace, and what a mountain with a pair of fleshings?) took up their allotted place within the picture plane and became gorgeously cynical.

And then, with quaint purloinings of the presidential mien, one retreated and with its infinitely removed back located the comfort of a chair. It slid downward; the silken covering on its back wavered like the fall of Rome. It telescoped some more, its gray ponderosity pulsed; it wobbled in rotund and slippery acres. It became, upon the moment that the chair held it, a monument of trust, vast tons of temerity.

And there it sat.

A man out in front in a frock coat laughed; a child in the gallery stood up and felt his youth. The elephant opened its mouth, swinging its trunk from side to side, and winked a regular masher's wink, for which policemen's clubs are made, a slippery Beau Brummell oscillation of the orbs. Its wink produced terror; its smile bred doubt.

Young men in the front row took a lesson. For this was

banter in the bulk, the jeer from the jungle, the hint of a possible knowledge of those corners of the human mind supposed to be secret. Upon beholding such a smile, you feel deeply inadequate.

An elephant, like an uninhabited mansion, is majestic. It is the religion of the acre. It has the unproductiveness and the austere presence of a sand dune. It is implacable and enormous.

Let me state here that as they came off to descend to the stables below, I turned my head away. I'm glad my mother does not know as much about me as those elephants.

As they passed out I noticed that Mr. Spellman, a sort of a joke in a high hat, with a sweet sense of humor and a sweeter, more valued sense of truth, was imparting knowledge.

"A bear, you know," he remarked, "never hugged a person in its life; that's a statement that some hunter returning from the wilds made to attract attention to his caressable anatomy. Teddy R. made the most of it—we all like to think of it, it is so romantic, so charmingly bourgeois; for only one of the rabble would take to his vest with such amiability and persistence any foreign element."

Note, for instance, their entrance. They come in as Kipling describes them in "The Truce of the Bear," on hind legs, with "paws like hands that pray"—aye, even so, passing across the dun-colored stage in file, twelve of them (numbering a Japanese sun bear, who demands his rice), straight across the open space with music of softly lurching flanks, with the deep security of padded feet—still with paws like hands that pray, held up before their charred, black snouts, in direct line with their "little swin-ish eyes," unblinking, cautious even of meditation; shrewd, enormously hypocritical, swaying to an invisible choir.

There is no rattle of the chains now; they are suddenly transported from the animals into the actors. They are a part of a system of joy termed the three-ringed circus. They could fulfill the three-ringed circus's mission alone if they wanted to. We feel that. You who sat in the fifth or the eighth or tenth row felt that, too; you are glad, oh, very glad, that you will not have to witness their ability; you have heard so much about their hugging and their general wickedness. You don't know that they can kiss as deftly as any human; you never have held their heads on your lap. "No," you say, "you bet we haven't." Well, I'm not going to say that I have, because it will, or at least it might, spoil the sale of seats to some degree; for when a menace boils right down into a mate, a sort of parlor companion, no one is going to get ecstatic spinal shudders.

Then the camels, the mountains of the desert (you've noticed how they resemble mountains in miniature), striding about like thin old men, like supremely indiffer-ent beaux in stiff collars, modestly shocked at the wild sky performance going on above; scornful of the upper attrac-tion—of darting female bodies on trapezes—animals who look indefinitely into Egyptian atmosphere as if with a lorgnette before their noses; desert dudes!

You hear the yapping of little dogs on little leashes, the crack of a whip somewhere in the distance. You see the alert face of Herr Max as he minces—all little animal trainers mince—after his canine conquests. Comets on a string are fox terriers, and he knows it. He is smiling blandly; he is deeply gratified at existence. He notes the faces in the crowd, and he forgets that there were displays before him and that there are to be displays after. He forgets that there are other things upon the stage; in fact, he is an organism given up entirely to satisfaction, preening with presumption. He passes on and out of our memory with his strings of dogs; but though forgotten by the multitude, he still is the display of the century to himself, long after descending into the monstrous and profound depths of the Hippodrome; long after the little door has closed on himself and his array of boxes, each labeled with a puppy's name; long after the pungent and overpowering medicinal odor has disappeared, for in him is still the act to come. He is training still, like the good German he is, ducks, hens, roosters, pigeons, and turkeys. Surely you will see him later in your life, bowing still smartly, still agile, with his newer offering.

After him there are the zebras, the seals, the donkeys, the kangaroos, the leopards, the lions, and the tigers.

You know I could not keep away from them.

There are flowers which are so sublime that they not only possess an odor, they possess a perfume. There are animals which not only possess a presence; they also possess a kingdom. Of these are the lions, and to my mind, as purely tragic is the tiger.

They have the drama beneath their pelts, tragedy in their souls, conquests in their stomachs, strategy in their eyes.

"Alphonse, thou art a clown."

"Aye."

"What do you think of a tiger, of a lion?"

"A tiger, a lion, my lady—I do not think; I retreat upon that subject."

"Not so bad, Alphonse, yet come you hither"—speaking rapidly into his ear with that first-act intonation left to Hamlet's ghost—"on your life as a gentleman, or as an artistic fool, how would you describe this wild, this truly ferocious, this almost pulse-pausing animal? In what words would you couch his soul?"

"Aye, lady, how would I describe a lion, a tiger? As rubber rage, as oiled energy, as systematic Samsons. Also I would say they are pretty, very pretty sarcophagi; as moving hearses they are birds—no one ever went to oblivion with such a cradled feeling."

I could have done as well myself, perhaps; I know that as a speech it sounded well. But had he really set forth with accuracy the true purport of the animal; had he done the death-dealing thing justice? Were there not some curves that, in his haste to become history, he might have forgotten? I gave the beasts the once over; I noted their noble poise, with front paw set forward like Sir Henry Irving in *King Lear* or *King Henry* or something, and I began to doubt but that perhaps this animal was playing to the gallery.

Had he not eaten a man practically out of life? Of course he had, but perhaps he appreciated notoriety. Perhaps it hurt him to do this; perhaps he knew with appraising eye that the suit he spoiled was worth, in its youth, eighty beautiful bones. Perhaps he knew, too, that the haircut he spoiled had been administered that very morning; but this only lent more prestige to the act. He is his own best press agent—how can we, or I, make fun of him? I'll tell you. In reality I was stunned, petrified, at his appearance, but I will not admit that he is the king; I will not add to the rest of the deeds in history and make him out a regular devil; I will not allow my typewriter to put down more in a million times the statement that he had all of a tragic gastritis and that his eyes pulsed with a purple or green doom. I won't—not because I did not feel it, not because I'm stubborn, nor because I'm mean or calculating, nor indeed because I want to be backbiting; but because the thing has been done; because the animal has long enough had human life upon its menu. I—I at last insist that it be fed lentils and classed among the vegetarians; it has been given too much notoriety as a man secreter, as a king, a lordly monarch. I won't accept it!

Let us not capitulate, let us not split the difference.

I went down afterward into the depths where the animals are kept, and slipping up to the cages of these animals at last privately—no longer before the public, no longer in the limelight or the footlight—I stepped up, paused without, looked around for any trainer that might be present, for any keeper, for any intruder, and finding myself quite alone with nothing but my iniquitous past, I slowly and softly raised my hand—in salute!

A Visit to the Favored Haunt of the I.W.W.'s

The Industrial Workers of the World, a revolutionary union formed in 1905 of forty-three labor organizations, chose direct action over arbitration and collective bargaining to work toward its goal of overthrowing capitalism. Its members, called "Wobblies," were numerous and unskilled and their union highly controversial, inciting numerous violent labor actions in the years before World War I. War provided the government with a rationale for suppressing it, and it did so successfully, arresting the union's leadership, including Eugene Debs, who later helped form the Socialist Party.

There are two classes of people: those who wear caps and badges and those who wear hats and canes.

There are two kinds of reform: that which is above the collar and that which is below.

Also, there are two types of resignation: that which is gained upon the knees and that which is gained by the fist.

God has become accustomed to both sorts—that of the middle class, which consists of a convex ambiguity, and that of the bourgeoisie, which consists of the contracted palm. Both demonstrations touch Him, but their effect upon society is entirely a different thing.

All revolt has a color; the revolt of the mind is the same tint as the revolt of the body and the revolt of the soul.

This color is red. Where one comes upon this color, one finds the hub of despair.

A man preaching that which he feels to be truth from a soapbox is upon a throne; a king speaking from a throne that which he feels to be misleading is speaking from a virtual soapbox.

Therefore the resignation of the man who said the other night at an I.W.W. meeting, "This is the way that it has been in the past, but it is not the way that it is going to be in the future."

When one wants to become cognizant of the color and the texture of the soil, one does not get a ladder; one gets a shovel. When one wants to get into touch with the texture of the universal mind, one does not go to Boston; one goes to the Bowery.

Despair betrays itself in epigrams; when one wants to build, one begins to gather. The Bowery boy gathers pictures that express his mind, clippings that express his heart, and phrases that express his education.

Upon the walls of the hall at 64 East Fourth Street, one sees this: "If war is hell, let the capitalist go to hell and do his own fighting." "Why should a man's belly go empty when ten men can produce enough to feed one hundred?"

Certainty always produces questions, uncertainty statements. It is a balancing law of nature.

"And now," says the man with a fifty-cent cut of suet but with a Tiffany interior, "what is wrong?"

When a man subscribes to God, he subscribes to an inner conviction; when a man subscribes to revolt, he subscribes to a conviction that gastritis has forced upon him. Out of the torpid realms of dyspepsia shot the torpedo of conviction. The strongest of leveling forces is the stomach. Stomach trouble is the emetic that looses redemption.

These men, these I.W.W., have starved. By way of the empty interior they came to the shut door.

What lies on the other side of it? They say, "The gate to plenty."

And what is the method by which one gets there? They say, "Not by a key but by a fist."

A boy ties a tin can to a dog's tail for the same reason that a man ties a consequence to a capitalist: to make him fear as the can resounds in like ratio to the speed he accumulates.

Coming into this hall, one has no illusions. It is as straightforward as a painted woman. At the windows there are iron bars; upon the floor there is nothing but the dust of congregation. That dust is as necessary to agitation as water to Jennings Bryan when upon the platform. The benches are wooden, hard, uncompromising. One sits upon the palm of labor.

There are no obscene jokes chalked up, for though these men may be vulgar in their bedrooms and their kitchens, they are standard in their council hall.

Upon the walls there is that multitudinous polyglot pasting of paragraphs, pictures, and epigrams that I already have mentioned. The people have gathered, and they have saved.

The low collar is here and the overalls—and though their methods are coarse and their colors vivid and their gestures wide, one remembers that their wounds are wide also.

At one end of the room, near the door, a large round office stove stands. I firmly believe that it has been around such stoves as this since the world began that the most of our problems have been hatched, from the affairs of Mirandy Ann up in Wyandanch to the problems of labor. While it is true that many an ambition has been drowsed to slumber by the heat of a stove, many a resolution steeped in the heavy lees of dreams by the application of the sole of the foot to the iron ring running around the middle of the burner as the halo of Saturn runs round the circumference—still, thoughts, like chickens, are sometimes hatched by persistently applied warmth.

At the further end of the room an improvised platform has been raised. A set of twin doors has been nailed together; about this is draped a yard or so of dirty sheeting. Upon the top of a little red stand, and upon that a bulging, arrogant, almost brutal gavel.

There is a noticeable absence of cigarette or pipe smoke; there is also a striking absence of tittering.

I have seen at these meetings but one girl. And she was not so much an audience as she was a query. She had those flat hips, those lank, slender arms, those uncertain knees, and that abridged face that one sees upon the second step of nearly all dwellings below Washington Square.

She had suddenly appeared upon the horizon of whatever family she represented as an interrogation point, and wherever she went she probably presented the same absorbed appearance of stupendous and acute astonishment, with all shock long past.

She leaned her thin chin upon the back of the bench in front of her.

This man was possessed of a sober sort of gentleness—
the one who lifted himself out of the congregation like a
paragraph out of a biography. His trousers fitted vilely,
his feet turned in, his collar and tie were labor-loosened.
They presented to view a slackened appearance that is
only acquired by one thing: by straining and bulging of the
neck muscles. His hair was unkempt, his face little
washed, his high tide, like that of so many others, seeming
to reach scarcely further than the back of the ears. His
vocabulary was immense but damaged: his "education"—a
thing much boasted of by the I.W.W.—was great, but
chipped; he spoke in sentences almost poetic in their
decay, almost subtle in their malformation.

He flung the gavel upward—it came down with a crash.
It was rapping every lax soul into tensity—that, at least,
was its supposed mission. It failed to fulfill it: each man sat
as untouched and as unstartled as a herd of dumb beasts,
but all were watching.

They sang a little among themselves and to the rafters
and to those of the listeners who cared to listen. They
seemed to read from little red I.W.W. song books, but in
reality they all knew the songs by heart. A man just
behind me even improvised acrid remarks in the rests.

Individuals become dangerous when paragraphed; here is
Oscar Wilde in the shape of a bomb: "It is easier to beg than
to steal, but it is finer to steal than to beg." On all sides the
jottings of brillant men are justifying their impulses.

And then sprung up one of those arguments that are as
certain to push their point through the sod of human
intercourse as mushrooms through the pasture in damp
weather.

"What," demanded one of them, "is the sense of being organized all winter merely to beat it in the summer and be plain, ordinary dusty Dicks? What is the sense of open-air speeches only to end their use by catching a train to ride belly up, like the flies, over perfectly good ground that it is our right to ride over decently? You know what you ought to do, yet I had to repeat so often: keep bunched—stay in the city—let Manhattan have us all the year round. Raid the restaurants in squads of fifty or so, not singly. Then they can't arrest all of you. For heaven's sake, don't be personal, be impudent."

Now, it's not that we particularly mind loafers—to continue the argument, they are decorative, simple, susceptible, standardized. Stupidity is the silhouette of brilliance. Such men are the shadow by which we perceive the light. That is not the objection; we only insist that they be professional loafers, acknowledged and proud of the fact, and willing, or rather insisting, upon staying in that club. We do object to their crawling in on the other organization, the I.W.W., which is another club altogether.

One speaker says, "There aren't any loafers in the organization; why do you try to locate forgers of an ideal—admitting that there are any?"

Ah, well, we won't, then; but such are the signs.

A little blond man, perhaps not over twenty-one or so, arises at the moment when the hall has lulled itself into approbation. A long, fusty, gray cloak hangs away from his long, thin neck, drops down to his belt line, where it is caught back with hands thrust into trousers pockets, and from there on it trails about his feet. The blond hair is very blond and as much too long for his head as the coat for his body, and his convictions seem as much too big for his soul. This hair, however, is the thing that has made the man. It falls over his eyes like the languid wings of a bleached eagle.

He speaks:

"There's sumf'in wrong when a man's so low down that he'd rather beg than take, when he'd rather stick to the Straus water wagon, and sleep in mooinicipal lodgin' houses. We fellers with the benefit of the orginized I-double-yer-double-yers [his pronunciation as nearly as one may spell it] with the social fabric mere pocket han-kerchers in our palms, and the remedies in our minds, to think that such should show up so ratten bad is enough to break a feller's beliefs in all that it teaches. Mr. Chairman and brudder woikers, I'll tell you where the trouble lies. In ourselves—in us I-double-yer-double-yers. We're most of us too damn lazy to work when we get the offer of a job. Philosophy consists in staying round the stove. 'Why should I woik,' he says, 'when I kin stay where I am and keep warm. Me eats assured, me legs in the standard seventy degrees, and me mind at peace.' Why in the woild don't he go to hell?"

The question is not put savagely; it is put sadly. It is not aggression, it is depression. He feels himself to be at least a thumbnail edition of The Great One.

Someone from somewhere leans down out of space and demands in a stage whisper, "Fellow worker, did you take that job Mrs. O'Hennesy offered you last Saturday?"

The blond hair settles down still more abjectly over the patient eyes. "No, brother worker," he answers. "I felt the proposition to be an injustice to the cause—I won't go scabbin'."

He lets his chin find his bosom; his eyes are packed beyond standing room limit with a great conviction and an organized wistfulness. There is a quaver of acceptance throughout the room. A man at the back, with his head in his hands, nods slowly; perhaps it is sleep, perhaps it is approval, and perhaps it is neither.

"You know," he says, "they don't call it the downward slide any more; it's our temperamental journey."

And so still society and societies find the earnest and the faker, the visionary and, sad to state, the vision. The remedy and the remnant.

Therefore, in these summer mornings, soon to creep in upon us with cool legs and fiery shoulders, may we not see promenading our avenue not only Mr. So-and-so from somewhere with his dark-rimmed monocle but that other? Those who wear caps and badges, and those who wear hats and canes? For with us this springtime and this summer are such numbered among the present.

And out in front of the procession, I'm sure we shall see a little blond man, hands in pockets, stamping out his creeds as his coattails wink round a corner between the Forties and the Fifties.

Fashion Show Makes Girl Regret Life Isn't All Redfern and Skittles

Barnes took the title of this article on the world of fashion from a British expression that life cannot be "all beer and skittles," referring to a popular bowling game.

The "resourceful Keiths" to whom she refers were probably the chain of theatres owned by Benjamin F. Keith, the father of vaudeville. Raised on a New Hampshire farm, Keith joined the circus world and first proved his showman's talents exhibiting Baby Alice, an infant weighing at three months only twenty-four ounces, for ten cents a look. Keith's success escalated with each new addition to the "act," until by 1885 his own show hall was running six performances daily of two hours each. By 1913 he owned a vast chain of vaudeville houses and theatres in numerous cities. His thirtieth anniversary show in a Brooklyn theatre in December 1913 featured a dramatic playlet starring Mrs. Fiske's former leading man, Volant and his flying piano, Camille's poodles, a twenty-minute musical comedy, dancers, singers, and a juggler.

Probably, had I a really thorough knowledge of the old masters in literature, I should discover that it had all been done before. But being charmingly and precociously ignorant, I indulge in phantasmagoria upon the mental horizon, to announce with bland and trite composure that there is something a little different happening for the world of fashions; in short, a beauty fashion show has been delivered to the public by the resourceful Keiths.

There were twenty of them, they were young, they were without doubt pretty; they all stood some five feet odd; they produced upon the spectator a sensation of orgy; they caused acute concentration, and they all so nearly approached the standard that one groaned for a flaw.

It brings one back so shockingly to earth to mention names, but it must be done. Miss May Tully started it; Sam Ash sings, ushers, and bows it in, and Audrey Munson, Selma Pittack, Peggy Hopkins, Betty Brown, Virginia Kelly, Edna Burton, Ethel Schaffner, Mary and Sadie Mullen, Kathryn Beach, Kent Jackson, Maude Mason, Kay Karey, Marjorie Demerest, Blanche King, Ivy Melzer, and Nan Foley trip it sweetly out. By the time they all have taken their positions at the sides—some standing with butterfly hands in clinging chiffon and tulle, in satin and in lace, or smiling over powdered bosoms—and by the time, we say, each creation has been drawled before your senses, languished before your longing, and hesitated upon your hopes, you feel so ultra ultra up your spine that your ninety-eight-cent near-linen waist suddenly perceives that it is passé.

With a shock you appreciate that you are not a la mode, that you do not Maison Maurice through life, that you do not negligee a la Bonwit Teller to bed. Ah, well! Life has never been all Redfern and skittles!

And, if we may ask, what next? Yet do not answer. I fear to hear. For surely we are becoming but the models to our gowns. I ask you what temperament could dominate such things as the swirling, truculent, commanding, belligerent, docile, and arrogant charm of this thing that is laced upon the body of a girl?

It does not matter we are glad; we scent temptation in the air, and we scent the odors of invasion. The styles have got us by the throat—we laugh as they hurl us to the ground. We exult as we sink into that deep peace, gently lulled into stupefaction by the burden of duchess lace upon our minds, tulle upon our hearts, and gossamer upon our senses. We should worry if we look beautiful in captivity.

After all, life is merely a matter of succumbing becomingly. Therefore, let us root out this fear; let us lean back and be ordained.

Well, take it from you, beauty parade, the sensations are simply great! Paw up the ground! Tousle the skyline with your arrogant headgear! Flaunt the trickery of foliage with the foliage of foot-kicked hems! Life hangs upon a thread—the drawstring of a chemise, the ribbon in a petticoat.

"There are moments in a woman's life when both love and hate must be suspended." The voice is plaintive, yet full of absolute certainty. One turns sharply, and there in the shadow of the wings you observe her drawing a fine line of distinction while she draws one equally as fine with the tip of a stick of rouge upon her lips.

"What! Is there, then, something a little out of place?"

She throws her arms out wide. "Everything," she says. "The rehearsals take all one's time, and when one is young they simply must have dates——"

"Dates? Dates, did you say? Dates, you little ninny! Why, this is your supreme chance. What could you be but a chorus girl if you hadn't been picked to be a star in a beauty parade?"

"What could I have been," she demands sharply. "Why, a model, of course. That's what I am. I'm not a chorus girl at all and never have been. You've bought my face a million times upon the current magazines."

"Not that picture of a girl trying on a poke bonnet?"

"Perhaps," she retorts mysteriously, "and perhaps not. Oh dear, I know I'll be late. Don't I look beautiful?" Naive to say the least.

And upon the psychological point of this I was engrossed when the stalking, heartbreaking calves of Beau Brummell walked into my vision.

"No one has mentioned me yet," said Sam Ash with a mid-Victorian dejection. "Not a single notice about me in any way, nothing about my voice, my satin suit, my yellow vest, my lace cuffs, my peculiar type of masculine charm, my simplified manner of looking upon events that pass me by—the girls, you understand. Not a notice about my entrance, and none about my exit."

"You're all wrong, Sam. We not only noticed you, but we thought your voice was exceptional and——"

He put up his hand, "Don't say it," he whispered, smiling beneath his greasepaint and confusion. "I know it, but that is an inheritance, and I'm in no way responsible for those qualities that also put me in the blue ribbon class. Enough, enough. It's a distinction to be the only male among this swirl of perfection, and neither do they make me wear a bell upon my knee as they did in a certain convent in Paris in the days of Victor Hugo. I come, I go; I am content."

"We felt that the public still found something wanting," May Tully said, as she leaned against a dressing-room door with her pocketbook clasped to her bosom. "The fashions have been getting a pretty tight hold on the world, and when one sees which way the mind runs, it's simple enough. What could be more entertaining to the average woman than a beauty parade? Well, if you ask me, nothing. Nor is it merely the women who like to look on. Observe for yourself, look out there: is every face in ten a woman's or a man's?"

I looked and by the way disproved that fallacy about an actor's being unable to see anyone out front. A thousand heads like a field of well-ordered cabbages broke upon my vision. Holy smoke! Did I look like that to the actors? Just an anonymous head stretching on an unperceivable neck with mouth slightly ajar, and with eyelids descending—a white blur in a dark distance—a person too intelligible for the social register and too fragmentary for a pedigree, and too lacking in foliage to be descended from any very luxuriant family tree?

"I don't like it at all," I said aloud.

"What?" asked Miss Tully, whereat I turned crimson and felt like Alice in Wonderland when the white queen shouted at her.

"Do you make your observations correctly?" she continued. "Did you notice for yourself what that house out there says? Listen—hear the hand-clapping. If I'm not mistaken, fifty percent of that at least wears no. 9 gloves."

"What attracts them most?"

"The sublime teamwork of it. That's what counts—they are all thoroughbreds, these girls."

Pet Superstitions of Sensible New Yorkers

Each of the persons Barnes interviewed for this Sunday feature in 1916 was well enough known not to require an introduction. Enrico Caruso had established himself as Italy's greatest tenor, introducing millions to the masterpieces of Verdi and Puccini. Mary Hunter Austin from Illinois wrote political articles for major newspapers, as well as novels and a play, The Arrow Maker, produced in 1911. Amélie Rives, a novelist from Virginia, had acquired a royal title when she married Russian artist Pierre Troubetzkoy but was better known by her maiden name as the author of romances such as The Quick or the Dead?

Chauncey Depew was everyone's favorite good old boy, twice elected to the U.S. Senate and a popular after-dinner speaker and author. Journalists frequently asked his opinion on questions such as why dinner guests are always late and what epitomized the modern American girl, as well as on significant political issues of the day.

The newspaper illustrations of James Montgomery Flagg exemplify the drawings we associate with serialized novels and product advertisements at the turn of the century. Flagg sold his first drawings at the age of ten for ten dollars and by fourteen was earning his own living. After studying abroad, where he specialized in portraits, he returned to New York in 1901 and worked for Scribner's from a studio on West Sixty-seventh Street. In 1917 the governor appointed him New York State's official artist.

A high school teacher named Henrietta Rodman enmired the city's Board of Education in controversy when she concealed her marriage *and then refused to retire after adopting a child. No woman with children was allowed to continue teaching, and when Rodman called the Board a group of "mother baiters," she was suspended for eight months without pay for insubordination. As President of the Feminist Alliance, she frequently spoke on feminist concerns, including her idea of a feminist apartment house providing daycare, dumbwaitered meals, and housecleaning services for working parents.*

Dr. Abraham Jacobi founded the study of children's medicine in this country. His German origins caused him some difficulties during World War I, though he had refused an offer from the Kaiser to head the pediatrics community in Berlin. An outspoken advocate of birth control, Dr. Jacobi received numerous honorary degrees and frequently spoke at banquets before his death in 1919.

A distinguished lady of the American stage, Jane Cowl had begun as a child star a career that would span nearly a century. A great beauty, she later broke a record by performing Shakespeare's Juliet 856 times. She was beginning to write her own plays as well and would produce nine altogether.

Barnes had met Frank Harris the previous summer at a friend's home and accorded him a respect and affection she reserved for very few fellow writers. Born in Ireland, Harris was best known at this time for having edited the Saturday Review *during the 1890s and for his books on Shakespeare. His scandalous memoirs,* My Life and Loves, *were long available only in expurgated editions and his periodical,* Pearson's Magazine, *was eventually shut down for its pro-German point of view. In 1917, Barnes interviewed him at length on his views of genius, art, and politics.*

One always looks up an authority to avoid quoting him. I looked up Sigmund Freud and so am in a position to go on with this story without further contemporary interruption.

It deals with superstitions, and it also deals partly with the subconscious mind, through which all material things of the body are directed—which sees to it that the heart beats, which is the master behind those indiscretions of discreet moments—that quality, in other words, that does the best work of most lives. To discover just how far the voice of the past has carried and into how many ears it has crept, I questioned the elite few.

I recalled to them that Napoleon always carried with him—or rather, had follow him, on a horse set aside for the purpose—a painting of his young son; how at night he had it placed beside his bed; and how, on the morning of the battle of Waterloo, he arose in the gray of the dawn and stumbled over something. Stooping over, he found the picture of his son lying face down, causing him to say with profound significance, "A very ominous thing has happened on a very ominous day!"

I told them also of Goethe's dread of his own back stairs, down which he was never seen to pass. The secret? In his childhood its carpet dotted with crimson roses had made him dream of blood.

I told them of Oliver Goldsmith, who was encouraged to finish what to him was a very irksome task—*The Vicar of Wakefield*—by the industry of a spider, and how upon completion of the last paragraph he raised his eyes only to behold the spider hanging lifeless in its web.

I ended with Gladstone, who kept a special valet to care for a pet pair of amethyst cuff links.

All of this by way of encouraging them to be brave and come out thus.

Said Chauncey M. Depew, leaning back in his chair and

broadening the mouth comforted on either side by the old-fashioned, mutton-chop whiskers, "I am an unsuperstitious man doing superstition grandly. I will sit down to a dinner where I am the thirteenth at the table, though I'd rather not. In three of thirteen cases, the guests have died within the year. In three hundred dinners of fourteen guests that I have attended, sixteen of them have died within the year. Of some four hundred dinners of sixteen guests, something like twenty of the participants have passed out in the following six months.

"So, you see, superstition keeps its hold on the people because statistics are kept of it."

Signor Caruso, who has a voice box in every gesture as well as in his throat, beamed. "Do I believe in superstition? Ah, no! Do I fear the evil eye? No. Am I susceptible to signs? Still no; and yet, to all of my denials I shall have to add, 'Yes.' Superstition is sense without a reason, reason without sense—what you will.

"Shall I illustrate? In Monte Carlo—a place, by the way, where nothing common should happen but where everything common does—I was very fond of motoring. One day my friends and I passed on the road some charming lady priests—those creatures who have sanctified lives. Said my friends: 'Ah! such horrible, such ghastly luck! We must turn back.' But I remonstrated.

"'Did you not see?' they retorted. 'Those lady priests—it will not do to proceed. We must turn back.'

"'My dear sirs,' I protested. 'For lady priests one turns back on nothing but one's past. This ride is still a thing of the future. Proceed.' And so they went on, but presently the car stopped of itself. They said, 'You see? The women, the priests.' I said: 'No gasoline.' But in my heart—ah, well."

The Princess Troubetzkoy—she who is haunted ever with the brackets (Amélie Rives)—handed a cup of tea to her tall painter-husband and quoted from a paragraph composed in her youth: "There is a grain of superstition in the stuff all men are mixed of."

She continued: "There is a certain quality in an old fear, which superstition is, that even I can admit; but if one believes in God, how can one believe in peacocks? To the actor there is nothing more portentous than a peacock; yet I have three in my play *The Fear Market*."

The strong face of Mary Austin seemed suddenly to awaken into a fire.

"Superstitions are things practiced after one has none," she observed. "We hold on to everything that we do not believe. Personally, I want no intellectual junk. It is utterly wrong, this separation of thought from action. To pick up a pin is absurd, and yet——"

She studied, her eyes staring before her, the attitude of one who believes and yet does not believe. And still I saw in her no realization that superstition is the very pigment of life, that it strangles the dull monotony of existence and reduces living to one simple system of profound and pangless pains.

Montgomery Flagg, on the other hand, was funny. It seemed utterly impossible for him to think up a thing. He could be neither naturally superstitious nor yet naturally unsuperstitious. He just wasn't anything at all, in spite of the fact that he vowed he'd like to be.

He has very long legs, and he kept walking about above

them and shaking his head. He was plainly quite crazy about the subject but could improvise no method by which he could break out into a rash of superstition. In the end, he called in his wife and asked her, comically, what the devil his superstitions were, anyway.

She answered promptly, "Women." He said that wasn't superstition, that was a faculty, and walked about some more.

"I know what," he said finally. "I wish they would get up a correspondence school for superstition. I think life is utterly miserable without a superstition. It's like a prayer rug without knees. Great cats! You've put a new zest into my life. I'm going to cultivate my superstitions. It's absurd for a man with an income to be without them. I don't know what I've been thinking of."

Henrietta Rodman, of the short hair and the brogan gait, came next.

"I refuse to live in a topsy-turvy world," she said flatly. "If it is as silly as superstition would have it, and if superstition is real, then at least I can refuse to see it. After all is said and done, it's only a hangover of yesterday, and I can't be bothered with it."

And so I went away from there. I passed out into the street, still looking, and came upon Dr. Abraham Jacobi, whose thin voice said:

"Superstitions? What are superstitions? I do not feel them; I cannot answer to their message. My body is one vast treble of sciatica."

"Ah!" said I, "my grandmother, too, suffered from that. I am sorry."

"Thank you; you are a good girl. And that about your

grandmother establishes a bond between your family and mine, thereby beginning a superstition for ourselves which will hold the world together."

"Not a superstition in me," said Jane Cowl, "unless a hunch is superstition. Once it was about a horse. The owner said he would give me an option on it for a few days. When I returned at the expiration of the period, he had a choice collection of excuses but no horse. Now I always listen to that small, inner voice. Also, I know that if I stay in the country I'll have better health."

Here the unsuperstitious Miss Cowl knocked on wood. Then she laughed, suddenly coloring. "It's only a habit," she said.

Vexed with travail that bore but scant fruit, I came into the golden room of one Frank Harris, a man with the gifted pen but the still more gifted tongue, and put the question to him also.

"The little atavistic superstitions, like skipping certain flagstones and touching parts of the fence, I must confess to. I confess that I am continually counting nine stones and hoping for luck. I find myself looking up, trying to play fair, but all the time acutely conscious just where that ninth one lies.

"I think this is the only superstition I can trace in myself. I rather like whistling, but that is to keep my courage up rather than a superstition."

And as he believes, so will those who do not and who shall discover that superstitions are put aside for the minutes to betray.

The Last Petit Souper (Greenwich Village in the Air—Ahem!)

I have often been amused—perhaps because I have not looked upon them with a benign as well as a conscientious glance—to observe what are termed "characters" going through the city and into some favorite cafe for tea.

The proletariat drinks his brew as a matter of pure reason; how differently does our dilettante drink.

He is conscious of the tea growing; he perceives it quivering in the sun. He knows when it died—its death pangs are beating like wings upon his palate. He feels it is its most unconscious moment, when it succumbs to the courtship of scalding waters. He thrills ever so lightly to its last and by far its most glorious pain—when its life blood quickens the liquid with incomparable amber and passes in high pomp down the passage of his throat.

I am not prepared to say that the one gets nothing out of his cup and the other all. I say only what a dreary world this would be were it not for those charming dabblers. How barren and how dull becomes mere specialization. How much do we owe to those of us who can flutter and find decorative joy in fluttering away this small allotted hour, content with color, perfume, and imported accents, and accompanied by a family skeleton made of nothing less amusing than jade.

The public—or in other words that part of ourselves that we are ashamed of—always turns up the lip when a dilettante is mentioned, all in a patriotic attempt to remain faithful to that little home in the Fifties with its wax flowers, its narrow rockers, and its localisms and, above all, to that mother whose advice was always as correct as it was harmful.

There are three characters that I can always picture to myself. Let us call them Vermouth, Absinthe, and Yvette—the last a girlish name ordinarily associated with a drink transmitting purely masculine impulses.

Vermouth I used to see sitting over a cold and lonely cup of French coffee between ten and eleven of the morning, marking him at once above a position and beneath despair. With him he always carried a heavy blond cane and a pair of yellow gloves. He would stare for long minutes together at the colored squares of the window, entirely forgetful of the fact that he could not look out. Undoubtedly he was seeing everything a glass could reveal, and much more.

Sometimes damson jam would appear beside the solitary pot and the French rolls, proving in all probability that someone had admired and carried off some slight "trifle," composed, written, or painted in that simple hour of inspiration.

He was never unhappy in a sad way; indeed, he seemed singularly and supremely happy, though often beset with pains and sustaining himself with his cane as he went out.

If he was sad, one thing alone betrayed it: that quick, sharp movement of the head given only to those special children of nature—the sparrow who cannot rest but must fly, and the mortal who cannot fly and is therefore condemned to rest.

Then there were Yvette and Absinthe. Yvette had his god in his hip pocket. It was unrolled on every occasion, and when it was at last uncovered, it turned out to be merely a "Mon Dieu, my dear!" whereat it was quickly rolled up again, only to come popping out as quickly, like a refrain, to do battle with Vermouth's patient "Lieber Gott!"

Yvette's coat was neatly shaped, frayed but decidedly genteel. It possessed a sort of indefinite reluctance about admitting itself passé. It had what must be called skirts, and Yvette's legs swung imperially beneath them, as the tongue of the Liberty Bell beneath its historical metal.

A soft felt hat was held in a hand sporting several uncut stones, standing in relation to jewelry as free verse to poetry. As he passed, one caught the odor of something intricate such as struggles from between the pattern of an Indian incense burner. And lastly, there came with Yvette the now-famous, silver-wattled cane.

This cane was tall, alert, and partial. It was to him what the stem is to the flower. It enhanced as well as sustained his bloom, while he meant to life what the candle means to the nun.

Absinthe was like this cane: tall, energetic, but acutely pale. He seemed composed of plaster, his lips alone animate and startlingly scarlet. He spoke with that distinct English accent heard only in America.

He had a habit of laying his hands upon his face, presumably for the same reason ferns are laid beside roses. The nails of these hands were long—longer than Japan had ever thrust beneath the cuticle of any native yellow jacket—and they were silvered or gilded with gold.

There are moments in the lives of all of us, or shall I say some of us, that must be lived in French. As these gentlemen had all passed through that stage, dust could, as a consequence, be discovered upon their discourse. They passed each other the snuffboxes of their thoughts as though they were antiques, each statement was as carefully preserved. In other words, they valued that hour.

These men summed up all those little alien things that in their mother country are merely the dialect of the physique, nor were these men ever so pleased with themselves as when they were recollecting.

Yvette had the most unmistakable traces of foreign sojourns of the three; that unconscious product of a conscious program. He was a leopard who had chosen his own particular spots, and this is perhaps that difference between what we call ourselves and those other odd ones who extend their travels beyond ours on into the mental world, on a journey of so-called nonreason.

Yvette was feminine—he could not only look the part, he acted girlish in much that he did. Yet one should have admired him instead of ridiculing him, for it gave him the ease to say: "But my dear fellow, you make a grave mistake. German women are not fat, they are merely plentiful." Or his "Ah me. I miss the reputations of the boulevards far more than their realities."

Vermouth would smile and answer:

"Yes, yes, I know, but just imagine living in a country where one can have miscarriages by telephone and bruises by telegraph."

Thus, one saw how inscrutable Vermouth had grown along with Absinthe. Together they had spent too many hours contemplating a black tasseled curtain, perhaps because of what it contained or because of what it concealed.

He contended that his head was forever in the clouds. To prove it, he ordered chocolate ice cream and tea, and this at twelve at night; for it is a theory of our dilettante that bad dinners make profound diners, and there he was.

And here also am I, at the identical point that I wanted to reach—the twelve o'clock souper and its significance.

In the most profound and religious moments of the philosopher Marcus Aurelius, he came to this conclusion, that each day should be treated as the last.

And there is the secret of the dilettante. He is always about to pass through that incomparable hour, the hour before and the hour after the supper that may prove the last. And so it is that he, dreaming his dreams, making a liquor of his tears to be drunk upon this last and holiest occasion, has discovered that little something that makes the difference between him and the you who have ordered supplies home for a week.

And I, who have been in the presence of this thing, have learned to understand.

Greenwich Village As It Is

In this second of four articles on the Bohemian crowd and their lifestyle in Greenwich Village, Barnes virtually catalogued the literary luminaries and lesser artistes who populated the area of Manhattan around Washington Square. Barnes herself lived in Greenwich Village from 1913 until her departure for Europe following World War I, and again from her return until her death in 1982. During these early years she traveled in a circle of poets, novelists, artists, actors, and playwrights, many of whose artistic reputations survived far better than her own. Some were publishing periodicals—Alfred Kreymborg wrote for Others, Allen Norton irregularly produced Rogue, and Max Eastman's rhetoric addressed The Masses—and nearly everyone tried a hand at playwriting or poetry. Another publisher, Guido Bruno, the sleazy garretdweller who commercialized the Village for uptown voyeurs, published Barnes's first book, A Book of Repulsive Women, in 1915 in his chap book series and interviewed her for Frank Harris's Pearson's Magazine in 1919. Socialism was fashionable, as was draft resistance, and battling the censors became a cause celebre for Bruno, Harris, Kreymborg, and Theodore Dreiser, among others.

The theatrical milieu of Greenwich Village, which itself had roots in Bohemian circles in California and Chicago, would shape the American theatre for decades to come, first with the casual creation of the Provincetown Players, of which Barnes was a founding member. Eugene O'Neill's early work and plays by Edna St. Vincent Millay, Jig Cook, Susan Glaspell, Floyd Dell, and Louise Bryant offered the serious playgoer the first real alternative to Broadway's showy melo-

223

dramas; Barnes's play Three from the Earth *was produced in 1919. Another response to the same need for serious theatre, the Washington Square Players were more commercial in orientation and would become more lastingly successful as they evolved into the Theatre Guild, which dominated New York's dramatic scene through the twenties and thirties.*

A friend once told me of an artist who had committed suicide because his colors had begun to fade. His canvases were passing like flowers. People looking upon them sighed softly, whispering, "This one is dying," while someone in the background added, "That one is dead." It was the unfulfilled fortune of his future. If he had been less enthusiastic, if he had studied what constitutes permanent color and what does not, he might have left some of those somber pictures that seem to grow daily more rigid and "well preserved." The earliest nudes executed with the most irreproachably permanent colors seem to be clothing themselves slowly with that most perdurable costume—the patina of time. Turner is among those who live by the death of his canvases.

And so people are standing before Greenwich Village murmuring in pitying tones, "It is not permanent, the colors will fade. It is not based on good judgment. It is not of that sturdy and healthy material from which, thank providence, we of the real Manhattan have been fashioned." There are a few who sigh, "It is beautiful in places!" while others add, "That is only an accident."

How charming an answer it was of Nature to make most of her mistakes lovely. Christianity seems to be quite a reprehensible experiment; yet what brings tears so quickly to the eyes as two pieces of wood shaped as a cross?

Why has Washington Square a meaning, a fragrance, so to speak, while Washington Heights has none? The Square has memories of great lives and possibilities therefore; while the Heights are empty, and Fifth Avenue is only a thoroughfare. Here on the north side are stately houses inhabited by great fortunes, the Lydigs and Guinesses and all those whose names rustle like silk petticoats, and on the other side a congeries of houses and hovels passing into rabbit warrens where Italians breed and swarm in the sun as in Naples, where vegetables and fruits are sold in the street as on the Chiaja, and ice cream is made in the bedrooms and spaghetti on the cellar floor. Here is the den where the gunmen conspired recently to shoot down the free-trade butcher and here the row of houses whose inhabitants provide the Women's Night Court with half its sensations. Satin and motorcars on this side, squalor and push carts on that: it is the contrast which gives life, stimulates imagination, incites to love and hatred.

The greater part of New York is as soulless as a department store; but Greenwich Village has recollections like ears filled with muted music and hopes like sightless eyes straining to catch a glimpse of the beatific vision.

On the benches in the Square men and women resting; limbs wide-flung, arms pendent, listless; round the fountains and on the corners children, dark-eyed Italian children shrieking now with Yankee-cockney accent, a moment later whispering to their deep-bosomed mothers in the Tuscan of Dante. Here a bunch of Jewish girls like a nosegay, there a pair of Norwegian emigrants, strong of figure and sparing of speech; a colored girl on the sidewalk jostles a Japanese servant and wonders whether he, too, is colored or if he is thought to be white like "dem dagos."

On every corner you can see a new type; but strange to say, no Americans are to be discovered anywhere. New York is the meeting place of the peoples, the only city where you can hardly find a typical American.

The truth has never been penned about Washington Square and Greenwich Village—names which are now synonymous. To have to tell the truth about a place immediately puts that place on its defense. Localities and atmospheres should be let alone. There are so many restaurants that have been spoiled by a line or two in a paper. We are in that same danger. What can we do? Nothing. The damage has been done, we find, and the wing of the butterfly is already crumbling into dust.

I, personally, have never seen one really good article on Washington Square. The commonest spot is not recognizable. The most daring designs in the shops have all been wrongly colored. As for the long hair of the men and the short hair of the women, that type is to be found on Broadway. Cigarette smoking goes on uptown just as much as it does here; the drinking of wine is just as public; the harmless vanities are displayed in other places quite as blatantly as they are here. The business of making love is conducted under the table beyond Fourteenth Street, but does that establish a precedent forbidding the business of holding hands above the table? Is the touch of kid more harmful than the pressure of boot leather? Of course there are pretenders, hypocrites, charlatans among us.

But where are the records that state that all malefactors and hypocrites have been caught within the limits of what we call our Bohemia? And as for crime, have all its victims been found murdered in the beds of Waverley Place and Fourth Street?

Oh! out upon it, this silly repetition about the impossible people living here. Because we let you see us in our curl papers, must you perforce return to your paternal oil stove crying that you never in your life have done your own front hair up in a bang? And must you play forever the part of the simpering puritan who never heard of sex relations? What little story is it that is ringing in your ears, told you one night by your mother about Dad as she sat in the evening yielding up reminiscences, which by day appear to be right or wrong but at night are only clever little anecdotes, timid or sweet adventures of a man now too old for his youth and too wise to try to repeat those things that have made youth the world over the finest and saddest part of life? So forever we rob ourselves of ourselves. We should be born at the age of seventy and totter gracefully down into youth.

Is the beggar of Paris or of Naples any better off than the beggar of Washington Square? And is it not by our beggars that the similarity of a race as well as a group shall be known? These beggars who are the city's finger bowls, wherein the hands of greed have dipped!

What then? We have our artists, but we also have our vendors. We have our poets, but we also have our undertakers. We have our idlers, but have we not also our scrubwomen? We have our rich and our poor. We are wealthier by a mendicant and wiser by a poet.

In reality, Washington Square and Greenwich Village are not one. They have become one above the pavement at the height where men's heads pass; but measured out in plain city blocks the Village does not run past Sixth Avenue. It begins somewhere around Twelfth Street and commits suicide at the Battery.

There are as many artists living off the Square as on it. Some shops are mentioned as these artists are mentioned, because they have caught a certain something that for want of a better word we call atmosphere!

We always speak of Daisy Thompson's shop, of the Treasure Box, of the Village Store and of the Oddity Cellar. Just as many pretty things, however, are to be seen in a small shop on Eighth Street between Fifth and Sixth Avenues. Why is it not also mentioned? Because it is in, and not of, the Village.

There is the pleasant night life of the Café Lafayette. The Brevoort is loved for its basement, where one can catch the lights gleaming between the shrubbery. There, too, is the waiter who has been serving you for ten years past. There is a certain familiarity in everything you eat. You can tell just where you are by closing your eyes. The cold cuts of the Lafayette are superior to those of the Brevoort; the New Orleans "fizzes" are abominable at the latter and delightful at the former. There is a chance that you may meet someone you do not like, as there is a probability that you will meet someone that you do. You decide beforehand what kind of a sneer you are going to throw Billy, just how coldly you are going to look past Bobbie or freeze the spinal column of Louise, who has been your next-door neighbor for months.

The cholera scare populated the place, but the atmosphere entered not much earlier than the advent of one Bobbie Edwards. In nineteen hundred and six he turned what was then the A Club into what later was known as the Crazy Cat Club or the Concolo Gatti Matti—at a restaurant run by Paglieri at 64 West Eleventh Street.

Edwards introduced the habit of pushing the tables back and organizing an after-dinner dance. He sent out cards of invitation to his friends, and they in their turn sent out invitations to their acquaintances. Leroy Scott, Howard Brubaker, and Mary Heaton Vorse were among its earliest members. Thus came the first filterings of what was to be Bohemia.

Yet what does one know of a place if one does not know its people intimately? I know of nothing that I can offer as a substitute that will fit unless it is an anecdote—the skeleton of life.

This is the story of a dancer who came down here on a bus one day last summer, to live here. What she had done in her past we did not ask—what her eyes did not tell we knew was not worth knowing—yet she was vastly frank. One night this girl arose from the table (it was at Polly's) to answer the phone. At her side sat a young Russian, and as she went out she said to him, "Now remember, none of your dirty Slavic tricks, don't you put your fingers in my coffee while I'm gone—mind!" and someone at the other side of the table called out to the boy thus addressed, "Well, you Cossack you, what are you going to do about that?" Instantly the dancer ran back and, flinging her arms about the boy's neck, cried, "A Cossack, how glorious! I have heard of your brutalities."

And so now, having eased my mind by having made at least an attempt to dispel some of the false notions, I can find heart to give this place a body.

On Macdougal Street just above the Dutch Oven is the Liberal Club. It is one more of those things that have come to us from uptown. Margaret Wilson was one of its founders, but needless to say it has changed its tone since its change of locality. Members may bring their friends if they do not bring them too often. Many people have met here, fought, loved, and passed out. The candles of many intellects have been snuffed here to burn brighter for a space until they, too, have given place to newer candles. Here Dreiser has debated and Boardman Robinson sketched, and Henrietta Rodman has left the sound of her sandaled feet. Harry Kemp has posed for his bust only to find on turning round that no one was doing it. Jack Reed and Horace Traubel have been seen here; Kreymborg, Ida Rauh, Max Eastman, Bob Minor, and Maurice Becker; a hundred others.

Whitman dinners are held every thirty-first of May in a private room of the Brevoort. Two seasons ago the heart of the Washington Square Players began to beat here, though the theatre itself was located uptown. A little later Charles Edison—who can really afford to be known for himself, only wearing his father as a decoration—started the Little Thimble Theater with the great Guido Bruno for manager. If they had no successes aside from *Miss Julia*, that was of sufficient importance to have warranted the venture.

Bruno started to make a personal paper, entitled *Greenwich Village*. Allen Norton soon followed with the harmless little *Rogue*, which went out for a while but which is scheduled to return in October or November. Kreymborg put out *Others*, a magazine of verse, blank— the moods of many; a sort of plain-bread-of-poetry— called *vers libres*; and though it was printed in the Bronx it was reeking with the atmosphere of the studios along the south side of the square.

Clara Tice burst into print, and so did Bobbie Locher. The Baron de Meyer began to be seen above a glass of yvette in the cafes, among a score of faces that may have had addresses out of the Village itself but were Bohemians. After all, it is not where one washes one's neck that counts but where one moistens one's throat. And still things are coming, expanding. The very air seems to be improving. There is a rumor that "King" McGrath—or otherwise Jack—backed by some society people, is going to open a tavern on Sheridan Square and, Jack adds to those who will listen, "*With* a license."

George Newton is also planning to erect a Toy Theatre on the same Square. Newton has started a new paper, selling at two cents. The first issue will be out in August. Ah, you see! after all you cannot put out the sun by spitting on its shadow.

And our studio buildings? Our apartment houses? The Judson on the south side of the Square, the hotel Holly, the hotel Earle, the Washington; the promised building where now stands the Village soda fountain and Guido Bruno's garret. The Washington Mews has already been partly demolished to arise again. And of recent past history, what of Louis's at 660 Washington Square South? It is held in the memory, as only a dead woman or a past hostelry can be held: the one for its clasp on the heart, the other for its hold on the mind. Louis's had not only Louis, it also had Christine, a woman who, had she not been born in this century, would have been some great heavy goddess whose presence would have been justice without word of mouth. Louis's was closed because it was running without a license. Perhaps that was one of its charms! Drink there was not mere drink, it was wine *libre*.

And there is the Candlestick Tea Room, and there is Gonfarone's, and there is the Red Lamp, Mori's, Romano's, the Red Star, and Mazzini's.

And so you of the outer world, be not so hard on us, and above all, forbear to pity us—good people. We have all that the rest of the world has in common commodities, and we have that better part: men and women with a new light flickering in their eyes, or on their foreheads the radiance of some unseen splendor.

Becoming Intimate with the Bohemians

Four o'clock in the afternoon and someone has spilled a glass of wine; it creeps across the tablecloth in a widening pattern of sulky red. It is morning in Bohemia.

In a little back room, with pictures hanging crooked on the wall, lies King McGrath, far from the tumult and shouting, his head in his hand, looking into the face of the Virgin painted on the church just facing his three-plank bed. Yea, for the King has a cold.

Now, while Jack lies there staring at the painted face of the Virgin—while the dusk of a musty hall creeps through an ever-widening keyhole set in a house that was once something, as the ever-widening lips of a drunkard who was once a man—out of her dainty sheets, arising in dimity glory, shaking loose myrrh, long stifled, from crumpled lace, the Queen of Bohemia arises, and I can't tell you her name.

Yes, the day for the Greenwich Villager has begun. The waiters in the Brevoort and the Lafayette begin to preen themselves, for they are the only waiters in the world who feel free to cultivate their innermost longings—in other words, to acquire an individual soul.

Well, isn't Bohemia a place where everyone is as good as everyone else—and must not a waiter be a little less than a waiter to be a good Bohemian? Therefore, say nothing, you of the Bronx, when he openly ridicules you for your taste for parsnips when there are artichokes on the bill of fare. He means nothing, it is only his soul caroling on to higher things. He feels that he has to be negligent before he can be Nietzsche.

Between this hour and six, which is known as Polly's hour or the hour of the Dutch Oven or the Candlestick, the tea tipplers and the cocktail dreamers gather slowly in the basement of the Brevoort. Upstairs is respectability, wife, children, music; a violin plays a sorry tune like melancholy robins on a telegraph wire charged with gossip. In the basement is all that is naughty: spicy girls in gay smocks or those capricious clothes that seem to be making faces at their wearers, such as the gowns of Gaugh. Wild, wild exotics of fabrics—effects of Bakst. Men with arms full of heavy literature, pockets jingling with light coin, resplendent in ties—hold, Allen Norton has described them:

. . . The arch cravat.
That maddens like the moon and once looked at
The moral soldier faints and turns his back.

And again—but no, you have an idea of those winking satin ties, the woven threnodies that make music upon the outside of the throat as the voice box on the inside.

"A liqueur, Tito"—this to her latest lover lounging beautifully, a handsome man of fifty summers, but not these summers; an Italian, perhaps, or a Russian or a Frenchman, for the Bohemians have a preference for foreign make. I personally am with them: the foreigner lies so bewitchingly; he is so cleverly bad. Perhaps it is because he is a better scholar of nature or a better liar—a scholarly man toward unscholarly moments. He has the secret of unalloyed happiness and unalloyed pain. Recognition of both, acceptance of both, love of both, that is all.

Tito orders the liqueur, fingering the coins in his pocket. Has he enough with which to pay? What does it matter? The room is full of just such predicaments as his: no one can pay, and everyone does.

An impressionist sits in the corner with a woman. I know the man very well; he is hawk-faced, thin, and comes into my mind as something worth telling about. He holds his head slightly up, exposing a soft, high collar in which moonstones sulk. On his fingers are red gems and green; these fingers lie over the top of his staff as though they were separate personalities and wanted to be taken notice of. He knows how to smell nicely, gesture tellingly, and above all, he has the art of looking mid-McKinley, with a touch of the frailties of the Louis period. He talks in breathless English, snuffing each little candle of thought one by one, going out in the end in absolute conversational darkness.

The girl I know, too. Her hair is short (a proof that the Bohemians are, after all, so much like others that they are not original even in this); she had a historic past. She is one of the best sports I know—she has all the maladies in the almanac, and she doesn't care. She was born laughing, and she will die that way—a boy's laugh, a laugh that springs up from the gutter like a flower. She smokes cigarettes, perhaps a hundred a day. I have seen her rummage among the ashes for "makings" while there was yet a faint perfume in the air of others but lately smoked at a

dollar a box. I have listened to her and have laughed, but way down deep I knew she was keeping things that she feared lived—children of memory, and those memories' children.

She is quite reckless; she dances through an evening, she gets terribly drunk, for she can no longer stand what she used to do when, some ten summers ago, she was a girl. All that life holds she has borrowed to hold once also in those long, thin hands; only the eyes never change. They are set in her face like a child's peering over a wall where all the refuse of life has been whirled and caught. It is a terrible and a beautiful thing; her name is—let it go at that.

But let us pass on; it is to laugh.

Sometimes a room gathers an atmosphere, and sometimes it gathers a crowd. These rooms, these studios, these cafes in some future day will fall to dust, but the dust will fall singing.

I stood on the corner of Sixth Avenue where it runs past Greenwich Avenue one night, and as I stood there a fur-trimmed woman, heavily laden with jewels, and two lanky daughters hailed me. In her eyes was a restlessness that was strange to me who have been used to looking into the quiet, often lazy, faces of those about me. Her eyes roved; so did the eyes of her daughters. There was a definite air of the loser looking for the lost.

"Where is Greenwich Village?" she asked, and she caught her breath.

"This is it," I answered, and I thought she was going to collapse.

"But," she stammered, "I have heard of old houses and odd women and men who sit on the curb quoting poetry to the policemen or angling for buns as they floated down into the Battery with the rain. I have heard of little inns where women smoke and men make love and there is dancing and laughter and not too much light. I have heard of houses striped as are the zebras with gold and with silver, and of gowns that—— Quick, quick!" she cried, suddenly breaking off in the middle of the sentence and grabbing a hand of either child exactly like the White Queen in *Through the Looking Glass* as she hurried forward. "There's one now!"

And so she left me in pursuit of a mere woman in a gingham gown with a portfolio under her arm.

I heard that she successfully chased her into Polly's and, once there, sat with bated breath—bated with the little giblets of the mind bantered back and forth between tables from the throats of Ada Foster, Adele Holliday, the perpetual and delightful debutante; George Baker, Renée Lacoste, Dave Cummings, Maurice Becker, Marney and Billy, while at another table Harold Stearns talked to Francis Gifford between bites of a fraudulent tapioca pudding.

But still Madam Bronx was not satisfied. She trailed away with her two daughters wobbling after her on uncertain Sheffield Farm-like ankles unto the Dutch Oven, where she listened to Floyd Dell explaining the drama to Max Eastman or caught what she thought might be risqué bits in the conversation between Marsden Hartley and Demuth. The girls ordered custard pie and giggled, for it is so that custard pie should be eaten in Bohemia.

Finally, Madam Bronx could stand it no longer. "Are you an artist?" she inquired of a red-haired woman who had somehow forgotten to cut her hair.

Marsden Hartley

The red-haired woman smiled; a twinkle came into her eye. "No," she answered, "I am a pamphleteer."

"What is that?"

"One of the birth controllers," the red-haired lady answered with immovable face.

And from there to the Candlestick, and from the Candlestick to the Mad Hatter, and from the Mad Hatter to the French pastry shop, and from the pastry shop to all the known haunts, ending up in Mazzini's. For this sad little fur-trimmed woman with her certified daughters was ignorant of those lost places that are twice as charming because of their reticence.

No, I shall not give them away, but I'll locate one of them for those of you who care to nose it out as book lovers nose out old editions. It is a basement this side of Sixth Avenue on the odd-number length of Washington Place. I lived there once, but on the night of the disaster to the gunpowder mill in Jersey I was confronted with a house full of wailing women, in the midst of which the rotund landlady, in bare feet, stood crying out upon Manhattan and broken windows in general and moaning for her rosary of beads and her rosary of children.

"They do not shatter glass in Boston like this," she said, and stood shivering until she sank upon the cushions of my couch, calling aloud for a drop of wine to forestall the chills, adding that dynamite was mighty impertinent.

And so I moved. But there in the basement, with pallid Latin faces, are a husband chef and a wife waitress who bring out molding tomes: a cookbook of the early Renaissance, or a favorite recipe of some baron written in his own hand long ago, fading now from the page as a blush from the cheeks of the love-stricken. Or monsieur the chef plays on a bulging mandolin, with twitching blond mustache, while the young composer who lately met with an accident, surviving with a broken leg, sits profiled against the wall, smiling with fine, kind eyes.

This is real—this is the unknown. Even a basement has its basement, and this is one of the basements below Bohemia.

Well, there is Bobby. We cannot forget Bobby, with his row of ukuleles hanging in his studio on Washington Square. Bobby has kept up the old tradition: he has proposed marriage to every girl in the place, hoping devoutly that she would not take him seriously. Bobby, with his hornrimmed spectacles that keep his eyes from stampeding into trouble as a fence keeps cattle from forbidden grounds; Bobby, who steps upon a table at the Black Cat to sing the now justly famous song, "Way Down South in Greenwich Village," and the still more pathetic "Song of the Camel" who desires to forgo the waters of a million pumps to be with his love.

Guido Bruno, in green felt hat, can be seen pondering over his vichy and milk while he writes a last edition on a paper napkin. Or Peggy O'Neill—not the actress, but the other Peggy—comes bouncing in to spill the latest dirt, her hands on her hips as she adds, "Watch me page myself a dinner," later ordering a "flock of lambs," which is nothing more nor less than chops.

A few Radical pests come in with flowing ties and flowing morals, walking from table to table, maintaining that Baudelaire was right when he said, "Be drunk on wine or women, only be drunk on something." Hippolite Havel

supports Baudelaire a little better than anyone else, keeping up at the same time what nothing can quite obliter-
ate—education that has been blunted into charlatanism of
thought through many, many hard knocks.

There are the evenings in the studios, blue and yellow
candles pouring their hot wax over things in ivory and
things in jade. Incense curling up from a jar; Japanese
prints on the wall. A touch of purple here, a gold screen
there, a black carpet, a curtain of silver, a tapestry thrown
carelessly down, a copy of *Rogue* on a low table open at
Mina Loy's poem. A flower in a vase, with three paint
brushes; an edition of Oscar Wilde, soiled by socialistic
thumbs. A box of cigarettes, a few painted fans, choice
wines (this here the abode of the more prosperous).

And then—a small hall bedroom under the eaves, a dirty
carpet lying in rags; a small cot bed with a dirty coverlet. A
broken shaving mug with a flower in it, a print of a print
on the wall, a towel thrown in a corner, a stale roll and a
half-finished cup of tea. A packing box with a typewriter
on it, some free verse, a copy of a cheap magazine with a
name in the table of contents that corresponds to the
name written at the top of the sheet of paper in the
machine. A smell of incense, perhaps from the hall downstairs, where the rent is higher, perhaps bought with the
last quarter. A pair of torn shoes, a man's body on the bed,
with arms thrown out, breathing slowly the heavy breath
of the underfed.

Then there are the theatres that have sprung up, the
Washington Square Players with a lease at the Comedy,
and now the Provincetown Players in a room next to the
Liberal Club—which, by the by, in spite of its liberality,

threw out a few poker players—and there are to be others.

Of small shops: Daisy Thompson's, the Jolin Shop, the Treasure Box (somebody took some jade rings from here—if they see this, please return). Helena Dayton has clay personalities for sale in some of them; Clara Tice's can be bought in others.

And then in the end, when everything else closes up and the chairs are lifted to the laps of the tables and the lights go out—all together—there is always the Hell Hole on Fourth Street and Sixth Avenue. A slit in the door, a face staring into your face, the dirty back room with its paper cutouts of ladies in abbreviated undergarments, the men at the tables, the close atmosphere, the sordid faces, the unclean jokes; straggling in of colored women and men, a colored sweetheart with a smile set in her face like a keyboard into a night—compliments from him, first embarrassment from her, then preening to end in a mincing exit. The deadening down, down, into a gray, drunken slumber, the still, dead beer; the heavy air, the inert bodies—daylight.

Life's little comedy: comedy's great tragedy—Bohemian night, Washington Square day. Melancholy, the only sign of loyalty to something they once believed. A few friends, a sweetheart playing with two make-believe fires. Real things that are beautiful mixed in dreadfully with that which is sham; a wonderful, terrible hash on the table of life. And the fan keeps on blowing through the world, winnowing the wheat from the chaff. And because the chaff is lighter it blows up and up and turns and shines in the sun, dancing a moment a mad, wild dance—a dance that turns the gaze from the grain lying there in a still, fruitful heap. But the chaff dances slower and slower, down, down, and down; it blows out of sight—it has never been.

Well, in the morning it will be funny again, the morning beginning at four or perhaps as early as eleven. There will be the occasional balls, the dances at the clubs, the dinners at the inns, the appointments for a theatre or a moving picture show; the chats in the evening about art and life, the theories as old as the hills and the newest fads that are new, the trottings uptown of the interior decorators to match a shade for a chair or a color scheme for a studio. Anton Hellman hovering above the legs of chairs arranging their tone as Ziegfeld arranges the legs of his chorus. The Italian restaurant keepers will begin to mix the tomato sauce for the evening rounds of spaghetti. Students will gather in the park. Somewhere out of the rattle of trolley cars will be heard the sharp, high cry of little bootblacks crying, "Shine, shine, mister; only three cents!" The policemen, swinging their clubs, will stroll past the Mews, talking together. The leaves crackle under foot, the grass dies, the birds grow scarcer and scarcer. The endless crowds of "slummers" looking for painted beads and black tassels will go by. A candle or two will gleam in a studio window to the south. A rattle of music through an open window, the weeping of a baby in a tenement, the click of a typewriter in a basement, then the Villagers hurrying to their favorite eating place; the cigarettes once more, once more the round of drinks, once more the hilarity, a few clever jokes, a jest at free love—night.

And back there in the little room where lay the King staring into the face of the Virgin, behind his bars now stands the King in full dress, for the tumult and the shouting has begun, and the King is going out into his day. Yea, for the King has forgotten his cold.

How the Villagers Amuse Themselves

After all, one must be faithful to one's bracelets, and there are so many little pleasures bracelets enjoy and so many social functions one must attend if one is to be in the whirl at all; and then what of those ten debutante wristwatches per season? They must have their chance.

Well, it's a hard life, for down here one has not only to live up to one's blue china—an occupation much lamented by Wilde—but they have also to live up to their jade and antiquities, not to mention their sullied reputations.

So the Greenwich Villager sets out to amuse himself. It's sordid and hard, but it must be done. There are those beastly early, taxing breakfasts in bed. There is the nerve-racking half-hour before dinner when the incredible folly of the world must be tabloided into wisdom; for down here one teaches more than one has knowledge of, one dreams more than one has power to dream, one hopes beyond hope. Music must be put in the arches of one's laughter and into the arches of one's feet, for the poet's footbeats must have both rhythm and scansion.

With manicure set in his hip pocket and his nails shining like a Venetian tumbler from much surreptitious buffing on his moist palm, the Villager walks across the tiled floor of the cafe. From his shoulders hangs a long Mephistophe-lian cape; this he unclasps slowly with long, white, convalescent hands. The cape slips back—ah, dear Lord, what have we done to receive so much beauty per flash! On his gaunt form is naught but a leopard skin, a little talcum, a string of beads, a garter of winking, seductive sapphires. A dawn of myrrh, a dusk of Hindu-colored grease paint.

His feet are sandaled, and in his pocket lie also the pipes of Pan, bursting with incredible music, heavy with frothy flutings; sad, bright, irregular tunes, untouched by either the law of technique or rule.

And as he breaks thus upon the vision:

Then all the long-prone dead arose.
And one was Helen of old Troy,
Still walking down the day at close
To find some yet-unconquered boy.

Or one a Persian king a-gloat
Who sat with foot half-raised and cold
For one last step upon a throat
That sepulchred a tongue of gold.

Or one perchance was Proserpine
With seven grapes caught in her hair,
Like little birds made mute on wine
Who knew of love but did not dare

To follow on where chase met chase,
And hunted, caught the hunting one,
And in the darkness kissed a face
That once had looked on Babylon.

Yes, that was the way it went, for it was party time, and the Liberal Club was giving a ball.

In the corner a player piano sang to a life much synco-
pated, and the figures in flowing silk and hasty chiffons
whirled round and round, while in the near distance the
president laid appreciative hands on an ebony beard.

A woman in an orange smock comes cooing across the
floor.

"You're marvelous tonight, Harold," she says as a Corsi-
can leans down to catch the compliment his ears have
grown concave for. "In that wig and that gray uniform
you are simply divine—you are a magnificent core on
which to hang the fruits of love." Again he smiles; they
trail off together into a one-step.

"Do you see that couple dancing there? Yes, the one in
orange and the other in gray. Well," continues a short-
haired progressive, in an undertone to the man who wrote
the first realistic sonnet beginning:

Six loaves of bread I hold upon my heart
For like six loaves your love feeds my desire. . . .

"What I know about them would make all other knowledge a sort of ignorance."

This amusement passes, and they go back to their dancing or sit around making tomorrow's scandal.

The lanterns sway in globs of yellow and red light; one
bursts suddenly into a quick, high flame, chars down. No
one notices that from the line of lanterns one has passed
out into nothingness. Only a man sitting at a table raises
his eyes a moment, the blue light falling on his red hair
and beard. He looks down again. The next dance begins.

Or it may not be the Liberal Club but Webster Hall on
East Eleventh Street. Perhaps Mike, the waiter of Polly's,

is taking in tickets at the door; perhaps Allen Norton passes by in Oriental splendor. Or one sees the Baroness leap lightly from one of those new white taxis with seventy black and purple anklets clanking about her secular feet, a foreign postage stamp—cancelled—perched upon her cheek; a wig of purple and gold caught roguishly up with strands from a cable once used to moor importations from far Cathay; red trousers—and catch the subtle, dusty perfume blown back from her—an ancient human notebook on which has been written all the follies of a past generation.

By two and two they come, pompous beetles in the web of an old desire. They pass up the stairs, are seen walking through the gallery arm in arm, painted faces and painted skins, painted limbs and painted fans, telling each other the things in life that mean little and much. In a corner Christine stands eating a meat sandwich; a woman goes jangling by, covered with trinkets—harnessed like a horse to the past. At the bar a gray mist floats over the heads of a man and woman drinking absinthe from one tall glass. Somebody else is singing a song. A party of three pushes by, two women and a man; by one of the round tables Beatrice lies in a Bohemian attitude in the cold and secure New England embrace of Albert.

Not long ago I sat through one of these balls myself. This particular night, a great deal of cheap beer had been drunk, and along about three-thirty some of it was carried out in a little human keg—a fainting oblong of pain upon the shoulders of a Polish woman, carried so out into the night.

Well, had not a lantern gone out also?

A drunken Swede reeled up to me, burned a hole in my veil, and pulled me out upon the floor. The bandmaster began pounding the stage with his feet, calling out some item of interest which each pair of ears let slide, depending upon the sharpness and curiosity of the neighbor ear. A boy in white flannels, white face, and rouged lips skipped lightly by, holding one perfect lily. Someone tore me from the arms of the Swedish man, and looking up, I found the tear-stained face of Alexis above me. I said:

"Wherefore do you weep?"

"Ah," he cried, "life has become so pure that it is no longer a pleasure to go slumming. What's the use of thrusting your hands into mud only to have them emerge cleaner and brighter, like a kitchen knife.

"Why," he continued, "one can sit in the gutters of Manhattan and arise covered with nothing worse than the shadow of a star. Jean Valjean could have passed beneath our city, gone through its most corrupt sewers and have found—what?" he demanded tragically, letting go of my shoulder blade in a moment of reckless forgetfulness. "Nothing but a lot of castoff ethics and two or three discarded points of view."

I took him, weeping, once around the hall.

"And what did you expect?" I asked.

"Do you suppose," he answered, "I left the lure of my student's lamps and my shelves of Rabelais and Moore for this? Do you think I came from upper Park Avenue, where every grocer knows delightful French jokes and wraps up the prunes with subtleties, to come here and listen to the baker's daughter talk about the possibilities of reform in New York? Or on the other hand, the charming decadence of Lawrence Hope: 'Less than the dust beneath your chariot wheels'—indeed! 'Pale hands I loved'—nonsense!"

I left him spilling his too-full soul like cologne into a perfect cambric handkerchief.

And all these nights, whether in Webster Hall, the Liberal Club, Fifty-seventh Street, or private studios, and as Angela ended in *The Genius*—they sink steadily and die.

To rise again. With differences.

To play poker somewhere and get thrown out. That is one form of amusement.

To enjoy the lovemaking of another woman's husband.

And again, to get somebody out of jail.

Well, and what of the other pleasures?

The amusements of those who have to "bat around"— they must be fed, and the only difference between a Bohemian and an ordinary slum-ite is that the slum-ite dies in a self-respecting way in some alley. The Bohemian is a man who knows how to enjoy his poverty: sponging, yes, but sponging among sponges. Not one but has taken, not one but has given.

But these are only the more obvious ways in which the Villager amuses himself.

It's amusing to kill a cat.

It's amusing to rip up objects of art.

It's amusing to wear purple ties and yellow bathrobes.

It's amusing to smoke cigarettes under the bed.

It's amusing to lose one's reputation.

It's more amusing to talk away someone else's.

It's still more amusing to watch the whole world going to the devil from the fire escape.

But all these things are child's play, thank you.

Listen. There is an idea going about that people enjoy themselves when they are happy. What a preposterous idea! How like the stupid world to think so.

These are not the real activities of the man who amuses himself when he is miserable. Had you ever thought of that? There is a certain room in a certain house for all of us where we live out the great comedy—alone. A moment when the fog has settled over the chimney pots and a feeling of autumn comes into the soul, leaving an ineffable sorrow behind it as deep and as portentous as the thing which gives it birth. This is the real way that the Bohemian amuses himself. How shall I tell you of it, or how should we any of us know? It may come from a line in a long-forgotten book, perhaps the color of a faded flower in an old vase. Perhaps none of these.

Nearly always a memory—a broken memory, a small thing of five seconds—and then——

Gathering his hat suddenly to his heart, he makes a dash for the street. Something had almost touched him as he stood by the empty grate. Perhaps it was only a shudder; perhaps it was a sense that "we cannot be living always, and we must be satisfied."

Found on the Bowery

Barnes clearly found a friend in Mimi Aguglia, the sizzling Sicilian actress whose voluptuous dance in Oscar Wilde's Salome *brought her overnight success in 1913. Barnes had interviewed her a week after the opening, and Aguglia appeared by name in several of Barnes's short tales of these years. After several revivals of her famous role, Aguglia found a career in Hollywood films.*

It pleases me from time to time to write of those people who, having gone around the entire circle of human feeling, finally end where they began. To write of a puritan, perhaps, who, having a birth in Brooklyn, leaves for the great metropolis to become eventually the inevitable Messalina, only to end once more in Brooklyn, to die at last at the age termed by the mourner rubbing his hands palm to palm with exceeding pleasure as "ripe". Just what age "ripe" may be, he does not explain.

Nevertheless, it is something of a satisfaction to find one race of people who have no circle and who disdain to call finality final. These people are the Italians, insofar as the Italian drama characterizes something of their soul.

In the midst of life, scorning beginning and acknowledging but a temporary end, these people lift themselves clear of love and hate and murder long enough only to make the return to them both profitable and spectacular—the art of the swordsman who wipes his rapier that it may lose none of the joy of new blood.

"Murder— how they love it!"

Whether I should ever have got alone to the Italian theatre or not, I do not know. Mimi Aguglia brought me there, forcibly. Not by hand nor by word of mouth did she direct me. It happened one night some years ago: I saw her on Broadway as Salome.

Ah, what a creature; a little heavy, not a woman who has eaten her food without so much as observing it, as many do, but a woman who has gossiped with it and become strangely familiar. Short, black curls weighed down with oils and perfumes lay on her shoulders; her eyes, those marvelous, extraordinary eyes of the ordinary Sicilian—set between the upper lid of ebony and the lower lid of bister, like jewels in bondage—looked neither to right nor to left as she advanced with curling feet to the middle of the stage.

One forgot her weight, her smallness of stature, her lack of lithe youth. True, she was not the high-born daughter of Herodias who forbade Herod to look upon this daughter. But then, is it only a king or a queen, after all, who can give life to such stupendous feeling and such command of motion as that indulged in by Salome! Nay, for before my eyes did I see Mimi growl and make moan, cupping her hands like leaves in a great fire that fail and break within the heat and die utterly. Mimi, if I am not mistaken, is a pure, great peasant. What she failed to complete with her hands, she did with her feet; that which her feet left unaccounted for, her back told. If indeed there was anything omitted that flesh could utter in that mad orgy of emotion, then I do not know what it is.

Subsequently, Mimi Aguglia played in Philadelphia and was censored. It was not only an artistic error to halt her on her beautiful and magnificent abandon, but it was also a great stupidity insofar as it kept her that much farther away from a proper recognition on Broadway.

But perhaps it is just as well; for while Aguglia is learning English, one feels instinctively that she will only be something alien bridging that alienation with the flimsy pontoon of a foreign tongue. If the roof of her mouth does not revolt at the tolling of English phrases as a church would sorrow under the tolling of a sheep bell, then I shall be much surprised.

Nosing around among the colors and the divine dirt of the Bowery, having discovered one real, good wine in a little Italian cellar where an old woman peeled onions slowly (standing to the work, thereby rendering it more of a serious performance by the labor required of the legs), while from behind a pile of lard pails and old glass wine decanters rose the white hood of the cook as he manipulated the languid, reluctant lengths of spaghetti—while, I say, browsing in among these things and the odorous fruit that is nowhere in New York so lovely as in the dray of the Italian, past strings of dried figs and stalls of nuts—once more I came before Aguglia; and this time it was as *La Luppa* ("The Wolf"). This time she was true to herself, in that she played the part of the supercommon and played it with such fire and with such spaces of silence as has ever pleased me to see.

It is not given to everyone to be important in their silences, but it has been given to Mimi. Well, and what of it? She knows how to cry. She knows how to menace with the back of her throat; strange, animallike cries set about the most primitive and the most civilized of all emotions: love and rare hate. She can laugh. It is to her we must grant the art of the doubled hand upon the hip, knuckles in. She has a period of wild weeping in *The Wolf* that is unexcelled.

Unfortunately, Mimi Aguglia made the one fatal mistake, and still more poignantly, a mistake was it in that she committed this error a few minutes after the final curtain of *La Luppa*, in which there is much of the solemn whirlwinds of common passion. She affected the part of a

Parisienne in *Uno Quarto d'Ora*. She was unspeakably bad; she had wedged all of a fine, voluptuous, Sicilian anatomy into a tragically ugly near-attempt at a modish gown worn by the women of Paris. She had thrust her head into an impossible blonde wig—she was frightful. Oh, if she had only been crockery, brittle chinaware at which I could have hurled the bricks of my despair and have shattered her to bits. There was no divine flame here; there would have been no kerosene spilt. There was no passion; there would have been no stain of blood. There was no understanding of the part; therefore, there would have been no death—it would merely have been an accident.

I can be so harsh only because I love her so when she is playing those things she is fit to play.

But there you have the psychology of the Italian immigrant. In Rome one must do as the Romans, we are told. Of course, this is utterly ridiculous, not to say preposterous. It is like bringing wine to a foreign table that has its own apricot brandy and, by way of patriotism, tipping a little of the wine into the said brandy, thereby getting neither the subtlety of a good affinity nor the pleasure of one of the drinks by itself.

So it is considered well to play the part of a Parisienne, just as they try to add a little "spice" to their vaudeville by introducing American mannerisms which are horribly out of place but which seem to be somewhat enjoyed by the second generation of Italians, American born.

However, of Mimi, enough!

It was also my good fate to see about this time two operas given in Italian, one of which was *Carmen*. During the performance they sold ice-cream cones between aisles,

"One ornate lady dies per minute."

shouting out its excellence in riotous glee, and to my left
an editor of a Jewish daily sat enjoying one of vanilla as he
discussed German opera with a music critic. Some of the
audience did not trouble to remove their hats, and children cried in discordant flats and sharps all about in the
galleries, making themselves vocally prominent as the
globes from time to time made themselves electrically
evident. Konrad, who was with me, said that at one time
the Italians used to bring their lunches with them, a sort
of picnic with music and play. I thought the idea charming.
He said that it was very messy, as the place was nothing
but a clutter of paper and bread crumbs when the performance was over. Still, I thought it very naive, fuller of the
real significance of life. Are not all tables set between
tragedies and comedies?

For Carmen, they had a woman who was built on the
grand scale. She revolved in every point possible, her head
was never still, her hips rolled incessantly. She snapped
her fingers beneath the astonished and finally charmed
nose of her sweetheart time and time again, until it fell on
the ears like the irregularly regular popping of chestnuts
on a fire, while she threw the bitter sarcasm of her wit
into the air as one tosses a shuttlecock—those verbal
plums of love that, when thwarted, turn to prosaic and
revengeful prunes. Really a delightful woman—so vulgar,
so coarse, and so full-blooded. Her gowning was historic:
she sported more plush and gilt per inch than a mid-
Victorian lounge, and her constituents were braided and
gilded and velveted within an inch of their lives. Sometimes the music was off-tune. It did not matter. One or
two of the soldiers were distinctly Irish or German. This

did not matter either. The crowd was evidently so good-natured and so hearty that one overlooked such slight things as tonal perfection and elegant costuming and professional acting. One felt, as is indeed the case, that these people had cleared the stage of their beds and their children just before the curtain went up and that in a few moments they would return to them and to a waiting bowl of wine.

The other was *Lucia di Lammermoor*. From her mouth fell speech like strange grapes in exotic ways where no man is; the thunder of her hate was only less gigantic than the lightning of her love.

The Italians view life in their drama like a passionate storm and die only to return again. In their own mysterious frankness, they slay incessantly that which they love and drag from its pit of oblivion that which they hate, for it is so that they seem to understand life. If only the state, based on such elements, could be ruled for a day not so much by the mental portion as by the purely emotional. What a charming thing it would be if indeed one could live each day apart, without the knowledge of the terrible continuance of days. Then, and perhaps then only, should we see something at once beautiful and real, or at least real and perhaps not beautiful at all. Only in such ways can real things be accorded the above term.

How the Italians love blood-jealousy! How they admire it; passion, how they revere it! Their drama is no less vivid than their vases. Even their piety is touched with the sun, not of that austere faith in which we of the north walk. Nor does devotion need a closed room, nor grief a tomb:

they place before their vision of the cross the fruitage of their speech and the flowers of their faith in great and colorful abundance.

They leave none of the bitterness of required loyalty; they cast before their god the offering of their homes as well as of their hearts—bread from their board and bread from their soul.

It lacks subtlety—thanks be to all the powers for a change! They stab and commit murder and suicide continually. They grind teeth and tear hair and wreck homes. They weep, they laugh enormously, they eat, they are fed, and they are bountiful. At least one ornate woman dies per minute, as at least one ornate male vows eternal love per second, probably because they know

> A little sorrow, a little pleasure,
> Fate meets us from the dusty measure
> That holds the date of all of us;
> We are born with travail and strong crying,
> And from the birthday to the dying
> The likeness of our life is thus.

The Italian vaudeville is much poorer than Italian drama proper or improper. It is considerably less entertaining than our own vaudeville, though in the matter of vulgarity they are children, thanks to their reverence for life from whence springs all fine feeling. A joke on love is taken very badly from such an audience as Majori gathers. And when the Italian prima donna of the place sings a song, she hardly attempts to enhance the effect with the calves of her legs as our actresses so often do. It is true she just touches her gown a little, dances a little, flirts a little, but it is in such a naive way and is so homely in its evident attempt to be American that one can laugh at it with all sincerity.

This theatre, formerly Miner's, is said to be the father of all drama. Now it is battered and old, and no one passing would think to stop there to see anything more lively than perhaps a store, a house, or a cafe, if it were not for its bills posted conspicuously all over it. Stout Italians, trying to look like Caruso (ah, how proud they are of him!), stouter *señoritas* trying to look Spanish and entirely dramatic but often failing utterly, looking so homelike indeed that it only needs a fork or an infant to make them purely domestic.

This vaudeville house has put the regular, legitimate Italian drama at least half out of business; the doorman says business is much too good here to make opera or drama profitable—the Italian flocks much more willingly into Majori than into Thalia.

And the Peoples' Theatre, which used to present Italian plays, has now passed into Jewish hands, where moving pictures and dramas are displayed to great crowds. Still another is used as a restaurant—one of those many where there is real wine and real food, not the embalmed death chambers that most of our uptown, so-called Italian tables d'hôte are. I am thinking of one in particular in which the owner's wife presides, smiling like the very smile of death that lies piled up on her kitchen table in the shape of chickens, chops, and weary and dead salad leaves. At such places one does not live; one can only say that one does not die, that is all.

But I have got away from my subject, which was beginning to get down to a description of the interior of these playhouses.

Well, they are dirty. What would you? Does not the foot of the laboring poor enter in? Does not the dust blown from the Bowery filter through the cracks? Does not poverty sit here hand in hand with the arts? The seats are hard, you say. They are of wood; so be it. So are the people: hard of endurance and simple of comfort. Then you whisper that there are fleas. Ah, my dear, well-regulated, and well-shaped philistine—of course there are fleas. England was a hog-wallow in the time of Shakespeare, and roses grow only in fertile ground. Fleas are not a nice subject, and they are not exactly on a footing with fertile soil, I grant. They are the portable commas in a life filled with many, too many, final periods of neglected streets and neglected drainage systems. Someone said that they were so large and stupendous that one bent beneath them where they jumped. Remember that they spring up from bent lives and warped hopes. But I do not wish to seem to be saying a word in your favor, little animal. Often enough have I longed to kill you where you stood between me and art!

Italian vaudeville consists mostly of songs, a small amount of acting, some aerial work in which a trapeze performer bows to himself every second for a very poor performance of agility and a poorer conception of daring. There is usually a one-act play in which someone speaks English. Indeed, a little space is given to the several Italian dialects—the Sicilian, the Piedmontese, the Neapolitan—and the English is no doubt interspersed with the Italian for the benefit of the American born, who are growing out of the ways of Italy into the ways of New York.

There is a little horse play: the inevitable tramp in tatters, who says nothing and makes a good deal of noise with the soles of his feet, which threaten any minute to come away from his shoes and to float out into the oblivious sea of humor along with the straw hats of the juggler—all of which seems to me to be too much of an attempt to be American again. I felt that much was lost in this unfortunate tangling up of races. However, as a whole, it seems to please the audience, which did not fear to hiss that which it disliked any more than it feared to clap, hoot, and stamp for that which really touched it, either in a sad or in a funny way.

During intermissions there was a great silence. The Italian, if he comments, must do it after he goes home. Here you could have heard the proverbial pin drop had it not been for an occasional question put in English to a little girl just behind me by a little boy who took great delight in the strutting form of an officer of the army who, to put it in the child's words, "was doing exceeding grand."

And after that I came out again into the day, the Italian day of the Bowery and its intervening streets. A midwife's sign caught my eye as I turned, and looking away from it again, I saw a funeral procession wending its way slowly across town. The Italian spends his life on death; his all goes for such a funeral. The dead man or woman may never have had a wagon ride before; the flowers on the casket are perhaps the first that have been within smelling distance of the now-incapable of appreciation. The horses who are trained to look sad are the first that have ever walked for the one who no longer can navigate. The procession passes a bakery window in which are marvelous cakes, pink and blue and red, cut into extraordinary shapes to represent fish, houses, boats, and so on— deathly things with a frosting on them that would rival the modern movement in the art world; past a fish market with its hanging carp, its tank of eels, its devil fish looking like a deadly cape discarded by some vampire. Past the pushcarts filled with raisins and almonds, figs and dates, oranges and bananas, olives and apples.

Life was indeed all a theatre and a play to them: a good performance at Majori, and a good performance of it on wheels, lavish to the last. They eat well, they play passionately, badly, spectacularly. And they die as they lived.

Crumpets and Tea

The casual stranger—if there are any casual strangers in New York—upon coming through the many side streets that have Fifth Avenue for their destination, would in all probability undertake the consumption of so many waffles and tea in these street wayhouses that the said casual stranger would not have any room for thought.

A wig maker from the Strand, a Chouan from Brittany, or a student from the Latin Quarter would discover in our tea shops that air, half-sad, half-pretentious, which comes near to being European. At the same time, these shops make a brave show of being antiquated, by a display of early periods in Connecticut furniture.

With what astonishment would our forebears look upon the portion of New York occupied in our leisure moments, when we have nothing better to do than consume crumpets and tea! I have in mind one tearoom in particular in which I learned to like Swedish wafers.

The room is situated at the head of a rickety flight of steps very weary of having been gone up and down so many years. Small brown teapots stand in a row on a shelf as you come in, like rotund gentlemen in evening shirts. The curtains are powdered with sprigs of flowers of the same shade of blue and white as the teacups. Sad-faced, angular women in white, ruffled caps ask you what you desire; ordering, you watch them disappear behind another length of flowered curtain into the distance beyond, where the murmur of steaming kettles purrs up between rows of buttered cinnamon toast and scones.

At a long refectory table at the back of the room, two white-haired ladies sit. The copper mugs hanging along the wall reflect the light from the flames of a small fire burning brightly, casting an occasional reddish spot upon their high, flaring collars. They whisper to each other, disturbing two large cameos that lie upon their breasts. In front of them is a ledger and a small pile of bills. These they take one by one, and straightening them out with their long, thin hands and bending them evenly first one way and then the other, they drone, "Thirty-four, thirty-five, thirty-six."

The visitor looks away to contemplate the high-backed chairs standing primly at the worm-eaten tables. On the wall hangs a tapestry—a lady on a prancing horse. A small velvet cap rests lightly on the rusting curls, and on her arm sits a falcon.

The place is twilight: the twilight of antiques, the twilight of age, and the twilight of soul. Great copper shields hang from the roof speared with lances, and in front of them on an oak table lies a Bible open at the Book of Job.

Below this room, which looks out upon a small courtyard filled with statues and basins, roaring lions and small cherubim with heavy grapes, is a large, dusty room filled with old chairs and with but a chink of light streaming in over a print of a jockey in a very red cap and a very bowed pair of legs riding low down upon the neck of his horse. A dusty bust of Shakespeare sits frowning down upon the rest of the room, with its high forehead and its small, compact mustache and its transparent eyelids. A long-armed girl stands ever behind these things with a feather duster that can never remove the grayness from her life nor the age filtering through her eyes. Outside in little boxes grow small pink and yellow flowers.

Sometimes middle-aged ladies with sensible heels on sensible shoes labor slowly up the worn stairs and into the room above, their black veils streaming. And there are happy, young art students with their tam-o'-shanters of red and green corduroy and their portfolios under their arms, or a little cast of something in a wet cloth.

Yeats looked out of this same window that the visitor now looks out of, and onto the same court paved with the same flag in broken cross sections, and smelled the odor of hot pickles and frankfurters coming up from the street in the heart of a summer noon, or thought perhaps

> Of some too dewy evening where
>   Great lilacs leaning peer and loom,
> A lady walks with skirts a-flare;
>   A hooped thing that spreads to bloom
> Each time her tiny foot moves out,
>   And shakes the foamy lace about.
> Stooping she picks a crimson phlox
>   The while a saucy catbird mocks,
> The silver laughter wedged in
>   Her little mouth. The soft cleft chin
> Trembles quickly: her bosom heaves,
>   One perfect tear shows much she grieves
> That gardens are such curious things
>   Until the tomboy catbird sings!

And then there is another tearoom somewhere near Forty-fourth Street East, where long ago a young Slavic

The tea shop type.

man used to be seen sitting, his heavy, large-booted feet standing up on the other side of his table as though they were his guests. Sometimes he would sing as he waited for the patted butter and rolls, and sometimes he would cast an approving eye over the high caps of the waitresses in their tight-fitting bodices and bustled skirts. Or he would make some remark to the effect that all tea shops were run by "Englishwomen, who could not seem to build up."

"They have a great contempt for food," he would go on to say, "and a great reverence for crockery," and he would laugh.

It is true, this proverbial slimness of tea shop keepers, their contempt for food, and their unending passion for china. These places are usually hung with plates, teacups, and mugs, while saucers of all sizes and patterns stand upon shelves displaying to ravenous eyes their sprays of varnished flowers and their glazed fruits and fishes.

What would Zola say to this? If his markets of Paris filled him with dismay and with nausea, if his stout, bourgeois shopkeepers brought horror to his soul, here he would be rested by the sight of little food and thin, quick-eyed women who do a great trade in aesthetic cakes and thin tea.

Ah, well, that was a long time ago, before the war started, when one sipped leisurely and had time for conjectures and description as well as an occasional thought; a long time ago, when the biggest news story was a divorce or a fire, and when there was a time for silence, too.

Those times are gone, but we return to our cups nevertheless and to our scones, and we talk about the latest novel and the poems of Amy Lowell and the batiks of Miss

Slade and listen in rapt attention to Sidney as he talks about the art of the short, irrelevant essay as produced in Lucas's time, or of the deterioration in the pen and ink line since Picasso.

Strolling off on Thirty-fourth Street, coming downtown, one turns abruptly to be confronted by pots of flowers in green boxes and a jockey in red cap and breeches. Turning in at the entrance, one comes face to face with the slender Englishwoman sitting behind her desk doing up the accounts with a fountain pen while the visitors stamp in the stalls impatiently waiting for their orange pekoe and buns.

This tearoom is frequented by middle-aged ladies who bring their impatience with them as well as their knitting, and other strange members of society. There are stout gentlemen in plaids, whiskered parvenus, middle-aged "men about town" who produce the effect of beauty with their little curls, business ability with the shrewd intensity of little eyes held close together, good temper with lips that fall easily into appreciative smiles, and a thorough knowledge of the world with those short laughs indulged in by our ancestors in the Elizabethan comedy when the hero asks the father for his daughter's hand, adding that he will treasure her and love her with uninterrupted and sublime devotion.

These and others carrying large deck rugs or shawls commit small treasons with the sugar and their eyes and fall together, elbows on table, to discuss the trend in politics—all save the man about town, who displays his great and overshadowing knowledge of a disappointing universe by sticking his thumbs in at the sides of his vest and fluttering the eight fingers of these two anchored hands. These stables never held anything quite so "horsy" as some of these gentlemen. On the other hand, nothing was ever quite so demure as some of the tea drinkers from Harlem who butter their buns carefully with an eye to the edges.

Another tea shop in the late Thirties, seeking orginality, shrouds itself in deep gloom, relieved by a back yard converted into a garden by much wicker and trailing vines and rustic tables where young men sit contemplating some decorative suicide, some harmonious manner in which to leave the world in debt.

And there is that tea shop which I shall never see again because it is lost at the end of a memory that even Barrie could not find if he were to go all the way back to youth again and should go down upon his hands and knees and search for it between his tears and his laughter. Well I recall the umbrellas under which we sat and the striped tablecloth of our table and the young man opposite me telling me about Plattsburg and how dreadful it was to get back to New York to the negligible manners of the bourgeoisie after the once-superior training of Plattsburg.

This man was very much of a gentleman of the type that deems it a slip in good form to be seen at his thoughts; who starts, blushes, and acts as though he had been caught not only stealing jam but enjoying it as well. This type always knows how to button a woman's glove, to tie her lace, and to kiss her fingers, but he would be utterly lost if his valet should leave the cuff links on the table instead of the dresser. He wears glasses, but one never suspects that they are worn not because the eyes are bad but because the glasses are good. He is at once troubled by foibles and social precepts and the hidden power that at the right moment sends him up where he dominates, or drives him into that sudden despair—that acknowledgment that the world is too unutterably strange—that we call self-destruction; a man who must inevitably destroy or be destroyed.

Well, and so it is that he and I and those many others have gone to our crumpets and tea, have come to know each other over our cups, or have lost track of each other in reaching for a lump of sugar. Places where no one ever returns, yet which are always occupied. Little shops where one occasionally comes upon a real personality among the unending nonentities that come and drink and, drinking, pay: a woman in a high-backed chair, with a pair of French eyes under a blond bang; a strange, flat-chested creature bent upon painting porcelain and miniatures after the manner of the Persian; a languid, hot woman who burns up in December and lives panting the summer through; a woman to be afraid of, for there is more than the spine in collaboration with the turn of the head; an odd, altogether unpardonable person who makes one begin to doubt society and evolution and a great many other accepted theories of being.

And ever and always the thin Englishwomen prevail, and ever and always the china predominates, and ever and always the curtains are of flowered stuff, and ever and always the window boxes are red with geraniums, as toiling up and up the flights of steps one comes upon the same detail, the same attention to old furniture, the same copper and the rows of bright mugs. The mirrors, the trapdoors, the Bible open at the Book of Job, the long refectory table, the pile of green bills, the two white-haired ladies with necks encased in flaring Flemish collars, the two cameos moving slowly up and slowly down as they count together, straightening out the pile before them, "Thirty-four, thirty-five, thirty-six, thirty-seven."

Or you make the mistake of turning in at the Plaza or Ritz and never see any of it at all.

Or you miss it by going up beyond the Forties or below the Twenties, or you walk on the wrong side of the street, or you go through your pockets and find you have only a fare on the bus, and taking that instead, you find yourself at its end, in that small section of the city that is nothing more nor less than a cave of lunchrooms and dens, a village of tea shops. Then, of course, you are lost forever.

Surcease in Hurry and Whirl—On the Restless Surf at Coney

There was once a woman who was born under the most romantic of circumstances—that is, between two countries, Russia and Poland—on one of those nights in December when the sky is too cold to move aside for stars.

This woman's blood, like her birth, stood midway between two races, Jewish and Norwegian; and as she grew up, her mind also balanced between two conditions, sanity and insanity.

She was large-featured without being coarse. She had a small, thin mouth which contracted at the corners, and she blinked. Her lids were very pale and without lashes; they never seemed to cover her eyes, they only shadowed them. Her hair was thin and parted in the middle like a Madonna's. She always wore an open blouse showing a firm throat of a strange whiteness. She lisped a very little when conversing in English, but she spoke both rapidly and easily in her own tongue.

She would sit with her hands in her lap saying nothing for a long time. The tale has been told of her that once in a remote corner of Switzerland she had not been seen outside of her hut for days, and a neighbor, becoming anxious, went in and found her staring at the wall. When she

275

was touched, she fell. There was food in the house, but she had not eaten. They questioned her, saying:

"What is it that ails you? There is food here, and you have all the time in the world to yourself?"

"Oh no," she replied, smiling, "I am much too occupied doing nothing." When asked what she meant, she replied shortly that people were not people, they were "dolls."

She had belonged to the revolution but had finally turned from it in disgust, saying, "You are not fit to be released—you do not wriggle under the whip. You are an insult to rage; you cannot suffer.

"Why should I break my body among puppets?" she would say, slowly blinking her eyes. "You would only find my blood upon you with annoyance, as you find mud upon your Sunday clothes. I will not throw the mob my head that they may learn how a thought is mixed—they are too dull to learn the trick."

Then she would lift up the little ends of her dark hair, placing them over her pallid ears. Sometimes she would say that she did not mind the baldness which was coming upon her; when asked if she was doing anything to prevent it, she would answer, "Nothing." She had ceased revolting against the loss of hair as she had ceased revolting against society. But sometimes at night she would sit up in bed and ask herself what was worrying her, and placing her hand on her head in her usual way, she would lie down again murmuring, "Ah, I remember."

This woman had for America a sort of gesture of pity which was at the same time the italics of mercy. She would say that we do not know how to amuse ourselves or how to be sad. She agreed when a friend pointed out the

truth of this observation by remarking that people ceased
to amuse themselves, relying instead on the amusement
offered them by watching the forced antics of a paid
individual who supplied this personal loss.

And it was of this woman that I thought as I went
through Coney Island.

Yes, she was quite right in some instances, but in others
she was quite wrong. There is about many a characteristic
hurry, a ferocity, a hustling determination to be amused
at any cost, even if it is painful. They will weep that they
may laugh.

Some of us approach Coney by boat. Deckhands wander
up and down looking disinterestedly at the water. A lonely
couple sits aft drinking pop and beer. A man steps out of
the salon looking fresh and cool in white duck, but his face
is sad. A baby with bowed legs chases its bonnet down the
deck, and a young girl stands at the railing eating candy
and laughing. But for the old iron steamboat it is the
winter of its glory.

We pass a bell buoy tolling sadly, softly, uncertainly—as
though the waves, upon reaching it, hurt. Its four iron
hammers roll against it, bringing forth a melancholy
groan; it is sad and sweet and patient. The boat passes on.

Reaching Coney, one struggles up the pier confronted
by the eternal grin of the Steeplechase man who has a flat
head and two perfect spit curls over his brow like a traveling salesman. A man sits by the pier side, fishing tackle in
hand and a basket at his side; his wife throws pieces of
bread into the water and looks up at the merrymakers and
down again.

As one reaches the Bowery, a strange mingling of sounds comes to the ear: a sound of bells, of dancing, of the hoarse cries of the street vendor, of young girls laughing, of boys throwing remarks at the passing throng in that voice which is a mixture of youth and age—the cracked cry of the adolescent.

A man in white apron and cap stands with his mouth open behind his flat-topped stove covered with hot dogs, a reddish-brown mass which he pierces from time to time with a long-handled fork as he surveys the throng. As the heads turn his way, he recollects what his mouth is open for and cries, "Here you are, get your dogs, all hot. Everything here but the bark and the license—here you are, get your dogs!" Somebody cries at this moment, "Wuf, wuf," and laughs.

Then, in a low guttural, "Get your roast beef sandwiches—ten cents apiece," from a stout woman standing to one side.

A little, red-coated, high-hipped man passes, twisting his moustache and looking from side to side as though he expected daisies to spring up about him; for as a boat has its wake of foam, he expects his wake of flowers.

An officer flanked by two boys in sailor dress stops before the shooting gallery trying the rifles. One of the boys makes a remark:

"Ah, this is the best dancing master after all." Nudging his companion, he aims at a duck and brings it down. They move on. On the face of one of the sailors there is a strange look, and he pulls at their arms. "Come on," he says hurriedly, "come on." They do not stop at the next gallery.

A sideshow attracts the attention. Great posters of THE
FATTEST FAT LADY, THE OSSIFIED MAN, THE SNAKE CHARMER, and
that unfortunate fellow who has legs like whips and who
is advertised as THE CIGARETTE FIEND. You look down upon
these people as from the top of an abyss; they are at the
bottom of despair and of life. The demonstrator comes
forward, cane in hand; he touches the nearest freak on the
shoulder and begins turning him around as if this turning
were all that the unfortunate had been born for. He begins to enumerate this man's misfortunes as though they
were a row of precious beads.

"An explosion in the mine, a falling of stones and coal, a
man pitching forward in the darkness, a stumbling foot, a
prayer to God, and then a pick through the body—you
see." He gives the young man another twist, tapping him
upon the stomach. "Here is where the pick entered." He
turns him again, this time tapping him on the back. "And
here is where the pick thrust its head out." He smiles,
rubbing his hands. The young man turns again, a fixed
look upon his face, neither pleasant nor otherwise—a cool,
self-possessed stare—a little uncertain, perhaps, whether
to be proud or sorry for the accident that has made him of
interest to the gaping throng.

The demonstrator has blown a whiff of smoke through
the young gentleman, where the pick has been, and now
he goes on to another—this time the ossified man. The
man has a mirror about his neck, and from time to time he
looks at himself as he lies there, moving his mouth, because this is all that he can do. Many rings with pale blue
stones adorn his strange, flexible fingers, and now and
again he kisses the side of a cigar pierced by a long stick.

We move on.

The noise increases. A throng of children hoots at the man calling out his wares. A thin little girl like an old woman steps up onto the sidewalk, both dirty hands on her hips, her short, broken, blond hair stretched back in two braids. She begins to cackle, copying the crowd; "Get your picture—nice pictures of baby and mamma"; and then in a more insolent voice than before, "A picture of your wife, right this way." There is something incomplete in her great, horrifying completeness; she seems to be an outcome of past cries, curses, shouts, laughter, music, dancing, hubbub, and merry insolence. She is a little girl who has collected herself from the gutter and molded herself into this saucy, angular body from the refuse of great noises—that are, alas, never grand noises, but the hue and cry of a thousand middlemen making a nickel. A handful of confetti and popcorn, a splash of soda water and beer, dust of a dime and a boot.

She has taken her shoes off that she may feel her connection with the world. When she walks in the gay, crowded street, she has entered her home; when she sits upon the curb, she has found the lap of her mother.

An ice-cream stall with shining bottles of red and yellow passes by; for at Coney one feels that the inanimate objects are the only things that are animate and that people are there merely to exclaim: "At last it is as it should be—characteristic with the rest of America's hurry and whirl."

As one turns a corner the sound of a dance comes to the ear, and peering into the darkness of a long shed one sees an old man executing an Irish jig. In a space no bigger than one's hand, he rises and falls. The floor is sanded, and as his feet strike it, the sand hurries in all directions, leaving a bare spot which is covered again by his descending foot.

This man is small, old, and very erect. When the crowd hoots, a short smile flickers about his mouth. Still he never stops; up he goes and down he comes, up and up and down, down, feet held close together or lifted a bit that he may pat their soles with one leisurely movement of his white-haired hand.

The man at the piano lights another pipe; the concertina stretches out. A pause ensues in which one catches bits of histories from the adjoining tables, has time to observe the faces as they dip in and emerge from foaming mugs of beer. Then another, taller old man comes out and, striking the boards in the same spot the little man has just left, takes up the next jig.

Instinctively one feels that this is something a little different—an air pervades this shed that is missing elsewhere. It is less pretentious, it is even dirty, but it is not afraid to be natural. Even the waiters appreciate the fact and stand smiling in the entrance or talk in French to some stout woman with rosy cheeks who sits nursing a baby, saying:

"Vous rappelez—vous notre douce vie.

"Lorque nous etions si jeunes tous deux."

And there is one other of these cafes run by the same man, where Irish songs are all in order and those who have had Ireland sometimes close to their hearts volunteer for their own delight.

In this later place I met Allen Norton, Bob Carlton Brown, and Rose Watson. We ordered, and Bob showed me a copy of the *Coney Island Splash*, a little magazine for

Coney Islanders and those enjoying a French flavor with their sodas and sandwiches. But Allen couldn't stay, and he took the copy away with him just as I was about to discover what Beatrice Wood and Clara Tice had drawn and what Harry Kemp had written.

After this Rose suggested Steeplechase. The lights of Luna were just springing up as we crossed Surf Avenue and stopped for a round of oysters before entering the doors of the "Funny Place."

The merry-go-rounds were packed when we entered, and a strange contrivance built in much the same manner but with a seesaw effect was covered with boys and girls like robins on a wire. How they were twittering and shaking their feathers!

Great polished slides lured us, and donning carnival costumes we took the dare down, down, with a sensation in the pit of the stomach as though the world has suddenly gone on a jag. Then a catapulting pitch into a bowl, where we whirled around and around, finally ended on a set of whirling discs that took all the dignity out of our lives as far back as our great-granduncles.

Next we ascended twitching steps that threw us forward and plucked us back again, till finally they ended by being satiated by our halting steps and landed us safely upon our feet at the top where a tower yawned, its polished spiral leading down into the depths of the earth.

Saying our prayers we sat down, shut our eyes, and began the descent. A flash of light and again abysmal darkness, through which with scorching clothes we whirled, waiting for the finish, with all thoughts of higher philosophy somewhere up there in the daylight and the air. Then at last we were out again, standing erect but trembling a little, looking for our hair pins and our friends.

Over upon a whirling platform I beheld Bob, going around and around like a nut on a wedding cake, smiling idiotically.

But it doesn't matter, that's what we are there for, and presently we shall go below and get a drink. We do and saunter out into the dark gardens like the gardens, perhaps, in some old novel, where lovers commit suicide in some old Renaissance way by nibbling violets—a garden spotted with lights from the moving-picture signs and the cabarets.

We enter a Ferris wheel. We are wound up into heaven and left there with two silly little girls who talk about "anachronisms," meaning anarchism. But it is all a part of the evening's fun and the twenty-five things you can or can't do, for the particular combination you first indulged in.

We gaze into the sky, and someone says, "Isn't it like the garden of the Tuileries?" Someone else answers, "Don't look over the side, you may get dizzy." I am thinking how beautiful are the shadows down there where the grass is and how strange the sky is in this wheel that might never come down at all.

But of course it does, in the stupid manner of machinery, thereby spoiling another perfect tragedy.

By the time we have descended, Bob and Rose have another idea to submit to Allen for the *Splash*, and they laugh as they walk across the park and out into the open air.

And then there was Luna with its incubator babies who are too small to bear names and too strange for adoption. There are the boats that plunge into water and the lights and the laughter and the pink tongues laid against the pink ice cream in the yellow cones. And there is the nice press representative smiling in the door of his particular house, and there is Surf Avenue all over again.

Walking down to the beach one hears the iron steamboat pulling out. Throwing back one last glance at the strange forms on the water's edge who are crying out to one another and making movements with their arms and singing, and with a mental picture of the little gold-haired girl who dried her locks in the sunset, we say farewell to Coney and catch the boat before the gangplank is hoisted.

Going home I see the girl with her arm around the young man's neck, the same girl who was eating candy; and the baby who was chasing its bonnet down the deck is asleep in its mother's lap.

And presently I hear the bell buoy tolling.

The Hem of Manhattan

In July 1917, shortly after the U.S. joined the war in Europe, Barnes wrote this account of a forty-mile boat trip around Manhattan Island for the readers of the Morning Telegraph. Up the East River—that isn't a river at all but a strait separating Manhattan from Long Island—through the narrow channel called Hell Gate, to Spuyten Duyvil Creek where on Manhattan's northern boundary the Harlem River meets the Hudson; south along the steep cliffs of the Palisades to Battery Park at the island's southern tip, and under the magnificent Brooklyn Bridge; past the first of New York's great skyscrapers, the wedge-shaped Flatiron Building, and the Woolworth Tower, at sixty stories the tallest when completed in 1913, magnificently Gothic and still one of the city's most remarkable buildings.

To take a yacht trip around Manhattan Island is to find yourself in the awkward position of one who must become a stranger in his own house that he may describe it with the necessary color.

How much easier, for instance, to have been sent to Russia to paint a word picture of their afternoon meal and their homes. Or to have gone to France, there to stroll among the ruins of what used to be the descriptive parts of Cousin Milly's letters home; to have walked awhile along the boulevards or to have coveted hats in a window in a street off from that cafe Jules talked of with me the other night. Or to have watched the smoking of French cigarettes, or to have visited Napoleon's tomb or walked

285

where Bernhardt used to walk, or to have tried to find the cafe where Verlaine and Baudelaire wrote their poems, or any one of the million and ten things that one expects to be seen doing when he takes a trip to a foreign country.

There one would notice how the buttons were made because it would be a strange, new person wearing them in a strange, old land. Here one's buttons are never missed until they fall off.

Here one looks upon things because one has eyes. There one has eyes that he may contemplate. This is the inevitable tragedy of being familiar with one's home. Here we live and go through the usual daily program because we must; but it is only when one travels—be it only to Kansas, providing Kansas is a foreign land—that one comes upon the discovery that to appreciate and to understand one should never be on anything but a friendly footing either with architecture or with people.

It's the saying of "How do you do?" that is the educational part of life. The goodbye is only the sad little period to a no-longer-needed paragraph.

Who was it who said, "My friend, you cannot reach into your home because it is from there you were found reaching out"? And so I am condemned with a thousand million unless I find myself in a lonely place, where I may be profitable in my crying for the echoes I set around me that have never called back since I was born; a place that will be as strange to me as I to it.

It's a pleasant thought, but still I cannot escape my ultimate task: the fact that Manhattan Island has passed before me in review.

"The gentleman who said, 'You cannot reach into your home.' "

I believe this trip is advertised as one of pleasure. Well, perhaps I am melancholy, as I have often been told, but what can one be when to reach the boat one has to cross Death Avenue first? And what is one going to suffer if not despair, when for three hours and a half there pass misery, poverty, death, old age, and insanity?

The two shore lines are separated by a strip of level, uncomplaining water, like two convicts who have between them three links of impassive chain: two terrible positives separated by a negative.

But as the storyteller would say, this is not beginning at the beginning.

I think it was something like two-thirty when I started. The boat was the smallest of its kind I have ever patronized, and as I climbed aboard, the upper deck was already covered with stiff-backed, Middle West school teachers and others, most of whom were bearded gentlemen with gold nuggets mounted and used as tiepins.

They all sat there in uncompromising rows as though they were in a classroom, and off and on they turned their heads just enough to look at the water with determination, because they were there to see, and they would see.

The sun was hot, and you could hear the cordage and the planking creaking. Let me mention that I did not see more than one child on this trip. And after all, this was quite the right thing. Children are taken to Bear Island, or up the Hudson to some camping ground, to some place that resembles at least a definite spot.

Presently, as the yacht pulled out and started moving in a side circle about the Battery, the megaphone man stepped forward and began chanting: "This building to your left is known as the Woolworth Tower, the largest building in the world; it stands so-many-and-so-many feet high," giving the exact number of feet and inches, as though it were growing, and then he turned in the other direction and added casually, "This is a transport steamer to your right, filled, as you see, by our boys in khaki."

Then we heard their voices, hundreds of them, coming to us over the intervening water. A strange cry, a happy cry, an exultant cry, proclaiming doom and death. They all rose up, calling aloud, waving their arms and their handkerchiefs. A few words drifted back to us as we pulled alongside and then moved on. "We'll get the Kaiser," and the often-repeated, "Come on, too." One of them standing a little forward kissed his hand lightly; others thrust their shaggy heads out of the portholes. It made me think of Coney Island and the voice that usually accompanies an outthrust head; "Three shots for a nickel."

I looked around me: everyone was sitting in the same passive manner, stiffly and conventionally and unemotionally.

Looking at the skyline as we rounded the Battery, New York rose out of the water like a great wave that found it impossible to return again and so remained there in horror, peering out of the million windows men had caged it with.

Boats, like pet dogs, were leashed to the docks, and one little tug looking like a spitz growled at our side, sticking its nose out of the green, loose water as though it were trying to bite.

The Brooklyn Bridge, the Manhattan, the Williamsburg, and the Queensboro came into view, stretching away into the distance. The megaphone man came back again, explaining that Steve Brodie was the first man to jump this bridge without loss of life; afterward he kept a cafe and was quite a character.

And then I thought of another trip I had taken once—a cheap excursion trip on a larger and dirtier boat. Somehow I had liked that better; there was something living and careless and human about it. Babies sprawled about the decks in Oriental attitudes crying for the bottle; young people in blouses and open shirts giggled together and sang songs; there was a great disorder about it, dancing, music, fun. Lunches in small uniform boxes, a sandwich, an egg, a piece of cake, and then the mugs of soda water, the bottles of ginger beer, and the occasional splash as one hit the water, thrown from the upper deck by some satiated youth. And I turned in again and looked at this boat's passengers, who sat with folded hands upon gingham and dimity gowns, murmuring to themselves at times that they hoped the educational parts of New York and surrounding country would be visible to the naked eye. Well, they were, but they didn't see it.

The only refuse that cannot be renovated seems to be the human mind. Here at the waterfronts, barges heaped with the city's garbage swayed in the greasy, dark water, great mounds of a city's refuse suspiring in the sun like a glutton lolling after an orgy. One felt that, had one listened sharply enough, one would have caught its thick, throaty breathing; the mounds seemed to move, rising slowly, falling slowly, a great stomach on a couch. Ah, our modern lily maids of Astolat are the unnamed dead from the morgue who are rowed up to potter's field past the hospitals and this great, unending, daily birth of the city's dead food. I never realized before that there are places more terrible than the cemetery. They are the dumping grounds, and like carrion birds that sweep over a battle-field, men move in among this filth and decay, picking out wood for kindling, paper for the mills, and rags for the paper factories, and God knows what else for what, and someone making a million upon this terrible resurrection.

It was from the water's edge that we crawled in the days of our oblivion and first started that slow ascent into the life of man, and it is to the water's edge that we are brought back again in the end, the great, wet tomb that dries all tears, that gives the raw material and takes back the finished tool and knows neither pleasure nor pain; for "This is the end of all the songs men sing."

And as I said, "Man is the only thing that has no further use after something goes amiss." Look for yourselves and see. Exactly opposite this line of refuse, these heavy-laden barges, is a home for the insane. There is no hand moving in these poor, disordered brains in search of some one thought that could be used again. No man pays the city for the privilege of saving some lost and beautiful thing among this sad refuse; no hired hands thrust their fingers in to save some little kindling from this wrecked house, nor is anything profitable to be found for the decay of the garden.

And side by side, the Old Men's Home. Gray figures bent like hooks move about the splendid lawns and pause beneath the great trees spilling their green bloom to the ground; Old men like futile pollen in a breeze whose scattering will bring no profit to the world.

And you will say, "Enough, enough; this was a pleasure trip! Pass on, and describe its beauties." How can I, when there was nothing beautiful nor pleasant to see, save the ever-lovely sky, the green of the grass and the trees, and an occasional handsome spire?

We progressed, the megaphone man cutting the trip up in two jokes, one to the effect that dogs wagged their tails up and down instead of sideways in the Flatiron Building, and another that no deaf man had been ever condemned— this as we passed a prison—for the simple reason that he must be given "a hearing."

And when I looked at this island with its old men and its prisons, hospitals, and home for incurables, I thought again of that day I had spent on a strip of land just on the other side of Hell Gate with a young boy who had found society too difficult to understand. It was a lonely, flat stretch of marsh, thick with wild, high grass set in water. Planking ran from the broken-down house to the edge of the bank where a boat was anchored. This island, with its broken bits of wreckage and its ooze and salty smell at low tide, made me think of these human beings. Sometimes nature has an ailment: this island was one of them. Across the water, late in the afternoon, came the cries of the mad—a wild, sad scream that was taken up by the others gradually, as though they were playing a game at madness—and a shiver ran through me, and I wanted to cry also, and I asked him how he could bear it. He was smiling. "Sometimes," he said, "I think we are the loony ones. You have songs on which to go to battle; why shouldn't they have their songs on which to go to death?" Afterward he said that often they swam across and played together quite amicably.

Well, that has passed—the island lies under the sun and rain now, and the boy has gone—where, no one knows—a tramp perhaps—an inmate of one of the houses on the other side of the island. But I know one thing, that wherever he has gone he has taken with him a little of the freedom of a wild life that no standard insanity can harm.

Presently we passed the last bridge in the Harlem series, where a soldier stood, gun over shoulder—and came out into the half-moon of Spuyten Duyvil Creek. Little naked children ran hither and thither in the wooded banks and dropped, sighing, down upon the leaves like acorns. Others looked at us with small, water-wet, squinting eyes and waved, diving off hastily that we might accord them due praise for their excellent agility.

We took the turn in Spuyten Duyvil Creek well, watching these children until we could see them no more. It was here that I drew my first contented breath. Up on the heights several handsome houses peeped between the trees, and in the coming evening the Palisades stood out no heavier than a puff of smoke.

There was a hint of rain in the air, too. A small motorboat shot past us, a brown-armed boy shouting hello as he steered. A three-oared canoe with a girl up front turned in from the creek behind us, the oars in steady, rhythmic motion dripping fine, silver beads of water.

A boy crying "Ice-cold soda here" came out of the hot cabin. A chocolate vendor stepped on my hat—I smiled.

The pilot, brown and lined of face, turned the wheel slowly, looking away into the distance. The megaphone man told us to pay strict attention to a white house on the drive: "Made possible by cigarettes," he said. We all leaned forward. Then he called attention to the college. All the Middle Western schoolmarms got to their feet.

"I wonder," one of them said, "if they discuss higher mathematics there." And another answered laconically, "Spinoza." They sat down again.

Somewhere, everywhere over there in that world that we had been around, and against which only one voice was raised—that of the megaphone man—actresses were getting their beauty sleep or were at school learning arduously a new dance. Somewhere a man was killing a gnat and somewhere else a man building a bomb. Someone was kissing, and someone was killing, someone was being born, and someone was dying. Some were eating and drinking and laughing, and others were starving. Some were thinking, and others were not. Waiters moved about in the great hotels, dragging their servility with them like trains. Pompous gentlemen in fat rings discussed politics amid spittoons, and handsome women read yellow-backed novels and gave their hands to be kissed by gallants. And there some were walking about, looking over at us as we looked back at them.

The tall buildings threw their shadows down on little buildings, great men on small men, joy on sorrow.

Someone was yawning at my side and buying postal cards, thirty-five views for a quarter, and I had a thousand for nothing!

And yet the city gave out only a faint sound of fabric being rent: one-half of the mass pulling one way and the other half in an opposing direction. Another self-sufficient tugboat hooted at us from the docks, and factory whistles shrieked back at them like masters calling them home. An electric sign stood up against the sky advertising some brand of chewing gum and beside it the steeple of a church. Great warehouses and grain elevators supported flaring advertisements; it looked as though the whole of Manhattan were for sale.

A dark line of boats to the left of us—Holland, German, Italian.

And somewhere in all this tangle of lives and tangle of buildings, inland out of sight of the sea and fog, there was my own particular little studio called home.

And "There's no place like home," chiefly because here we can best forget.

Commissioner Enright and M. Voltaire

Someone who believes that all old masters should be mentioned in a whisper whispered to me, "Do you know who has the largest Voltairean library?"

Of course, I shook my head.

"Police Commissioner Enright," he said slowly.

Therefore, I traversed Centre Street and mounted the steps of Police Headquarters and, sitting in the Commissioner's largest chair, awaited the moment when I could ask him about this somewhat strange passion for a man who is thought of only when one is about to die or when someone mentions religion.

As I sat there thinking of the Police Commissioner's functions and of the rogues' gallery and the whole dramatic side of life called crime, there came to mind a fable—the fable of the man who never knew when to end a thing while it still held a little something of beauty. When he reached the age of twenty, he discovered what was indeed the most beautiful thing: irrevocable finality. Three months later he invented a button which if pressed at the right moment would end a situation as a knife cuts bread. He could with only a little pressure keep a situation at that point where it had reached perfection. He was happy, saying, "Now it is in my power to have one really tragic

296

and marvelous moment in my life undefiled by those incidents that always come after."

The point of the fable is that he never learned when to press the button—died without learning it.

Yes, somehow I could not help thinking of this as I realized how many people die in a year because they do not know where to stop, because the murderer, for instance, does not know where to find his period.

Later I spoke of it to Commissioner Enright as he sat in his office in Police Headquarters, and he, looking from under his head of white curls, answered:

"Yes, but then that is the most difficult thing in the world to do. It can only be done by those lower animals who know a higher life, or to be more accurate and less poetic, who find the climax the only necessity and after-knowledge not merely an unknown quantity but one with which they cannot possibly cope."

I answered. "Well, of course, crime is not acknowledged as such among animals. With them it is instinct and very good instinct, though of course it always acts for self-preservation or the preservation of their young; it never reaches into the realm of the fraternal."

"Civilization always brings its troubles, and added good always accompanies added evil," Mr. Enright rejoined.

"There are good and evil again," I said. "But what are they?"

"One needs only to define good to define evil also by comparison."

"Anyway, this is plunging in much too deep to start with," I said. "Let us talk about literature."

"Well, now, there's Voltaire."

"I have heard about your great interest in Voltaire—tell me the secret."

"Voltaire was the man who wrote the first detective story," he answered and lowered his lids, awaiting my surprise.

"Really?"

He went on. "Do you remember reading the story of Zadig, or rather a set of sketches concerning the life of Zadig, a Babylonian who when disappointed in his love for Semira married Azora? In the end she attempted to cut his nose off for the sake of an admirer, thus driving Zadig to the conclusion that life on the ordinary scale was not right and that thereafter philosophy and loneliness were profitable alone.

"Well, one day as he was reclining against a tree, a eunuch of the royal house and some officers ran by, calling out, 'Hast thou seen the Queen's dog?' And Zadig answered, 'It is a she-dog who has just delivered herself of young; she has long ears and runs a little lame.'

"The same thing occurred about one of the Queen's horses, and Zadig made answer: 'He is the fleetest horse in the King's stable. He is five feet high, with very small hoofs and a tail three feet and a half in length; the studs on his bits are gold of twenty-three carats, and his shoes are of silver of eleven pennyweights.'

"He had a lot of trouble proving that he had gathered this information not from having seen the animals but through deduction. Finally he explained thus:

"'I observed traces in the sand of an animal and knew them to be those of a little dog. The light and long furrows impressed on the little eminences of sand between the marks of the paws made by the beast gave proof that it was a dog that had but lately whelped, and the other marks on the outside of the paws were plainly those left by the dragging of long ears. I knew that she was lame because one foot left a lighter impress in the sand.

"It was the same with the horse. The dust on the trees of a road seven feet wide was a little brushed off at a distance of three feet and a half from the middle of the road, proving his tail, which had whisked off the dust, to be three and a half feet long. I observed under the trees that formed an arbor five feet high that the leaves of the branches were newly fallen; therefore the horse must have touched them. As to the bit it must be of gold and twenty-three carats, for he had rubbed its bosses against a stone which I knew to be a touchstone and which I have tried; the same of his shoes also.'

"Thus we see the whole essence of the detective story of the future. Poe, Doyle, Anna Katherine Green—all of them are probably indebted to this one story of Voltaire's."

"Do you consider detective stories of any value to the detective in real life?"

"No use at all. They are only good as tales of amusement, of suspense and ingenuity. A real detective, however, does not go about it in that way."

I looked out of the window at the long, gray heights of the city, and I thought of the forty-three thousand pictures in the rogues' gallery downstairs, and I looked back at the Commissioner, who was turning over the leaves of a book.

"They say," he continued, "that we have no art in America. No paintings of value, no poetry of worth. Well, it is true that I love my Balzac and my Hugo; but we have our Richard Harding Davis, and our poets are many."

"But you don't mean that seriously, do you? Surely you wouldn't put R. H. Davis on a footing with Balzac?"

"Yes, I would. Because Davis wrote in English and was an American and might be seen in any of our clubs, the people do not value him. Yet I say without hesitation that some of the stories written by him have not been very far surpassed."

"Why should we be the only nation to disregard our art?"

"Because we have learned to value money more. It is a terrible and a shocking thing, but so it is. Until that time comes when we will turn around saying, 'There goes a poet,' instead of 'There is the richest man in New York,' our artists will not be encouraged, and without encouragement of some sort no art attains to its greatest and best. Instead of endowing homes for the feeble-minded, why doesn't someone secure those of great minds a living? The feeble-minded get a home and care and a burial—those of great mind sleep in the gutter and are the gracious unknown dead that line the earth in potter's field.

"For instance, let us think of the matter in a really large way. Take the criminal. What do we do with him? Kill him. What an absurd waste of material, what a scandalous treachery to the potential good in all flesh, what a monstrous blunder! When you stop a heart and a life, strike out forever the little breathing that is in a man, you have by that much crippled society. There are surely things that this same man might have done. I say, Put him to work, do not kill him and thus end his good. Make him support those he has wronged, let him help sustain the poet and the painter, let him be of value to the state."

As I have said before, the Commissioner has very nice white and curling hair; here he stroked it and smiled. "Let us talk of less gloomy things," he said.

"Can a Police Commissioner think of less gloomy things?"

"I should go mad if I couldn't."

"Yet it is not so very melancholy, Mr. Enright, for some of the nicest people I know are either potential or real criminals."

He shrugged his shoulders. "I believe in the soul."

"And?"

"Well, if you believe in the soul you know that this life is only a preparation for a next."

"To what avail," asked I, "if we go through this, so unrelated each to the other, on such different levels, a chasm apart?"

"Wouldn't it be deadly if we were all on an equal footing?"

"I'm not so sure."

"I am."

"We will both have to be convinced," I laughed.

"You will have to be," he answered.

"How shall I begin?"

"Go to the stars."

"You believe in the stars?"

"I do."

"That they make the person born under them, that they rule?"

"Emphatically."

"Are you serious?"

"I have never been more serious in my life."

"But this is incredible."

"Nothing is incredible. I don't know, no one knows—but I have a strong suspicion that the stars make us what we are."

"And the criminal is he who has been born under a star ordaining that he should be a murderer?"

"I think so."

"In that case all people born under that star would be criminal and alike."

"No two are born under the same star—or if they are I don't doubt but that they are very similar, that is, so far as their surroundings permit. Each is modified according to his birthplace and circumstances."

"But this is quite frightful; this puts us beyond the reach of ourselves. If we are good, it is the stars; if we are bad, they also are to blame."

"Were you under the delusion that good and bad were self-willed?"

"To some extent—yes, I even know it."

He shook his head. "You don't know it, you think you do. I'm not saying that a person cannot do a great deal himself toward becoming either good or evil, but I am saying that the stars have a great deal to do with the initial impulse."

"This makes me quite miserable. I shall have to have my palm read or turn to tea leaves or the cards."

"Those things I don't believe in."

"Why not, if the stars——"

"The stars are a matter of God, the cards a matter of crooked sharpers trying to make a living—bits of pasteboard conceived and executed by a human brain."

"And in the next world that you speak of, will we be ruled by stars?"

"No one knows."

"And would you be willing to live through successive generations?"

"I would be willing not only to live through successive generations but to go right back over those that I have known."

"You are the first person—or is it the second?—who said he would live his life over again with pleasure."

"Why not? I think it is a wonderful world. I have had a good time, and I have suffered. I am willing to suffer again, and I would like to go through all the moments of joy that have been mine—I am not afraid."

"You must, indeed, have been very happy."

"Not so happy—well, yes; very, very happy at times. At others——" He again shrugged his shoulders.

"But you who are so near to suffering, to the down and sad side of life, how can you——"

"That may perhaps be why. I can see something greater coming out of it. Such things cannot be for nothing. There must be some purpose behind it all, some divine power that will set the wrong right."

"But in the meantime?"

"In the meantime, we must do the best we can for those who come nearest us. For me it is crime, for you——"

"Ah, and for me also, perhaps."

He looked at me, puzzled.

"You see," I continued, "I have a lot of friends, as I before said, who are either potential criminals or criminals in action; and these somehow one likes—why?"

"Why? Well, you see, we all love the specialist," he answered and broke out into laughter.

Woman Police Deputy Is Writer of Poetry

Imagine a day on Centre Street, overcast and threatening rain; a day through which shuffle flickering tramps like wicks that are dying. Centre Street with its hurrying businessmen, its thin clerks carrying brief bags, the Criminal Courts Building, that edifice of anticlimaxes on whose steps people are obscured into a sameness of sorrow—men with hurt mouths, women in black talking in Italian and children playing noiselessly, as if they were the innocent ashes of some despair. Imagine the cries of someone in a vacant lot raised high above the multitude on a soapbox with wide, imploring, heedless arms crying for volunteers. Then imagine the long, cold corridors of Police Headquarters, the uniformed men with their badges winking sleepily above their hearts, the rows of prize beakers in a glass case, and then the room on whose door is the sign FIFTH DEPUTY COMMISSIONER. In here, by an imposing and legal desk, in a blue serge dress trimmed with lace, sits a well-built woman, her face at once stern and humorous. Imagine all this, and you have the environs and the person of Mrs. Ellen O'Grady, Fifth Deputy Police Commissioner.

Her eyes are set close together and slanting, the nose is of gentle modeling, and the mouth one of which one would say, "That moves for the state." My first impres-

305

sion was of a woman who was afraid of being too homelike in an office of business.

She is a woman to whom you put impersonal questions
last. Therefore I asked her about her immediate work.

"I am interested in the saving of girls before they have
taken the last step," she said. "I do not mean that I am not
also interested in and careful of the girl who has already
fallen—that goes without saying; but I do think that more
things should be done to prevent and less to attempt
cures. It is better far to save a girl before she is in dire
need of saving than to try to save her after it is too late.
Not but that girls can be reclaimed, but is it not better
never to have made a mistake than to have made one?"

She went on, turning over a ruler. "True, I believe in the
benefits of suffering; the worst of us are always better for
having done something for which we can truly suffer. But
there are some who can be saved and yet gain their knowledge and be as purified as if they had gone through the
last fires and out on the other side of Fiddler's Green." For
the first time she smiled a little.

"I believe in women; I love them; there is a kindliness
and an understanding and a sympathy in women that no
one, not even an animal, possesses. Oh, you needn't smile
at the animal; they are unequalled for blind devotion—
which, of course, has its limits.

"Because of this love of beauty, because of this reaching
out for something better and brighter and of more worth,
our girls fall into trouble. It is for this very reason that
those cast into the shadow by poverty and ignorance, by
pain and suffering, by neglect and misfortune, grope toward the only thing that they know as beautiful: love. It is

for this reason that since the war began there have been more cases of small girls going astray. Let me explain."

She turned around in her chair, facing the window.

"Somehow a uniform has always appealed to a woman—it appeals to men also, but they can wear it, you see. She connects it with something holy and something to be investigated, something at once to be venerated and to be familiar with. For a girl of fourteen—and the girls who go astray are younger than ever—nothing has ever come so close to her dreams as these uniforms. Anything she might do is jumbled up with a sort of patriotic fanaticism; thus, she pretends to herself that her feelings are somehow made divine and noble."

"How then are you going to prevent it?"

"I look into those conditions which are likely to lead up to such a climax. Now take, for instance, the girls doing messenger service. They have to go through the back entries of houses, or so I have been advised. When such a case is brought to my attention, I write to the company employing them and ask that they be allowed to enter through the front.

"And then, too," she continued with some firmness, "there is the problem of the 'masher,' a man who is not only a nuisance to himself but a menace to humanity. I mean to see to it that young girls are shielded from the attention of these men.

"The first thing to do is to watch furtive sweetmeat shops, with their rows of bottles filled with brilliantly colored soda water fruit syrups and the little back rooms; the pseudo motion-picture schools, which help to recruit the great army that Lecky spoke of as the 'sacrifice on the altar of the nation's purity'; the spurious 'theatrical agency'; and all the many other forms used to lure young girls to their ruin.

"You will realize that there could hardly be a more important thing to tackle—unless, of course, you mention the matter of national defense."

"Do you think that general public service is unfit for women?"

"I most certainly do. Such work as that of the streetcar conductor and running an elevator is very bad for women; they are subject to the passing insults of the crowd. You will say that women are subject to this anyway; that is quite true, but in ordinary life they are in a better position to protest."

"And," said I, "what do you think of crime in general? To me personally it has a strong appeal—I like crime, provided it is well committed."

She smiled, shaking her head. "That sounds nice, but of course that is the artist's point of view. Crime, murder, love, hate, all appeal to the artist; but you see," she added, "there are only a very few artists in the world, and the unavoidable crimes will always be enough for them.

"The criminal who is one through a moment's great feeling, through a sudden climax of passions, I forgive always in my heart. There is so little feeling in the world that even when it takes the wrong method of expressing itself it is something that the world cannot do without. There is too little love and therefore no really great and profound hate; too few people move with a 'certain somber fury.'"

"Will crime ever be uprooted? That is, will the court and the judgment seat and the prisons ever be done away with?"

"Never, not so long as humanity is inhuman. The gallows tree has not shut the mouth of all the angers, nor has the rope strangled the universal cry of despair."

"But the cause of most crime, is it not poverty?"

"Oh, yes; poverty is the greatest of all evils, because people do not understand how to be poor. Poverty drives the children into the street, we all know that, and from there to the saloons; but why? Because their own homes are not only poor but dirty."

"But soap costs money, Mrs. O'Grady."

"I know, I know, but some there are who have proved their divine ability, some who reach heaven little but skin and bones; but this kind He loves best."

> The sum of thy past agony shall shake
> The very marrow of thy bones, and move
> The oblivious skin upon thy nerveless veins

—I quoted.

Mrs. O'Grady looked up sharply.

"What is that?" she inquired. "I, too, love poetry, but there!" she added sighing, "I must learn not to speak of poetry in business hours."

"But you yourself write it, I have heard."

"Oh, yes; I write it, but I do not speak of it excepting to those nearest me—my daughters, a friend or two, and that is all."

"Yet," said I, "what of:

O marvelous man, must thy heart beat high
As with frozen limbs 'neath the northern sky
You planted the flag Old Glory there,
Your thanksgiving hymn, your voiceless prayer,
Was freedom's flag at the Pole unfurled;
The Stars and Stripes at the top of the world.

"Yes, yes," she said, coloring a little. "Those naughty boys on the papers got that. They played a trick on me, but I don't mind. The papers have always treated me kindly and justly; though I would like you to say for me that the newspapers no longer mold the public opinion, as was proved by the last election."

"But, for goodness sake, do not let us get away from our subject—crime and death. Now, death is something I am really keen about," I interrupted.

This time she laughed heartily.

"You're a funny girl," she said. "You love crime and now you adore death—I see you have the artist's soul.

"The saddest part of it all is that it really takes a lifetime to understand a person, and no one can spend a lifetime judging a criminal. Crime takes but a moment but justice an eternity. Therefore the best that we can do, the best that the judge can do, is to be as good a character reader as possible, a person who has almost occult powers, one who can discern at a glance all the little complexities that have gone into the making of the mistake."

"What of psychoanalysis—Freudism, you know?"

"I don't believe in it very much. It goes too far—digs down too deep; but I do believe in the psychological moment. Take a person at the edge, just before he goes over—a person with the knife lifted, one with the poison to his lips, he who is about to shoot—and you have a chance for redemption such as you will never have again and which you could not have had before. One always saves and loses the most at the edge of things."

"Do you think that Osborne's prison reform would have worked out well for the criminal?"

"I don't like to say yes or no to that. I do think that his ideas were good ones. I do think that prison reforms are good things. But the prisons as they were before were not as bad as they were painted."

"What about a colony for criminals: a whole town, if you like, walled in as China is walled in, through which the criminal could express himself; a place with libraries, public squares, town hall, opera house, movies, and garden—a place where crime could be developed into something beyond crime, beyond good and evil?"

"Ah, what a dreamer's idea that is!" she said.

"Yet, cannot criminals and fallen women teach things that none of us know, such things that we might be the better for?"

And now she rather surprised me.

"Yes, very many things," she replied. "I know of no honor that is at times more beautiful than that among thieves. I know of nothing more terrible and more tragic and more splendid than the feeling of fallen women for another who might fall. The honor among thieves reaches very often a sublime point; the effort of a fallen woman to save a sister has often brought tears to my eyes—but yet such honor and such unselfish feeling cannot enter our world, cannot mean anything for the great masses, cannot save or make better or count in the great world which, at large, is honorable and upright and fine."

"Yet, at any moment any one of us might commit a murder."

"It has been said quite truly that we are all potential criminals. It is true that environment makes most of us what we are; then we must change the environment."

"How? Through Socialism?"

"Certainly not." She looked displeased. "Socialism has nothing to do with it. Socialism is another dream of a class of people who see wrongs but no rights. No, I think it can only be attained by education: education of the senses and of the mind, education in what is desirable because it is best, education of the heart, teaching it to reach that point where it will not be an effort but a pleasure to respond to those things which are fine in themselves and which neither outrage the heart nor the theory."

"But is such a thing possible?"

"It becomes impossible only so soon as you give up all hope of the human race—and that I have not done."

"And what of death?"

"But that is a subject of which I know so little."

"That is why I want you to talk about it—it is the one medium by which one has to come to a conclusion through feeling and not theory."

"Well, death has always touched me very deeply. Why? Because it is so inevitable, so lasting, so unexpected, so imminent. Why do you regard it as you do?"

"Because it is so terrible to see all the gestures gone."

She half closed her eyes, turning a golden whistle over and over in her palm. Leaning forward, I saw that it was a police whistle and that on the table lay a badge.

"My jewelry," she said. "The only jewelry one should wear—the symbol of one's labor for humanity. Jewelry, by the way, is the first mistake made by mothers. They should forbid their children the wearing of rings and necklaces—thus many a girl has been led to her ruin. Jewelry is vanity, and vanity is destruction."

"And now, tell me about yourself."

"I am Irish; you can tell that, can't you? Yes, Irish all the way from Ireland. I married in 1888 after having studied to become a teacher. My husband, who was an expert accountant with a firm of importers, died in 1898, leaving me with five daughters. I took up dressmaking. Two of my daughters died. It was a hard struggle, but I have never been afraid to work.

"About this time I grasped the civil service idea, passed my examinations, and was appointed probation officer and served so for eleven years in the New Jersey Avenue court, Brooklyn."

"But most women left without support and with a family could not have done as well. Too many women are ignorant of life, and too many are without a practical means of support."

"Very true; that is the tragedy of it. Women, you know, I have great faith in, especially women who have borne children; for through the bearing and rearing of children comes wisdom. My advice to all women is first to learn a trade, have something at their fingertips and then to marry and have a family. A woman who has not had children knows no more of life than one blind. This does not mean that I am advocating the rearing of six or seven children. It really does not matter so long as you can say, 'I have borne.'

"I think that women are fitted for a great many things. There are plenty of places in public life where they can serve. They are excellent secretaries; they make good waitresses; they are librarians of the most careful type. There are hundreds of things that they can do besides vote.

"I do not like to see them doing work, however, that is entirely unsuited to them, as I said before. Housework is, after all, their master art. Did you ever see a man who could keep a house in perfect shape? No, and the state, the world, the entire administration and public life—what is it if not housekeeping on an immense scale? This does not imply that they must necessarily run cars any more than one would expect them to bring in the coal or kill the hogs.

"In my work there are many things that only a woman could understand. It takes a woman to know the temptations of women. That is why I have women detectives; that is why I would like to have women at every dance hall and every moving picture and along the beaches in summer. That is why I should deeply regret the removal of women from the outside world."

"And your daughters, Mrs. O'Grady—what do they think of their mother?"

"They think it most scandalous," she said with bright eyes, "that a woman of my age should be sitting in Police Headquarters at the beck and call of every unfortunate.

Yet I love the work, and I don't think I have an enemy in the world."

"And now," said I, reaching for the door, "tell me what you think of the Russians?"

"Ah," she sighed, turning to her papers so that I saw only the parting in the pretty white hair, "I enjoy Tolstoy a little more than anything else in the world."

City's War Camp Community Service Gives Our Boys Home Comforts

Walking through Manhattan one notices small signs reading FOR SOLDIERS AND SAILORS ONLY, and below, the words NEW YORK WAR CAMP COMMUNITY SERVICE. On inquiry, one learns that these places are clubs where soldiers and sailors may read, eat, write, and pass the time away, listening to the talk of their comrades and the latest jazz records and otherwise enjoying themselves.

I asked Rowland Haynes, director of the committee in charge, how the enterprise was being received. He began:

"What we are attempting to do, what we have done, is somewhat different from other war work. We are merely executives in a clearing house in which to bring together the enlisted men who pass through New York.

"We grew out of what was formerly known as the Playground Association. The funds that were to be used to build playgrounds for the children are now used to make a playground for our soldiers. Our enterprise was organized by representatives of the War Department and Navy Department Commission on Training Camp Activities, and it has only one aim: to entertain and care for the man in khaki.

"We have been running only since last September, and yet ten thousand men pass through our hands weekly. I don't want to bother you with figures," he went on, "but figures go here as they would seldom go in other cases. The war is a matter of figures, the Army is a matter of figures, and it is only by figures that we have thought of anything for the last few years.

"From the middle of September to the middle of January, over three thousand enlisted men obtained lodging at the four National Service clubs of the W.C.C.S. at a cost a night of from twenty-five to fifty cents. Over seventy-one thousand have made use of the clubrooms, and over thirty thousand men have enjoyed wholesome, home-cooked meals at a nominal price.

"In a few moments I am going to have Mr. Cupp take you down to Unit Number 5 at 55 West Twenty-seventh Street, the hotel that used to be known as the Earlington, which the Metropolitan Life Insurance Company turned over to us for the cost of insurance and taxes. And now here again I will have to mention figures. This hotel has nine floors and on every floor are ten baths, beside one general bath. The capacity is 900 guests, though on Saturday nights there are sometimes as many as twelve hundred accommodated." He laughed a little. "They particularly like the nice, soft sofas that belong to the restrooms."

"Don't you ever have an overflow?"

"Oh, yes. Then the churches come forward and give up their gymnasium space. We supply the cots, and some ladies offer to make them up and to see that everything is shipshape."

"And what," said I, "do you find the boys like best of all?"

"Dancing."

"Their pet books?"

He shook his head. "They aren't much on reading. They are in town for only a short while, you must remember, and reading seems to be the one thing they don't worry about."

"Isn't it rather strange?"

"Not so very. The boys are mostly out-of-town chaps. They are here to see New York. They are pleased with very little; they think a bus ride or a show about the best thing in the world."

"But the city boy?"

A gleam of humor came into his slow eyes. "He calls up Mamie or Mabel, and that's the end of that. All the city boys have their parents and their sweethearts, and that takes them out of our hands entirely."

Just at this moment in rushed H. D. Robins, a little quick man with gray hair and a long, black ribbon attached to a pair of impressive eyeglasses that insisted on coming off. Gesticulating energetically, he directed a group of very young girls to "finish that budget before lunch," and then turning to Mr. Haynes he asked something hurriedly about a poster, about a man from Washington, about Mr. Taft—at least I was sure I caught the name Taft— about the latest pictures of the club writing room, about the theatre tickets for some free performances for the boys, and finally darted out again with the exclamation, "Gosh, and the Army is growing every minute!"

"Four big holiday affairs were put through by our service in the first four months," Mr. Haynes continued. "We gave a Thanksgiving dinner at the Twelfth Regiment Ar-

mory and three dances at the Grand Central Palace. Now
we have so arranged it that each Saturday night finds a
khaki and blue dance in full swing, with an average attendance of from 1,200 to 1,500 men."

"How do you manage the partners for the boys?"

"Some ladies volunteer, some are from the Girls Patriotic Service League, and some are from other clubs. All
are properly chaperoned, and all of them, both girls and
boys, have a splendid time."

"Tell me about the free Sunday vaudeville."

"We began at the Forty-fourth Street Theatre, went
from the Harris to the Casino, and now we are at the
Astor. Our only admission fee is the color of khaki; our
motto is, 'Your uniform is your pass.'

"We have had such names on our bill as Percy Grainger,
now a member of the Fort Hamilton band; Louise Homer,
Laurette Taylor, Frank Tinney, George Cohan, James J.
Corbett, and Constance Collier. And speaking of Corbett
makes me think of our first effort to amuse the boys: we
gave a boxing match at the armory, and it did not meet
with the success we expected."

"How do you account for that?"

"It reminds them of camp, and they are not on furlough
to remember the camp, believe me! They have come to the
city to have a good time, to be amused, and wrestling is a
thing they can have any day. It is the natural thing for
men who are en masse to wrestle and box, so when we
put up this match they turned their heads away and
yawned."

In my mind I went over something that I had read about
this affair, ending with the statement that each boy got a

bag of candy. It seemed to me then that there was something strangely unusual about boys who when home always refuse candy with a superior sniff.

Finally Mr. Cupp did take me down to the hotel, and there I met Henry F. Lutz, who has charge of the establishment. He was sifting a soldier—or in other words, he was putting him through a cross-examination to discover if his plea for railroad fare was an honest one or if he was one of the many fakes.

"A lot of men are wearing the uniform who have no right to do so," Mr. Lutz said. "They are taking the services of our committee and are grafting on meals and free amusements, and these we deal with severely. But there are often others who have been robbed, who have parents who need to see them on account of illness or death, and these we help out of what is called our emergency fund."

But I wasn't listening, for my eye was traveling over my surroundings. Long, swaying posters with such sentiments as YOU BUY THE BOND, I'LL FIGHT and NO QUITTERS HERE moved upon the walls. By the open bay windows of the parlor sat three sailors, one reading, one dozing, one just staring out into the street; a phonograph was playing variations from *Pom-Pom*. A Negro porter passed with a pail, swaying a little as he went. A desk clerk sorted free tickets, while another gave a man in khaki a letter from his folks.

In the dim recesses of a long back room, about an immense table, sat five or six soldiers. One showed the pathetic droop of the man who must think and write; on the face of another was that vague, happy expression that is common to everything in spring. Suddenly the voice of

Mr. Lutz broke in on my meditation with the remark that
here were six boys we might not see again.

"See that table?" he went on. "That was given to us for
the use of the boys by a very rich woman. On it has been
spread many a banquet; many a cup of wine has been
spilled on its mahogany surface, many a whispered word
of love has floated over it, and now——" He paused. "And
now——?" The deep rhythmic snore of a private filled the
lobby with a sad yet peaceful murmur.

"He's not thinking of the U-boats," said a voice at my
side. It was one of the boys.

"Tell me," I said to him, "what you all think of now;
what change has come over you since you entered the
service? What do you think when in camp, when on furlough?"

He grinned. "Well, some of the fellows think of the girls,
but not me. I think of having a good time, going out to
some nice home for dinner—we are often invited, you
know. That's what pleases most of us best."

"But what else do you think of? War?"

He grinned again. "I should say not. What would we be
thinking of war and death for until we have to, until that
happens as will make us think. And when that does come
off—well, thinking is taken out of our hands."

"But don't you see life differently? It is a very strange
thing that has happened to you. You may be a driver of a
delivery wagon, and perhaps your chum is a chemist, and
his chum may be a day laborer, and a fourth may have
been a beggar; doesn't something happen to your concep-
tions of life when suddenly the hand of fate flings you
together in a heap for the first time?"

"Not much," he said. "We do or don't like each other; that's about all, just the same as we did in ordinary, every-day life."

I couldn't accept this and put the question to Mr. Lutz.

"They don't think anything much," he replied. "They are not philosophers, you know, or dreamers or artists. They are ordinary, healthy boys that we mean to keep healthy, for the army that goes over the top has to have the best, and no mistake."

"Do they become more or less religious?"

"They don't change."

"We leave that for the folks at home to do," the boy said.

"Church attendance has increased since it has not been forced on the boys," Mr. Lutz went on. "A church may give them a dinner and an entertainment, but because of this not a boy needs to stay unless he really wants to, and since that many more boys have wanted to. The idea is not to make the boys feel that they have got to do this or that. The sole idea is to supply them with amusement and occupation, thereby keeping them out of trouble."

Here he gave me an armful of literature, explaining, "These are given for distribution to railroad officials, to policemen, to clubs, to men who give the boys leave, so that the boys may know where they are going before they start, so that they may feel welcome when they arrive, and so that they shall be happy and well when they depart. In these pamphlets are the addresses of all those places where the only pass necessary is the uniform; addresses of churches, theatres, clubs, public baths; addresses of all kinds, where they will feel themselves welcome.

"We have many calls every day from families who want

one, two, three or more soldiers and sailors sent up to them for dinners. Theatres send down seventy or a hundred free tickets at a time for distribution, and the boys only have to pay the war tax."

"And do the boys prefer to go singly or in pairs to these dinners?"

"A boy hates to go alone to a strange house. They always say, 'Well, that's nice, but haven't you someone that can go with me?'"

"What kind of plays do they like best?"

"Oh, vaudeville, burlesque. I gave one lad a free ticket to a violin recital, and when he got back I asked him how he had enjoyed himself, and he answered, 'Fine; I slept through the whole list,' adding, 'Say, that man must have been a great violinist, he fiddled the whole hour and a half I was sleeping.'"

Presently, when he had dictated half-a-dozen letters, attended to a score of boys, and written the last names in the book of addresses, Mr. Lutz took me up to see the boys' rooms.

Long hall after long hall smelling of antiseptics, corridors resounding with the footsteps of a colored man with the eternal pail and mop, and then the rooms with their six, eight, or ten cots, with a towel lying on each. There were small iron beds with sheets and army blankets, a few lockers in green along the walls, and to one side a bathroom with its white, shining tub.

"This is where the boys sleep," Mr. Lutz said.

A thought came to me. "Do they all always sleep well?"

"War never keeps them awake—and death doesn't worry them much. Sometimes, of course, they get melancholy and won't eat, but that's only when they have been discharged from the army as unfit and they are mad to get into the fight.

"We had once a case like that. A young fellow, awfully nice chap—sort of idealist, I guess—got where he wouldn't eat, wouldn't sleep, and finally he had to be taken to the hospital. It wasn't any use, there wasn't anything we could do; he had lung trouble, and he would have hindered his fellow soldiers."

Traversing long vaults that had once been the hotel's wine cellar, we came to the canteen bar, which was once the bar without the canteen. A pile of plates and cups, of knives and forks, of paper napkins and glasses stood on one end, while a case of cigarettes flanked it. On a pillar there was a sign to the effect that for thirty cents a breakfast was served from five to nine-thirty consisting of bacon or ham and eggs, oatmeal and milk, rolls, butter, and coffee. For those of lighter appetite a breakfast consisting of oatmeal and milk, two rolls, butter and coffee could be had for ten cents.

Seeing New York With the Soldiers

At ten minutes past ten, the starter of the rubberneck wagon pushed in the last passenger, a little woman from Utah with green and black striped stockings, and we shot out into the mysteries of New York.

The French officer in his tight-fitting uniform turned his small black nodding head this way and that, singing through his mustache a song heard long ago in some cafe near his heart. As we turned into Broadway on our way up Fifth Avenue, he sang still louder as the megaphone man, who was advertised on the circular as the "educated lecturer," began shouting: "On the near left-hand corner, midway of the block, you see the spot where Hoimen Rosenthal was murdered—right here, madam," pointing with a back-turned thumb.

Two Canadian boys with their arms about each other leaned across the seat in front of the Frenchman and whispered to the "lecturer," "Is this Fifth Avenue?" The lecturer, moving his head toward them, answered in the affirmative, though there was cotton in his ears.

The smell of hot tar reached the nostrils, and the faint, far odor of vanishing gasoline fumes, while the little lady in the green stockings who hailed from Utah, in shaking out a small lace handkerchief as she turned to look back at the spot where Rosenthal was murdered, shed an odor about us of home-grown lilacs.

Women in white blouses and trailing skirts were left on the mind's eye like a blur of fancy seen by a Whistler. Ornate shops and heavy golden signs winked and spread thin in the memory like long wires holding together immense edifice after immense edifice. Through the open door of Sherry's, one caught a glimpse of small, smart women in white aprons pinching with long silver tongs the brown and placid sides off rotund Italian creams, while the megaphone man kept singing away into his nose the information that was warranted to set the heart afire.

The four soldiers on the back seats were smiling and looking this way and that as the thumb of the man up forward shot first over his right, then over his left shoulder: "The house of Willie K," then, "To your direct right hand the biggest church in New York, taking up four city blocks and holding thirty-six hundred praise givers."

The great doors were ajar. A woman in a red skirt and a plume stood in its shadow. Far away a stained-glass window shed little drops of holy colors upon the drab backs of supplicants. For a moment before we were gone, the white hands of some statue reached out of the darkness, folded, lifted.

"Shoiman on his ride to the sea"—a clatter of horses' hoofs crossing the square, the faint, opulent sound of rubber tires, the whine of a bicycle siren, and the deep, rich, and arrogant note of a horn on a long, black car nosing its way through the traffic, hurrying swiftly, uncannily, like an animal that does not breathe.

The little Frenchman could be heard singing through his mustache, "Très jolie figure d'amour."

"And you?"—leaning forward to speak to the boys from Canada.

"We're here for twenty-four hours. But say, lady, let me tell you something about Toronto. There's a place. You can talk all you like about New York, but I know something dearer, sweeter."

"Yes," smiling.

"It's about your own Walt Whitman. You know, you're pretty proud of him, but you're no prouder than this man back there who kept a stationery store. Well, he had pencils——"

"Here we enter Millionaire's Row," chanted the megaphone man.

"And he used to tell the customers about one special red pencil with six sides——"

"This is the house with the solid onyx steps——"

"And," went on the boy from Canada, "this pencil he would show to any customer who lingered a little over his books, his papers. He would say, 'Now here is a pencil that was held by Whitman on the twenty-second of August in the year eighteen hundred and ninety-nine when he was passing this way and a poem came into his head.'" The boys laughed a little, nudging each other before they could come out with the joke.

"Well?"

"Well, he never knew the difference between that pencil and the other six-sided red pencils we used to put in its place when he wasn't looking."

"Oh, but that's a shame—think what you did in removing a historic pencil from your town."

"Central Park——"

The soldiers behind the Canadians were staring at the green on the trees and the green of the new-cut lawns, and watching the babies falling and picking themselves up in the pathways.

"What do you think of New York?"

The little French officer in the tight uniform paused in his singing and looked at me. "New York," he laughed, showing large, good teeth. "It is very amusing—chic. It has such big feet and such small hands—and the sights in the windows are very funny. I was going down Fifth Avenue in the hot afternoon yesterday, and I see a sight, a most amusing sight, an intriguing sight." He slapped his knees, doubling forward. "I did not know you had such men and women in America. I thought we only had such people in Europe. It was a window on the first floor, it was on Eleventh Street. A little tree stands in the yard. The curtains are yellow. Dyed in tea, yes? And through the window one could look a little way, a very little way, into the room. Antique chairs stood about, old carvings, an easel with a dirty canvas on it. But that is not the funniest: a man, a long, thin man with tremendous mustaches, blond, lay sideways in an antique, asleep. His lips were colorless; his eyelids were colorless, as if they might be hiding white, colorless eyes. His heart beat a little, pulsing under his white chin, and on a long chain hung two great seals. The chain was amusing, too: it fled from pocket to pocket, it was afraid and hid its head; it was terrified to be on such a calm stomach; it was stretched with agony. And in a chair beside this young, sleeping man sat an old lady, bolt upright, with tea-dyed lace about her throat, with her hands folded in her lap, with dust in her hair, with wise, sleepless eyes. So," he raised his hands, breathed down his mustache, and ended: "These things you see only in Europe. Now, Balzac would have known what to do with that. Here in America it will be wasted, not noticed, lost. It is very sad."

I nodded, thinking.

"What was going on in that woman's head, no one knew. What was awaiting the awakening of that man with the blond mustaches, that also you do not know. But I'll tell you: I, a Frenchman, because I know, and I coming to America can tell you about such Americans."

"Very well."

"So. The old woman was his mother, probably, and probably a widow. She sits in bed most of the day with a cup of cold coffee on a little, stained table—is it not probably so? And she calls out aloud from time to time, to some hiding and aging maid, 'Jenny, Jenny, bring me my mirror, wind the clock; has the picture of Father fallen in the night with that heavy wind we had?' So she talks, sitting in bed in her tea-dyed lace, never any fresh air. Then toward four in the afternoon she calls again: 'Jenny, get my slippers and stockings and my black dress, and open the doors into the parlor, my son will be coming.' And presently her son comes, the tall man with the blond mustaches. And what of him? He wants to carry his cane just so, and he cannot carry his cane just so without a manner, and he cannot have the manner without sufficient money in his pockets; therefore, she must pawn something again.

He sleeps at the window until she shall have sent Jenny
out and until Jenny shall have returned with the money,
the noiseless, faded, overhandled bills of some obscure
broker—the bills that never crackle, that never whisper
their affluence to each other, hundred dollars on hundred
dollars without a word, like people accustomed to their
good fortune. They say nothing, and presently he will
wake up and go out, after kissing the old woman in the
tea-dyed laces, and he will walk with his cane held just so,
and he will enter the barbershop, and they will take his
cane from him a moment to dress his mustaches—so." He
broke off, sighing between his lips.

"Is that not it?" he questioned.

I nodded.

"The home of Hetty Green—she couldn't take it with
her——"

"And you?"

The four American soldiers from out of town did not
hear the question. They were looking at the home of the
famous, dead Hetty.

"Did she get decorated by the Pope?" one of them asked.

"Yes," thundered the megaphone man through his megaphone, forgetting to remove it to answer.

"Who has the house now?"

"A famous count."

"Is her son living?"

"He was, last time I heard of him."

"He was pretty close-mouthed, wasn't he?"

"I don't know; I guess so; most rich people can afford to
shut up."

"Oh, I see."

"No, you don't," grinned the megaphone man. "None of us folk do.

"Temple Beth-el, richest Jewish congregation in American worship," he went on, moving his thumb but not his eyes. "The Pickard Folly House, the show palace of Fifth Avenue, open three times a year to the public, home of ex-Senator W. Clark, the copper king. All the copper used in this building was quarried from his own mine. . . . Home of Andrew Carnegie. . . . Mount Sinai Hospital, where the Divine Sarah had her limb amputated. . . . Mount Morris Park, Seventh Avenue. . . . Highest point in the elevated tracks, called Dead Man's Curve. At this point we enter Morningside Drive." The bus, laden, turned, tossing the soldiers into each other's arms. Swaying, it came to a dramatic halt. The little lecturer stood up on the running board and turned, facing the Cathedral of Saint John the Divine.

"This cathedral," he said, without the megaphone to his lips, "has been twenty-five years going up and at the present rate of construction will be another twenty-five. It has seven chapels for seven languages, and Bishop Greer speaks here. There are several tablets to the memory of the dead, and the men who worked on it as children have grown up on it to maturity—watch them become senile." He removed the cotton from his ears for a second and, replacing it, told the chauffeur to go on.

"What was the matter with it?" one of the boys in the American uniform asked.

"Don't know—the roof, I guess."

"Why the roof?"

"Well, the roof looks most improbable to me," joked the lecturer, turning away.

"Struck a mud pocket," whispered the little woman from Utah, kindly.

"Panoramic view of New York here," shouted the lecturer. We all turned.

"Columbia University." A young girl in white tennis shoes was running down the interminable, short steps leading to the street.

"The little red house on the hill used to be an asylum. This is Barnard College for women—note the danger sign."

POISON, it said, KEEP OFF. We laughed, but still I don't understand.

We turned into Riverside Drive. Moving slowly downtown again, we watched the water and the great camouflaged ships. We paused; the car came to a stop. "Grant's Tomb," he said. "We stop here eight minutes, that you may go inside and visit the tomb. It's open to the public."

And as we climbed down and began our ascent of the steps, I thought back to the day when, as a child, my father had brought me here. He had taken me in and lifted me up and let me gaze down into the darkness where two bodies lay in state. And I wondered if I should feel that same awe, that same unconquerable feeling of vastness that death gives, when again, for the first time in fifteen years, I should look over the edge of this pit into the darkness below.

There was something cold, casual, unheeding, in the way the soldiers filed in, removing their hats, and the green stockings of the little lady from Utah shone dully in the purple light. Six or eight people were there before us, hats in hands, one holding a child as I had been held, by its blue sash, and I approached also, and I looked down.

The same darkness, only now the purple, mysterious light gave it a less somber and a more artificial aspect. There, side by side, lay the two great boxes like loaves of immense and precious cake, like a sunken confectioner's, with flowers and with ribbons and no air of death at all. And it seemed that there was something less than death in these two dead and a something less profound than the meaning of the tomb, and the moving figures, hats in hands, seemed like strange, inhuman things crawling around a stranger, more inhuman hole, a pit filled with darkness and death, and yet somehow less melancholy and inspiring than the depths of a cistern that sound with the low droppings of rainwater.

Round and round we went, looking down, and outside, faint but clear, we heard the voice of the guard calling: "Postal views of New York, ten cents a dozen," and above that the sound of ships leaving dock. Someone whispering through the silence broke an oppressive quiet.

"He died right," the officer was saying through his mustache.

"Yes," answered the boy from the West. "He died, let us say, in the great attitude of joy."

The little woman from Utah crossed herself silently and as silently tiptoed into the flag rooms and began peering, with silver-rimmed spectacles held firmly, at the faded flags, at the funeral service with its quaint directions— "Junior Vice Commander John A. Wiedersheim" (laying a rose or other flower)—at the framed proclamations and declarations of grief, and finally at the embroidered picture of the dead general, flanked by Victory and Justice.

And presently the ride began again. Turning down

Broadway, the soldiers from out of town looked wistfully at its length and sighed. The Great White Way: a blank array of electric globes crusted every building's side like the very skin of some immense and glowing thing that had left its shell behind, and the revolving doors of the lobster palaces seemed little more than the doors of some office building in Tacoma. In the faces of all of them, there was a look of finality; they had come, and they had seen, and they were going away.

The little Frenchman was still singing "Très jolie figure" as we came to a halt in front of the Flatiron Building, and the megaphone man, climbing once more up to a position of vantage, began telling about another trip, through the Bowery—"The Bowery, with its endless procession of human wrecks, old and young"—and smiling up into his face, the boys from Canada shook their heads.

"You can't frighten us," they said, turning in the direction of the subway, "we've seen a bit of life ourselves and will see more."

I turned to the little French officer as we crossed back to Fifth Avenue, saying, "Well, the boys were not as surprised as I thought they would be."

"That is simple," he answered, stepping out briskly with his small, foreign legs. "Those western boys come from the place where these things are made. Now, that house on the avenue built from the stone and the copper of that chap's own mines—well, the boys have seen it when it lay in the fields, when it rose up before them bigger, more imposing, as hills, mountains, mines, deep holes, abysses wherein lie all that now stands on either side of us. They were present when the city was only a dream, and they knew the texture of it before it was planned, cut."

He threw up his shoulders: "Well, au revoir, mademoiselle." And he went, swinging his legs briskly, singing, "Très jolie figure d'amour."

To Sublet for the Summer

SCENE: A charmingly disordered room. In the bed propped up by many colored pillows, with her head in a beribboned cap, reading a copy of a fashion magazine, is the figure of EDITH O'TOOLE. Remnants of a biscuit, a pot of jam, and a cup of tea on the table to her left. On the edge of the bed in a yellow gown sits FRANCINE LECLUSE. Telephone rings in room to right.

EDITH O'TOOLE: Answer the telephone; it's about the ad, dear.

MISS LECLUSE *(stalking over like a panther to the phone):* Hello, hello; yes, this is Miss Lecluse's apartment. What? Yes, we—I mean, I want to let it for the summer. Oh no, we—I—couldn't possibly give you the lease at the end of October. Wait a minute. *(Shoves the receiver against her chest.)*

See here, a man and his wife want this apartment after October for good. What will I tell them?

EDITH O'TOOLE: Tell them to ring off.

MISS LECLUSE *(disconnecting):* That does not seem to be the proper approach if you want to sublet this place. *(Telephone rings again.)* I wish you hadn't advertised it in my name. Why did you, anyway? *(Answering):* Yes, this is Miss Lecluse. No, three flights up. Oh, I'm so sorry you are lame, it's the war. Oh, I beg your pardon, your voice was so deep I thought—oh, you're the mother of four, have rheumatism—that's a shame. Yes, we have five rooms. No, it's not an elevator apartment, so it

336

wouldn't be much use my going into details, would it?—
What?—you live out of town, a long-distance call, and
you hear so few things of interest—you want a description of it because it's in Greenwich Village? Oh, really
(stabbing her chest once more with receiver). There, that's what
you get for advertising this place as four doors from the
square. *(Returning to phone.)* Well, anything to oblige. Oh,
yes, we have yellow chairs. Manners? Oh, very bad. Oh
yes, very bad. Charming, you say, so sweet of you.
Candles, yes, we burn candles. Why, the apartment is
done in gold and black with Beardsley medallions—no,
Beardsley was an artist, one of a chain of artists like
Butler's stores—oh, certainly we have incense burning
most of the time. We do light housekeeping over it; it
makes delicious Oriental eggs. Well, goodbye—no, I said
goodbye.

(Coming back.) I'm sorry I ever saw you. Why in the
world don't you get up and answer your own calls?

EDITH O'TOOLE: It's in your name. My name wouldn't look
so nice; there's something recherché about "Lecluse."
They might have family and all that. It's a name you
can't do much with. It's slippery, while mine is too
prickly and too historic. I can be traced back, way back
to the days before Marie Antoinette was beheaded. In
fact, it was the real name of one of the royal families
just before ascending the throne. But that's a secret, a
state secret, and you mustn't whisper it to a soul. Absolute silence. It's because of this that O'Toole has become
what the common people deem—well, a name to be
whispered only after sundown. It's those after-sun-
down names that have put the blue blood into families,

but as yet America isn't educated up to the qualities that make a real family. Some little taint of theft, some subcellar murder or a face gone forever from the high chairs of Europe, that's the stuff of which the royal purple is made. Whereas a noble line, some splendid craft, some belief whispered to the printing press stored away in some obscure and forgotten corner, where are such names, such people? In ignominy, my dear, dark and utter oblivion, while the name of O'Toole rings round the world. *(Telephone rings.)*

MISS LECLUSE: Hello. What? You're coming right over? But wait a minute.

(Telephone again to breast.) A man and wife—speaking in the terms of "we"—are coming right over. They are across the street now. They were going to take the apartment, but the baby there had measles and cries and Mr.—*(returning to phone)*—what's the name, please?—Mr. Mullius sleeps—he must be a night watchman—what? No, he says he's the night shift in a prison—turnkey; that would be so safe. What shall I tell him?

EDITH O'TOOLE: Tell him to keep away.

MISS LECLUSE *(sweetly):* Come right over.

(Before she can get back, the phone rings again.) Hello, hello. Yes, this is Miss Lecluse speaking. Oh yes, we did have an ad in the paper, by mistake. But it's all right. We might like to get out before the first of August though. Wait a moment. *(Putting receiver up to her chest once more.)* Do you or don't you want to move out of here before the fifteenth?

EDITH O'TOOLE: I'd like to move, but I'm afraid of coast towns since the raid. I do hate to be disturbed by noises alien to my education. Still, when does she want it?

MISS LECLUSE: No later than the fifteenth.

EDITH O'TOOLE: I can't leave so soon. There are the boy's rompers. I've got to change them; they are too small. The O'Tooles always grow faster than is really comfortable for summer plans.

MISS LECLUSE *(returning to phone):* Oh, I'm so sorry. Yes, it's not really my apartment. You see, my friend has twins; they cry alternately. Yes, no one ever sleeps. It might be a little difficult for you. We enjoy it—it's a new cult, the Stay Awake Club, or missing nothing. Yes, it's American. Quite American. Goodbye.

    There, now that I've made a perfect fool of myself for your sake, will you tell me why you put that ad in the paper and how long it's going to run?

EDITH O'TOOLE: Saturday, Sunday, and Monday. But it can be discontinued any day before six o'clock. If you call up before six it will be removed. Why did I put the ad in? *(Looks plaintive.)* I wanted to know if I could rent it if I should want to.

MISS LECLUSE: Oh, really. Well, I refuse to answer the next call. *(Telephone rings.)*

EDITH O'TOOLE: Answer it, dear. I can't. It makes me sneeze to get out of bed without my purple slippers, and you're wearing them.

MISS LECLUSE *(seizing the telephone):* What, are you there? But yes, yes, yes; this is the apartment of——

EDITH O'TOOLE *(in an excited voice):* Don't let them have it. Don't let them have it!

MISS LECLUSE: Come right over. *(Telephone rings again.)* Yes, what? No, the apartment faces due north, toward the uptown side. The elevated—between the park and Sixth

Avenue, you know. You're in the Secret Service and thought this a good part of town to do your first work— your best work—in? I beg your pardon. Why, yes; there are no end of things here that should be stopped. The pump, for instance, on the house opposite: coughing up the Minetta River; in fact, the Minetta River is running out of water, I should say. And then there's a lot of places here that need hindering—the Purple Pup— that's gone, you know. But there are other places just as vile, just as worthy of being—what do you call it?— raided. Yes, candles, incense, piano and dancing, black coffee and all that. There's a lot of things to see, too. A new headwaiter has come to the Brevoort; a fine family, I hear; come from that part of France where they take water for their health—they might start that movement down here. Oh, all right, come right down. When? Two o'clock? Dear me, I'm afraid we may be out. Very well, we will stay in. You don't mind a crowd, do you? You are a good mixer. That's well, there will be a few people here.

(Coming back toward MRS. O'TOOLE.*)* I refuse to see those people when they come. The maid will have to answer your questions. As for you, my opinion of women has shrunk to nothing. I always suspected them of being idiots, and now I know it.

EDITH O'TOOLE: *(composedly):* How can I be expected to know my mind from day to day? You talk like a man. It's only a rigid mind, a mind already formed into cubes, like bouillon tablets, that can always tell what it will do under certain circumstances. I am a person of tempera- ment, intellectual and physical. Temperament runs all

through my system. It ran all through my father, and
his father before him planted what are now the most
beautiful of the many beautiful trees along Main Street
in Middletown, Connecticut, so that proves that he also
was touched with that spontaneity that breaks us up
into many moods, many minds. I cannot and will not be
static; thus death comes.

THE MAID (*putting her head in at the door*): Callers, ma'am.

EDITH O'TOOLE: Show them into the reading room. You,
dear, go to them. You are dressed and I'm not. Put on
your beaded slippers and speak softly.

MISS LECLUSE (*going into next room*): How do you do?

   (*Six people file into the room with raised or depressed eyebrows.*)

VOICE OF THE OFFICER WITH GRAY HAIR: I think I'm first. At
least my foot passed the lintel before yours. Pardon
(*turning to Miss Lecluse*), this apartment is for rent, furnished, for the summer, I take it?

VOICE OF FEMALE IN MARY PICKFORD CHECK, WITH GOLDEN CURLS
FALLING OVER SHOULDER: Oh, Mother, look. They have
books on psychoanalysis and freedom of thought with
an introduction by Kuroswami; (*whispers:*) probably one
of those Russians.

VOICE OF THE TURNKEY: I suppose we might be permitted to
look at the apartment?

VOICE OF EDITH O'TOOLE (*through closed doors*): Don't let them
have it. I cannot possibly leave before the fifteenth, and
perhaps not until the thirtieth. I told you I had to change
John's rompers. They are a size too small—gingham is
going up, and John is still ahead of the gingham.

VOICE OF MISS LECLUSE (*conducting a personal tour—whispering
through the keyhole to* EDITH O'TOOLE): Be prepared to move

from room to room. *(To the would-be tenants):* This way. This is the kitchen, overlooking at least seven squalid back yards. You can sit here of a summer evening and enjoy the poverty and misery of your neighbors. These are the tubs, this the sink, this is the china closet. You will find everything in perfect order, and you will like the colors, patterns, and improbability of the tea set, bought in Chinatown on one of the rubberneck wagon rides when the bus stopped for eight minutes to give the driver time to smoke a cigarette. This is a small bedroom to the left, and to the right a large icebox; both of them hold a good deal. This is a hallway that we use for storing purposes. At the end of the hall is another room. It might be used as a den, any kind of a den, intellectual or moral.

(As she proceeds, the faint, soft sound of EDITH O'TOOLE *moving in bare feet from room to room can be heard.)* This is the living room, or tea parlor. This is the reading or drawing room. This——

VOICE OF SECRET SERVICE AGENT: I thought you said there were only five rooms. Why did you say that?

MISS LECLUSE: Why, er, that's a bit of humor on the part of my friend. She thought seven would be too many. Oh, it's too big to clean. Well, I'm sorry. Goodbye. *(Calling over the banisters):* If there is a letter in the box for me, will you ring the bell three times? Thank you.

(Going on in an even voice): This is a small aviary, or it could be used for ferns if you prefer the cry of the eggplant to the melodious warble of the catbird; and this is the street that you are looking down on. You recognized it? Well, what do you think of America?

(Pauses defiantly and yet a little tiredly in front of the remaining five. The telephone rings.) Hello; yes, yes, yes.

VOICE OF EDITH O'TOOLE: No, no, no!

MISS LECLUSE: Why, no, we have removed the advertisement—that is, we are going to. What is the time? It's half past three. It will soon be four. Oh, you didn't want to know that? Sorry; I have been giving so much information that I have gotten into a habit. I wasn't trying to be rude. Well, yes; you can come down and look at it. Yes, I'm Miss Lecluse, but my friend really owns the apartment and she was going away, but she is afraid to go now when she sees what a demand there is for her rooms. She suspects there's buried treasure; yes, she's hunting everywhere. There would be hardly a moment to spare for you. She is turning out the contents of an old hair sofa. *(Laughs hysterically.)* You had better take a room at the hotel. Oh, no trouble at all——

THE MAID *(putting her head in at the door once again)*: Three gentlemen and a lady, miss, to see the apartment.

MISS LECLUSE: Tell them it's already let—oh, how do you do? *(as they push in.)* Yes, it's let. These people here have taken it. Rather a large family, yes, but it's a large apartment. No, they don't know each other, but they are going to fight it out.

VOICE OF EDITH O'TOOLE: No, you're not. Wait a moment, Francine. If these people have seen the place, why don't they go?

MISS LECLUSE: It's their training. They haven't learned how to act in the congested districts.

THE LADY WITH THE BUSINESS WALK: Well, are you or are you not going to let some one of us have it?

EDITH O'TOOLE *(through the door):* Send them away. Why are they lingering?

VOICE OF THE TURNKEY AT THE DOOR: It was just the situation I wanted, and I have taken a great fancy to the wallpaper; however——*(Goes.)*

VOICE OF THE ART STUDENT JUST IN FROM WYOMING: I must have it. I love sublets. There is an atmosphere of old age and soiled linen about them that's perfectly entrancing. It's like a Greuze or a Dutch painting—full of genre——

MISS LECLUSE *(sitting down):* Well, do as you like—it's entirely in your hands.

VOICE OF EDITH O'TOOLE *(through the door):* Really, my patience is about given out. Are they going or aren't they?

MISS LECLUSE *(looking at the clock):* Why, it's a quarter of five. I must have made a mistake about the time.

OFFICER: Well, then, it is mine from the first.

VOICE OF FEMALE SECRET SERVICE: Oh dear no; I'm the lady here. I'll consider it mine from the first.

VOICE OF EDITH O'TOOLE: I've changed my mind. I'm not going until early in September.

(The crowd moves slowly toward the stairs with general expression of annoyance, displeasure, and astonishment. They murmur as they descend the steps.)

CROWD: It's the unreliability of the atmosphere below Fourteenth Street—is a well-known item in the instability of artists.

ANOTHER VOICE: But I don't think they have a thing to do with art.

A THIRD: I know, but how can one help it? Chicken fleas have been known to leap from the back of a Wyandotte into the hackle of many an enraged bull pup, and it seems to me that something strange was the matter there. Now I, for one. . . . *(They disappear around the third bend in the banisters.)*

MISS LECLUSE *(coming back, rushing for the phone)*: Hello, is this the *Evening Clarion*? This is Miss Lecluse. Yes, I inserted an ad for a sublet for the summer to run three days. I want it removed. What? It's one minute past six and it will have to remain! *(Sinks into the outstretched arms of Mrs. O'Toole.)*

BOTH TOGETHER: Oh, my Gawd!

There's Something Besides the Cocktail in the Bronx

Someone said to me the other day, "Now, there's the Bronx; so very few people think of the Bronx, even those who live in it, aside from the occasional fact absorber, who doles out statements that it is sixty-four miles square and that it is the city of babies."

And something further that he said brought back to me suddenly a memory of when I also lived in the Bronx.

Funny, the first thing I recalled was a stonecutter, an artist of his kind, who worked in a tombstone yard all day long with hammer and chisel: a gray-haired man with keen, melancholy eyes, who hardly ever raised them from his stone save occasionally to speak to me, lamenting the change in people's taste in carving. He used to say:

"There were days when tombstone engraving was as much an art as sculpture. I have carved many a superb leaf and cut many a weeping figure and child; none seemed to be weeping in their souls as mine seems to be weeping. One cemetery keeper told me that on a certain monument the sod was never dry; this was the one on which stood my veiled figure. That may be exaggerated, but you get the feeling. Now," he would make a slight movement with his chisel, "they only want fancy lettering, ugly and deformed and in bad taste. I shouldn't say only, but it is in the majority."

He was a good man and a clever man, and when the day's work was through he used to stand at the gate at the top of the little hill and, turning his eyes toward the town, sniff the evening air.

But surely, thought I, this is not what that gentleman meant by the Bronx, and again my memory played into my hands. It began at the Bronx Botanical Gardens. It was early morning—oh, very early morning, hardly more than half past seven. The grass was still wet, and the man who swept the steps was on the third stair. In the distance the soiled white jumper of the park wastepaper gatherer winked in and out between bushes and hedges as he went back and forth with his stick with the sharp end, searching for yesterday's newspapers and love letters.

It was the meeting place of some suburban society of bug hunters. They met once a year at the Botanical gate, and I was going with them. Presently they appeared. The first, an old gentleman thin to the point of snapping, carried a large butterfly net and an overcoat. He wore spectacles far down on his nose and talked in heavy, grammatical polysyllables about "any further impedimenta" and the like, and walked with a slight limp. After him came a middle-aged woman from South Carolina, who wore a tight bodice, mittens, and a pair of easy juliets. She was very round of face, jolly, and determined on specimens. She said, indeed, that she had not found a really good specimen since last year at this same time and that it was still in alcohol, much to the disgust of her unbotanical parent.

Then a stout gentleman, with very tight breeches and a very red face, who struggled with three immense volumes in which he was going to press his discoveries, came up behind the lady from South Carolina. A fourth and a fifth and a sixth and a final, very thin small woman ended the procession.

It seemed they were going to Clason Point.

I shall never forget that ride. It was the most mysterious and formal affair. Everyone was being introduced to everyone else. They seemed to have met for several years, but in the space between times they forgot each other, and some of them giggled on being reintroduced, saying things like:

"Well now, I do recall, you are the man who had an aunt who had water on the knee; and how is the dear old lady?" Or, "John Matthews, John—oh, yes, it was you who discovered that cryptogamous plant." And bowing with great pride, the gentleman addressed would answer, "I am."

Finally, they all climbed out, flinging themselves like bombs into the landscape. One gentleman immediately started a cry of "There's a specimen!" and kept it up for the rest of the afternoon. Two of them sat down among the rushes and began a discussion on the merits of love and hate. One maintained that love was stronger and therefore better than hate, and the other became enraged at the mere suggestion and said that he had been concentrating on hate since the hogs had been found dead in 1900 and that his teeth had only lately been successful in coming together on edge.

Suddenly, the little thin lady screamed, "Fiddler crabs, fiddler crabs!" and John Matthews rose slowly and menacingly and approached them. They were whirling around on uneven claws at the bottom of a very shallow pool—almost a mud puddle, nothing more.

This caused a great deal of excitement for a few moments; they seemed to have quite forgotten that fiddler crabs could hardly be called rare objects or real discoveries.

One or two of them had wandered away into the woods; one got lost and only wrote to another member of the party six months later that he had reached home safely.

Then there was the stop at the inn, a low-ceilinged house with six mounted deer heads and a stuffed snake under a glass, and a barkeeper with an immense set of whiskers.

Here I paused again in my memory, saying, "Is this, then, what they mean when they say the Bronx?"

And I dropped this memory for one when I was quite young and sneaked into Poe's house and, creeping up into the garret, found a little child's boot thrust away behind a beam; a dirty, worn little shoe with turned-up toe and worn-down heel; a shoe made of red leather with two buttons missing. And I thought of the "Fall of the House of Usher" and of the "Telltale Heart" and shuddered with unbecoming pleasure, thinking, This is the shoe of that man who made my brother scream in his sleep last night.

But when I got home, Mother laughed at me and said dozens of families had lived in Poe's house since his day, and no doubt it was the shoe of Mrs. O'Connor's baby, the one who died of the colic last spring.

And then I thought of the quarries of Fordham. Would Fordham be considered a part of the Bronx? I couldn't quite get away from Fordham without a memory of a great and beautiful Negro who used to squat with a drill all day, turning and spitting on his hands, with a background of cranes and swinging buckets and dust.

Up in the trees above these quarries a black box stood chained to a willow, with the word DANGER written in red across its tar paper: a box that we used to run past with frightened breath, a box that our father had told us contained dynamite.

"What for?"

"For the blasting."

And in the afternoons standing on our porch we could hear the warning cry, "Fire!" as the rumble of torn rock filled the air with a low moan and the odor of powder drifted up through the ravines.

And could this be called appropriate to the suggestion?

And there was the reservoir. We used to walk around the rim of the reservoir waving our hands to the babies that passed below on a lower and far less exalted plane.

And Pelham Bay, where Sydney went when he got in the Marines, and Fleischman's Cafe, where Alex and Courtney used to spend too much time—well, all of these places were supposed to be in the Bronx. But a man at my side kept saying, as I walked down Mott Avenue looking for the Italian gardens that dot the railway tracks, "That isn't what they meant by the Bronx at all; it's the 'Hub,' 149th Street—the 'cattle chute,' the great transfer point. Give them something about that, or about the floor of Hunt's Point Palace; it's the biggest dancing floor in the world, you know. Then tell them about the Park Hotel, that would surely interest them; that's where their businessmen dine on finnan haddie and alligator pears. Or if that won't do, tell them all about the bridge system: the Willis Avenue bridge, the Third Avenue bridge, the 129th Street bridge, the 135th Street bridge, the 149th Street bridge, the 155th Street bridge, the Washington Heights bridge. Tell them about the civic centers at Tremont Avenue. I saw a man run over on that avenue by a garbage cart——"

"Wait!" I cried in horror, holding up my hands.

"Tell them about O'Hara's Hall, at 200th Street; tell them about almost anything, but give them facts."

"Facts," I said, slowly. "My God, have we come to that?"

"Well, at least give them a little talk about theatres; there's the Art Theatre, the Empire Theatre, Miner's, the Follies, Loew's—at least tell them about the Bronx Opera House and where it is situated."

"Where?" I inquired.

"Four hundred and thirty-six East 149th Street," he answered.

"These things mean nothing," I said. "The real Bronx has nothing to do with facts, as the real Greenwich Village has nothing to do with facts, as no real good woman has anything to do with facts. Why, the only reason people consent to live in cities at all is because there, at least, you may get away from facts."

He looked troubled. "Tell them about the clubs then—now there's——"

"No!"

"Well, then, the asylums and homes."

"Again, no."

"Homes for the blind, the irreconcilable, friendless, demented, aspiring, incurable, enraged."

"Do not jest," I warned.

"I'm not. The banks, then; you must not overlook the banks."

"No banks."

"Well, at least, then, you must write something about schools—about the Hall of Fame."

"Why should I? I never went to the first and will never get to the second."

"Oh, indeed," he said scornfully. "Are you going to be purely personal?"

"I am—everyone is who writes well."

"What about the convent schools? Are you going to leave them out?"

"At last," I returned, "you have mentioned something that is almost personal to me. With a clear conscience I may write about a convent school, one that stood up on a slight rise—quite a grim affair—where a lovely girl, a red-haired creature, was brought up. Ah, truly, she was a lovely thing. So pure, so white, so sad. She had the most sorrowful mouth I have ever seen, yet she was quite gay at times. But off and on she wanted to die. Sometimes she thought of being a nun; once she wanted to run away to the West and become a gold miner's bride—'Because they need some of my despair,' she would say. Ah, yes," I continued, "I could write endlessly about that Bronx school. I can still see it, quite a distance away from where I first stood when I looked at it; a few figures, about the size of a well-used pencil, were walking around, and my friend of the beautiful red hair was no longer there."

"Where was she?" he said in an awed voice.

"Married," I answered, "married, and can be found at almost any mass, dropping pennies into the poor box or lighting a candle."

"Have you seen the mothers checking their babies outside of the department stores?" he said, changing the subject.

"Yes," I answered, "but before you go on about that I want to add that she had a head of hair like a murder—you know what I mean: it lay all over the pillow like blood; sort of divine, like a Rossetti. What were you saying about babies?"

"There used to be more Irish up here than there are now."

"Ah, the Irish," I enthused, "what wonderful people they are. You know, I would rather go to Ireland than to Paris. There's little use saying, 'Let you come now, I'm saying, to the lands of Iveragh and the Reeks of Cork, where you won't set down the width of your two feet and not be crushing fine flowers and making sweet smells in the air,'" said I, quoting. And then I recalled what an old washwoman had said to me once: "It's demure they were in them days, looking neither to right nor to left, and the horses and the dogs following them, and the doves dying as they flew for their high envy."

"There are still farmers, though," he answered, "and farm papers, too."

"And them driving into market," I said, nodding. "Ah, it's well I know them. As my washwoman used to say, 'There they do be coming in the light of the dawn, with their fair heads of cabbage and their waving bunches of onions and them an hour out of the dear earth only, and them a-bumpin' and a-joggin' down to the streets where those will eat them as has no notion of the great beauty is in the earth and air before they could taste them at all, and men laboring and women a-toiling and children a-growin' up to make more vegetables for the bad at heart.'"

We were almost back at the Hub, and I said that I thought the best thing to do would be to visit a cabaret— "Sennet's," I suggested.

We pushed open a green door and entered an empty hall, and backing into another door we peered into the gloom where a waiter was dusting the tables.

"Cabaret?" I inquired.

"Bartender tell you," he answered and went back to his dusting.

We walked into the bar. The bartender shook his white head. "At eight tonight—not now."

"No four o'clock teas?"

"No, ma'am."

"So much for the living," I said. "Let us hunt up my old friend the stonecutter."

"He's gone; they have a young man up there now who sells the old man's work at a bargain; hard luck, eh?"

"Heavens, what became of the old gentleman?"

"He married one of your Irish women and keeps a farm."

Back at the cattle chute, I ran for a train and bumped into a woman reading a book of poetry.

"The days are gone, the fair good days are past;
And in their place a leisure all distraught
With hurry and with unimportant gain."

Also by Djuna Barnes

SMOKE AND OTHER EARLY STORIES

First published in New York newspapers between 1914 and 1916, these fourteen incisive tales wonderfully evoke Greenwich Village Bohemia of that time. Sketched with an exquisite and decadent pen are lovers and loners, schemers and dreamers, terrorists and cowards, and many, many more. There's the terrible 'Peacock', a 'slinky female with electrifying eyes and red hair' whom all men pursue but cannot entice; Paprika Johnson softly playing her pawnshop banjo above Swingerhoger's Beer Garden, and Mamie Saloam, the dancer who 'became fire and felt hell'. There's Clochette Brin, who 'knew that love and lottery went together', the silent Lena, whose stolid appearance disguised her animal spirit, and the cunning Madeleonette, whose lovers enact the most dramatic rite of all.

I COULD NEVER BE LONELY WITHOUT A HUSBAND
Interviews by Djuna Barnes

In this collection, nothing is sacred – and no one is safe. Ostensibly 'interviews with the stars', these pieces are more reminiscent of Barnes's own novels and plays than of conventional journalism. 'Have you been making notes?' asks Helen Westley, founder of the Theatre Guild. 'I don't have to,' replies Barnes. 'My memory always makes a paragraph out of a note automatically.' We encounter James Joyce, 'the head turned further away than disgust and not as far as death' and 'the substance, the ether, the haze, that goes by the name of Ziegfeld'. 'I Could Never Be Lonely Without a Husband', says Lillian Russell, while 'Nothing Amuses Coco Chanel After Midnight'. In this 'distorted but highly revealing record of one of the greatest eras of American arts' (Douglas Messerli), we read Djuna Barnes at her quirky and brilliant best.

EMILY COLEMAN
THE SHUTTER OF SNOW

'A work which has stirred me deeply . . . compelling' – HAROLD NICHOLSON

'A very striking triumph of imagination and technique . . . The book is not only quite unique; it is also a work of genuine literary inspiration' – EDWIN MUIR

'An extraordinary, visionary book, written out of those edges where madness and poetry meet' – FAY WELDON

After the birth of her child Marthe Gail spends two months in an insane asylum with the fixed idea that she is God. Marthe transports us into that strange country of terror and ecstasy we call madness, a twilit country where the objective and the subjective are fused, where perspective is lost, logic absent and only pain remains . . .

Emily Coleman (1899–1974) was born in California. In 1925 she moved to Paris, where she became an important figure in the legendary literary life of Paris in the '20s, a close friend of Djuna Barnes, Peggy Guggenheim and John Holms. She spent the '30s in London, involved there in the literary circle of her good friend Antonia White, Dylan Thomas and T. S. Eliot, and others. She published *The Shutter of Snow*, her only novel, in 1930.

JANE BOWLES
TWO SERIOUS LADIES

With exhilarating wit, *Two Serious Ladies* follows the decline into debauchery of two very different women: Christina Goering, a wealthy spinster in pursuit of sainthood – she ends up as a high-class call-girl; and Frieda Copperfield, who abandons her stick of a husband for love of Pacifica, a Panamanian prostitute – *she* ends up more or less permanently under the influence. Though they might seem to end on a low note from certain points of view, from another their glorious independence, unlimited lust for doing exactly as they like and hilarious eccentricity in pursuing the paths of their choice triumphantly celebrate the joys of female freedom.

EVERYTHING IS NICE
The Collected Stories

With her idiosyncratic combination of high style, comic acuity and disquieting strangeness, Jane Bowles captures those slips between the lines – the silences, alienations and uncomfortable juxtapositions – which comprise the dislocations of life. An awkward widow and her shy neighbour fall in love via silence and anger; an American traveller, caught in the shabby exoticism of a Guatemalan town, has an affair with his landlady; a small girl drills imaginary troops, but finds she can no longer command them when she makes friends with a young boy; and an Algerian woman carrying a porcupine in a basket insists that a European woman accompany her to a non-existent wedding. These and other tales create an atmosphere of surreal tragi-comedy, where the ordinary is bizarre and the grotesque is everyday.

Jane Bowles (1917–1973) produced a small but remarkable body of work: a novel, *Two Serious Ladies*, the play *In the Summerhouse*, and the laconic, distinctive stories published in *Everything Is Nice*, including six fictional pieces discovered after her death, and three stories which have never before appeared in book form.

H.D.

BID ME TO LIVE

It is 1917 and Julia Ashton lives in a shuttered room in Queen's Square, Bloomsbury. A young wife, no longer happy, she mourns the loss of her baby, and lives that war-time life of love and death as her poet husband, Rafe, comes and goes from the trenches of the First World War. Then into her trancelike state breaks Frederick, the writer with the flaming beard and the driving, volcanic genius.

HER

It is 1909 and Hermione Gart is in her early twenties – "a disappointment to her father, an odd duckling to her mother, an importunate, overgrown, unincarnated entity that had no place." Having just failed at her college, Bryn Mawr, she stays at home, stifled by her family, struggling for an identity, waiting for her life to begin. Then the wild poet George Lowndes returns from Europe, expanding her horizons, yet threatening her new, fragile sense of self.

GERTRUDE STEIN

BLOOD ON THE DINING-ROOM FLOOR

In the spring of 1933 Gertrude Stein and Alice B. Toklas were living in their country house at Bilignin, France. With money earned from the best-selling *Autobiography of Alice B. Toklas* they installed electricity, had a telephone put in their house and bought a large car. But with these improvements came trouble. Servants came and went. Finally a man named Jean and his Polish wife were employed. A friend came to stay, but her car was tampered with and the telephone no longer worked. The servants were dismissed. Later that summer in nearby Belley, Madame Pernollet was found sprawled on the courtyard of her husband's hotel. Five days later she was dead. Was it an accident? Suicide? Murder? And what of Madame Caesar? As Alice B. Toklas said, 'there was no denying one could become accustomed to murdering . . .'

Gertrude Stein (1874-1946), one of the most important and influential writers of the twentieth century, combined a strong comic sense with a lifelong interest in violence and crime. Following this 'unnatural summer' of mysterious events and crimes she wrote *Blood on the Dining-Room Floor* – her one detective novel (first published in America in 1948). Published here in Britain for the first time, it is a perfect example of her work. There is no explaining the obscurities of her writing, no simple key which will unlock the secret of her outpouring of words. This, *Blood on the Dining-Room Floor*, is a *real* mystery.

Also by Gertrude Stein

EVERYBODY'S AUTOBIOGRAPHY

'. . . like it or not autobiography is easy for anyone so this is to be Everybody's Autobiography,' wrote Gertrude Stein; and this sequel to *The Autobiography of Alice B. Toklas*, first published in 1938, is indeed one of her most accessible works. Beginning with her life in Paris, she writes about the famous (Picasso, Braque, Marie Laurençin) and the not-so-famous whom she meets and observes in the streets and salons of her adopted city. But when in 1934 her opera *Four Saints in Three Acts* is performed to great acclaim in New York, America wants her back, and with Alice B. Toklas she undertakes an extensive tour of the country from which she has been absent for thirty years . . .

LECTURES IN AMERICA

Published in 1935, these six essays collected here provide an intriguing, warmly personal portrait of Stein's theories of language, literature and art. Considered the cornerstone of her critical thinking, *Lectures in America* presents her own history of English literature; her thoughts on painting, which she illustrates with personal experiences of specific paintings and museums; thoughts on plays and the theatre, and reflections on English grammar, punctuation and her own experimental writing. Written with verve, perception and humour, *Lectures in America* has become a key volume in understanding Stein's view of her world and her art.